Sibilant Fricative

Essays and Reviews

Adam Roberts

Sibilant Fricative

Essays and Reviews

Adam Roberts

Steel Quill Books
An Imprint of NewCon Press

First edition, published in the UK August 2014
by Steel Quill Books,
an Imprint of NewCon Press
41 Wheatsheaf Road, Alconbury Weston, Cambs, PE28 4LF

SQ001 (softback)

10 9 8 7 6 5 4 3 2 1

ISBN: 978-1-907069-75-8 (softback)

Cover art © 2014 by Aty Behsam
Cover layout by Andy Bigwood

Minor Editorial Interference by Ian Whates
Text layout by Storm Constantine

Contents

Part 2: Fantasy

Disagreeing with Adam Roberts

An Introduction by Paul Kincaid

Book reviews are not holy writ: you don't have to agree with what the critic tells you. That is not what it is about at all. There is no one way of reading a book, there is no single interpretation that must hold for the text. All that any critic can do is offer you possible readings, possible interpretations.

A good critic will back up their interpretation with evidence, experience, the fruits of wide reading. If the critic is really good, all of this is likely to be convincing. But that doesn't mean it is the only reading. A diametrically opposite view might work just as well. Which means that any critic is open to disagreement, but that is not necessarily a bad thing.

A counter view opens up different perspectives, may reveal more than was originally noticed, may even persuade the original critic to change her mind. On the other hand, the way that disagreement forces you to reconsider your own arguments may also reinforce those arguments. At the very least, disagreement is a way of testing your ideas and that is something that should be welcomed.

As a critic, I have often found myself disagreeing with Adam Roberts. I know, from his review of my book, that he has disagreed with me. I like to think that I was invited to introduce this collection of his reviews because of those disagreements, not in spite of them.

Now I happen to think that, apart from those occasions when he is clearly and plainly wrong, Adam Roberts is a good critic. That is, for my money there are three qualities to which any critic should aspire. Years ago, I put it like this:

> A review should be honest (any reviewer who allows her opinion to be swayed by friendship, bribery, peer pressure or whatever, is not worth reading), defensible (I don't mind if people disagree with my judgement, I am quite used to being the only critic to hold a certain position, pro or con, on any particular book, but I want to be sure the readers can see why I reached that particular judgement), and, so far

as I am able, well written (a review is also an entertainment, the reader should be rewarded for taking the time to read the piece).

And Roberts nails all three of them as often as anyone, and more often than most. However, that very quality can make it difficult to disagree with what he is saying. Yet I firmly believe that you should approach this book, as you should approach any book of criticism, prepared to disagree, ready to argue.

So, how do you disagree with a critic like Adam Roberts? Well, to start with, you could try reading a lot. These reviews cover everyone from Martin Amis to Thomas Pynchon, from Ursula Le Guin to Connie Willis, so you'd probably want to be up to date with those authors, of course. But as you read the reviews you'll find references to lots of other works beside, from Beowulf to H.G. Wells and on. As a critic, he likes literary context. Now, I'm not saying you have to have read as much as he has before you can argue with him, but the more you have read the more weapons you'll have in your armoury. There's a side effect to this, of course. The more you read, the more you recognise the references that litter these reviews, the more you'll appreciate them.

Tied in with this is what is technically known as putting in the legwork. The book concludes with an epic undertaking, in which Roberts reads his way through every volume of Robert Jordan's *The Wheel of Time* sequence in order to write about them. Personally I believe this is above and beyond the call of duty -- that way madness lies -- so I wouldn't necessarily suggest that you do the same. Actually you can witness the exercise having a debilitating effect upon Roberts as you read your way through the reviews, so maybe we should take this as a dire warning. Nevertheless, taken together these reviews offer some interesting insights into the nature of generic fantasy. (Compare them, for instance, with the pieces on Tolkien earlier in the book, a writer for whom Roberts clearly has a great deal of affection; the contrast is revealing.)

Now I'm not about to suggest that you need to read everything by Robert Jordan in order to disagree with Adam Roberts. But it helps to recognise that he has done the hard work, so you are going to have to pay attention.

(Parenthetically, I repeat that one of the hallmarks of a good reviewer is that the review is entertainingly written, and the Robert

Jordan reviews are very funny. It takes a rare talent to make serious points and be funny at the same time. That is one of the things I admire about Roberts's reviews.)

Let's assume, then, that you are keeping pace with Roberts' wide and thorough reading. That gives you the tools you need, so it's just a matter of mustering your counter-arguments. I'm not going to do that for you, there's no point. The likelihood is that you will find yourself agreeing with the things where I think he is wrong, and disagreeing with those places where I'm sure he is right. But here's something you may find useful: look for patterns. In my experience, finding a pattern in a book may give you part of the picture, but it is rarely the whole thing, especially when the critic is picking up on a pattern they have found elsewhere. So a critic returning to the same pattern may indicate a chink for you to explore.

Roberts, I have noticed, has a soft spot for binaries. Anyone who follows him on twitter will have noticed how fond he is of puns built around Kierkegaard's *Either/Or*. Actually, anyone who follows him on twitter will have noticed how fond he is of puns, period. And notice how he keeps returning to yin and yang in his preface to this volume. Of course, an awful lot of science fiction and fantasy is built around simple binary patterns: good and evil, them and us, and so forth. But keep an eye on the binaries, they may open something up for you.

Above all, have fun. Roberts clearly does. The review of M.D. Lachlan's *Wolfsangel* is one of the shortest and most entertaining reviews you're likely to encounter. I'm not sure how much it actually tells us about the book, but it's a thing of wonder in its own right. And there are many more moments throughout this volume where you'll either laugh out loud or slap your head because he's pointed out something blindingly obvious that you'd never noticed before – sometimes both at the same time. For me, that's the mark of a good critic, and these are good reviews.

But remember, don't take my word for it. It's your job to disagree.

Paul Kincaid
October 2012

Preface: On Reviewing

This is a collection of essays about SF and F, hence its title. The sibilant *s*, the fricative *f*. The better-informed amongst my readers will have noted that the second of these terms is actually a form of the first of these terms, but that strikes me as appropriate since the 'science' and the 'fiction' in 'Science Fiction' exist in a properly dialectical, yin-yang way.

Fricatives are consonants articulated by pushing air through the narrow channel formed in the mouth by putting two articulators in proximity to one another, as (in the present case) lower lip and upper teeth. A sibilant is a particular sort of fricative and affricative consonant, made by using the tongue to divert one's exhalation towards the sharp edge of the half-closed teeth. Uttering a sibilant as a constituent phoneme of ordinary words is a thoroughly unexceptional part of every language spoken on Earth. But uttering a sibilant in other contexts – let's say, by an audience member at the end of the performance of a play – carries rather different connotations. I love SF and F both, and often (it seems to me) I write reviews that rise almost to dithyrambic heights, but by the same token I have been known, on occasion, to hiss, and this collection certainly contains a quantity of the geesier sorts of articulation. As for the fricativity: well, it has always seemed to me that *friction* is absolutely core to SFF. Ordinary (sometimes they're called 'mainstream') literatures aim to reproduce the world in textual form. SFF aims to do that too, although with key differences (*novums*, these differences are called) that have the necessary effect of introducing friction into the mode of representation. That's what makes it all worthwhile.

'SF', when spoken aloud, is sometimes pronounced 'ehsef', sometimes 'sky-fy' or 'skiffi', sometimes deacronymised into 'Science Fiction'. It is never, I think, pronounced as it is spelled, in part because there is something tongue-twistish about the cramming together of a sibilant and a fricative after this fashion. A plosive and a fricative (lan**df**all) or a sibilant and a plosive (pa**st**ime) go more naturally together because of the mechanics of coordinating tongue, palate and teeth. But the difficulty of juxtaposing sibilant and fricative appeals to me as a small symbol of the larger, creative difficulty of the genre as a whole. SF ought to be difficult. The melding of science (technology, philosophy) and fiction (aesthetics and narrative) best not be facile, and SF in which this blend is too painlessly presented is generally bad SF. In genre terms, this is more likely to be because the science is taken as self-evidently more important than the fiction, although it might be for the contrary reason –that the aesthetic task has overwhelmed the scientific one. I have doubtlessly written novels of this latter sort myself. Above all, critics and readers of SF, and Fantasy too, *ought* to value difficulty. It's hard to say why, often, they don't.

Some years ago, John Lanchester published an essay about video games called 'Is It Art?' [*London Review of Books*, 1 Jan 2009]. It's an essay that deserves to be better known than it is. Lanchester considers gaming intelligently as a sort of invisible seismic shift in culture, and one of the things he's good on is the *difficulty* of most video games. Here he is on Ken Levine's 2K Boston/2K Australia game *BioShock*, which he likes a great deal:

> As a video game, *BioShock* fully subscribes to the conventions of the medium, and if you as a non-gamer were to pick it up and give it a try, it is these you would probably notice most. Not just the conventions of which buttons and levers you press to move about the world of the game (annoying and hard to recollect as these often are) and not just the in-game mechanics, such as the 'plasmids' which you have to inject to give your character the powers he needs, or the tapes which are conveniently left around for you to discover and play back to hear the story of Rapture; but also the whole package of conventions and codes and how-tos which become second nature to video-game players, but which strike non-gamers as arbitrary and confining and a little bit stupid. Northrop Frye once observed that all conventions, as conventions, are more or less insane; Stanley Cavell once pointed out that the conventions of cinema are just as arbitrary as those of opera. Both those observations are brought to mind by video games, which are full, overfull, of exactly that kind of arbitrary convention. Many of these conventions make the game more difficult. Gaming is a much more resistant, frustrating medium than its cultural competitors. Older media have largely abandoned the idea that difficulty is a virtue; if I had to name one high-cultural notion that had died in my adult lifetime, it would be the idea that difficulty is artistically desirable. It's a bit of an irony that difficulty thrives in the newest medium of all – and it's not by accident, either. One of

the most common complaints regular gamers make in reviewing new offerings is that they are too easy. (It would be nice if a little bit of that leaked over into the book world.)

In the spirit of that sentiment, I say: often, Science Fiction and Fantasy are too easy. As to why this should be – why, that is, many of the same fans who actively prize 'difficulty' in their video games spurn it as they might spurn a rabid dog when it crops up in their novels and short stories – well, that's a profound and unsettling question. I have a go at addressing it, in various ways, with what follows. At the very least, one of the aesthetic crotchets that informs my own reviewing is a preference for the difficult over the easy. An active valorisation of the friction of the best art, not despite the fact that I am reviewing SFF but precisely *because of it*. The problem with Realism, it seems to me, is that it is almost inevitably superficial. But the problem with the metaphorical modes of fiction, Science Fiction, Fantasy, 'Magic Realism' and the like, is almost that they are *too* deep.

It is only fair, mind, that I lay out the principle upon which the reviews have been written. American critic John Leonard has a six-point desideratum for the attention of reviewers. The context here is that Leonard was reviewing a collection of reviews by the famously (in some quarters, infamously) aggressive Dale Peck. Peck is the sort of reviewer who calls a spade a fucking terrible spade, and a widely-liked author 'the worst writer of his generation'. Personally I enjoy reading Peck's reviews (I especially recommend 2004's *Hatchet Jobs*, although it covers no SFF at all). Leonard dislikes Peck's reviews very much; his term for what Peck does is the excellently sibilant-fricative-nasal 'smashmouthery'. Basically, what Leonard wants is more respect in reviewing:

> First, as in Hippocrates, do no harm. Second, never stoop to score a point or bite an ankle. Third, always understand that in this symbiosis, you are the parasite. Fourth, look with an open heart and mind at every different kind of book with every change of emotional weather because we are reading for our lives and that could be love gone out the window or a horseman on the roof. Fifth, use theory only as a periscope or a trampoline, never a panopticon, a crib sheet or a license to kill. Sixth, let a hundred Harolds Bloom. [Leonard, 'Smash-Mouth Criticism', *New York Times*, 18 July 2004]

Certainly it looks fine, written down there like that, not least because it implies something genuinely uplifting— –that literature is not merely a pastime, a distraction or a subculture; rather that literature is life, and it is love, and we should treat it with something approaching vibrant reverence. On the other hand, Leonard's review begins by quoting one particular point-scoring, ankle-biting, single-sentence review that, it seems to me, approaches genius:

> Although Robert Southey was the poet laureate of England from 1813 until his death in 1843, and a Lake District buddy of Coleridge and Wordsworth, he is hardly read at all today. A wisecrack by Richard Porson may have done some serious damage. About Southey's epic poems, Porson said, "They will be read when Homer and Virgil are forgotten, but – not till then."

As one-line reviews go, that *rocks*. It so happens I have read Southey's epics which puts me in the position of being able to vouch for the truth at the heart of the wisecrack: *viz*. not that the poems are hopeless, just that it's hard to justify reading them when there are many better epics around. But it's also hilarious; which is to say, it's a really good piece of writing (timing a punchline is the trickiest bit of comic writing). And that's worth something too. Reviews are not merely secondary, or parasitic, things. They are texts in their own right. No reviewer should to be excused for writing poorly, or being dull, any more than any other writer.

My cards, here, down they go, onto the table: the reviews in this collection are sometimes negative, and a couple may even merit being called smashmouthy. To quote another eminent American critic and thinker: "'Will Smith don't got to cuss in his rap to sell records' – well I do, so fuck him, and fuck you too." The anxiety, of course, is: *am I rude?* I'm English.Rudeness to my people is what murder and blasphemy and cannibalism are to other cultures. On the other hand, rudeness does not correlate very precisely with outspokenness. Speaking personally, I have been wholly marinated in the cultural milieu of repressed English middle-class strangulated politeness and self-deprecation. There are ways which every Englishwoman and –man knows, by which the most withering dispraise can be communicated by a string of seemingly blandly approbative words. I quite often find myself slipping into that idiom in face-to-face communication. I try not to do anything so cruel in my published reviews.

And anyway, all this sort of discussion of reviewing tends to put the question the wrong way around. Trollope (in his *Autobiography*, published in 1883 and as good an account of being a jobbing novelist as I can think of) recalls that when his first novel came out a friend told him he'd arranged for a positive review to appear in the *Times*. Trollope was, as any author would be, pleased at this. Thinking a little more, however, it gave him pause.

> It set me thinking whether the notice, should it ever appear, would not have been more valuable, at any rate, more honest, if it had been produced by other means; if, for instance, the writer of the notice had been instigated by the merits or demerits of the book instead of by the friendship of a friend. And I made up my mind then that, should I continue this trade of authorship, I would have no dealings with any critic on my own behalf. I would neither ask for nor deplore criticism, nor would I ever thank a critic for praise, or quarrel with him, even in my own heart, for censure. To this rule I have adhered with absolute strictness, and this rule I would recommend to all young authors. What can be got by touting among the critics is never worth the ignominy. The same may, of course, be said of all things acquired by ignominious means. But in this matter it is so easy to fall into the dirt. *Facilis descensus Averno.* There seems to be but little fault in suggesting to a friend that a few words in this or that journal would be of service. But any praise so obtained must be an injustice to the public, for whose instruction, and not for the sustentation of the author, such notices are intended. And from such mild suggestion the descent to crawling at the critic's feet, to the sending of presents, and at last to a mutual understanding between critics and criticised, is only too easy. Other evils follow, for the denouncing of which this is hardly the place.

Facilis decensus Averno is from Virgil's *Aeneid*, and it means 'it's easy enough going *down* into the land of the dead.' Not only can anyone do it, in fact we all will, at some point. The tricky part, Virgil is saying, is coming back up again.

The world of SFF is a narrow one. I am very likely to know, perhaps even be on friendly terms with, the authors upon whose works I am opining. At the very least I am likely to bump into them at publishers' parties, conventions, award ceremonies and the like. It would be foolish to deny that this puts pressure on a reviewer to moderate the invective. Some of these SF writers are not small. I have seen bears with less heft.

Surely, though, this only makes it *more* pressing that reviews do not mislead potential readers. (Isn't the flipside of Leonard's 'do no harm' agenda a kind of reviewerish moral pusillanimity?) The Trollopean phrase that really nails, I'd say, is the one pointing out the intensely reasonable fact that puffery 'must be an injustice to the public, for whose instruction, and not for the sustentation of the author, such notices are intended.' John Clute is a leading light in this regard. Perhaps the most widely respected of current SFF reviewers, he operates by a principle of 'excessive candour':

> Reviewers who will not tell the truth are like cholesterol. They are lumps of fat. They starve the heart. I have myself certainly clogged a few arteries, have sometimes kept my mouth shut out of 'friendship' which is nothing in the end but self-interest. So perhaps it is time to call a halt. Perhaps we should establish a Protocol of Excessive Candour, a convention within the community that excesses of intramural harshness are less damaging than the hypocrisies of stroke therapy, that telling the truth is a way of expressing love; self-love; love of others; love for the genre, which claims to tell the truth about things that count; love for the inhabitants of the planet; love for the future. Because the truth is all we've got. And if we don't talk to ourselves, and if we don't use every tool at our command in our time on Earth to tell the truth, nobody else will. [John Clute, *Look At The Evidence* (1995)]

Clute does not pull his punches, certainly, although he has the advantage of a writing style so ineffably effulgent that, on occasion, it is hard to tell whether his point is one of praise or dispraise. But truthfulness is the only criterion. A review must justify its existence as text on its own terms, not merely in parasitic relationship to another text. It needs to be entertaining and thought-provoking, whether or not you have read the book being reviewed. It should be a good piece of writing in its own right.

Writing novels, as I have good personal reason to know, is hard work. Nobody sets out to write a bad book. Maybe there *is* something fundamentally disrespectful about writing negative reviews. Of course, we might want to argue that respect is earned, not given away for free. But then again I don't believe that I would review bad books so mercilessly if I didn't also write fiction of my own. I don't mean, when I say this, that I consider the writing of books a necessary qualification for the reviewing of books. Not at all: Johnson's observation, that a man need not be a cobbler to know that his shoes pinch, seems to me spot-on. No, what I mean is the fact that my own books are liable to be reviewed, perhaps by the very people I am negatively reviewing, licenses me to a candour I might otherwise feel to be unsustainable. It's the difference between on the one hand standing in a field, like Pushkin, aiming your pistol at a figure aiming *his* pistol at *you*; and on the other hiding behind a wall to snipe at a passer-by. I suppose, since my own books have received some pretty swingeing reviews, there's a danger my own reviewing might look like redirected fury. I don't think it is. Rather, I think my own books being in the line of fire makes me understand that bad reviews are part of the *heat* to which the wise old saw concerning staying-in or removing-oneself-from the kitchen refers. I try to imagine what a literary culture would look like if its reviewers strove to *do no harm*. I can't say I like what I imagine.

One final point, about reviewing, before I bring this too-lengthy preface to an end, and it has to do with irony. Following on from that, and related to that, is the question of irony. This is another reason why I love SF so much: because it is the ironic mode of art *par excellence* — its the closest I'm prepared to come to a definition of my beloved mode to say that its relationship with reality is ironic rather than mimetic. Irony fascinates me, both in its 'serious' and in its laughable modes, and irony informs everything I write. You can tell that, you know, if you read what I write in this collection or elsewhere. And whilst I'm aware of the danger of projecting my own individual crotchets onto the world at large, I also tend to think that irony in the broadest sense is one of the great achievements of the best 20th- and 21st-century fiction. James Wood, a critic of no small insight, howsoever blinkered his larger perspective, says something along these lines in *The Irresponsible Self*, although his nomenclature doesn't precisely map onto mine: 'the comedy of what I want to call "irresponsibility" or unreliability is a kind of subset of the comedy of forgiveness; and although it has its roots in Shakespearian comedy (especially the soliloquy) it seems to me the wonderful creation of the late 19th and early 20th-century novel. This comedy, or tragi-comedy, of the modern novel replaces the knowable with the unknowable, transparency with unreliability' [p. 8]. A little later he says 'this kind of comedy seems to me the creation of modern fiction because it exchanges typology for the examination of the individual, and the religious dream of complete knowledge or stable knowledge for the uncertainty of incomplete knowledge' [p. 14]. But many scientists and engineers are closely attached to ideas of typology and complete certainty of knowledge (typology underlies algebra and Linnean categorising, I'd say), and many of them like their SF to cleave closely to the typological and a kind of rectitude of knowing. This isn't the SF I write, any more than it was the SF that Lem, or Dick, wrote. Now, many people dislike irony, and some of those people dislike it with a righteous and furious vehemence. Indeed I'm not sure I'd realised until fairly recently, in my general myopia and self-absorption, how actively hostile many people are to irony today; a reaction, perhaps, to the dog-days of Postmodernism, now decades behind us. A couple of things recently reminded me of this. One was the (very successful) China Miéville conference, hosted by the Institute for English Studies at London University in September 2012. Amongst many other things, Miéville's plenary expressed his sentiment to the effect that he disliked irony, or as he put it 'whimsy', in art. Personally I'd see 'irony' as a very different quality to whimsy, but I don't doubt this to be a connection, and an animadversion, shared by lots of people. David Foster Wallace, for instance, hated it. It's one of the fascinations of his literary career, that he employed postmodern forms to articulate a very unpostmodern heart's-yearning.[1] Wallace craved authenticity, especially emotional authenticity, with an almost painful intensity. But irony is more than a knowing wink, and more than a snide put-down. Irony is the logic of the world we live in.

Kierkegaard was right when he identified irony as a necessary qualification of modern subjectivity ('Irony,' he said in 1841, 'limits, finitizes, and circumscribes and thereby yields truth, actuality, content;

---

[1] "Make no mistake: irony tyrannizes us[…] Irony's useful for debunking illusions, but most of the illusion-debunking in the U.S. has now been done and redone. Once everybody knows that equality of opportunity is bunk and Mike Brady's bunk and Just Say No is bunk, now what do we do? All we seem to want to do is keep ridiculing the stuff. Postmodern irony and cynicism's become an end in itself, a measure of hip sophistication and literary savvy. Few artists dare to try to talk about ways of working toward redeeming what's wrong, because they'll look sentimental and naive to all the weary ironists. Irony's gone from liberating to enslaving. There's some great essay somewhere that has a line about irony being the song of the prisoner who's come to love his cage."

it disciplines and punishes and thereby yields balance and consistency.'
Or more precisely, he said something like that in Danish). More to the
point, Kierkegaard was right when he insisted, in his concluding
'Unscientific Postscript', that 'the presence of irony does not necessarily
mean that the earnestness is excluded. Only assistant professors assume
that.' Indeed, nowadays not even assistant professors believe that.
There's no outside to irony, no place from where we can stand with a
perfect *Embassytown*-style access to true, genuine, authentic,
winsomeness-purged Real Thing. Of course there *are* real things, and
they matter very much, but the Real Thing is both Coca Cola *and* being
present at the birth of your children, and the two things can no longer
be neatly separated out from one another.

One of the reasons irony and whimsy aren't the same thing is that
irony is more than just a mode for saying serious things, it's actually the
only mode left to use nowadays. One of my personal gods of writing is
Nabokov, an ironist to his marrow whose attachment to 'bliss' was
both genuine and playful *at the same time* (because of course those two
things are not opposites). The end of *Lolita* is extraordinarily moving –
I don't mean Lolita herself dying, sad though that is, so much as the
scene in which Humbert's realises belatedly that he has fallen properly
in love with her at exactly the moment he understands both how much
he has damaged her and that he will never see her again – it's
moving *because* the preceding 300 pages are so complexly ironic in their
unmimetic European-poetic intensity of apprehension of 1950s
America. It wouldn't work otherwise. It's precisely the real thing,
emotionally, that is also complexly compromised.

Maybe you and I don't think of the same thing when we say the
word 'irony'. Maybe you see irony as a kind of superciliousness, or
Pilate hand-washing, or, indeed, whimsy. Of course art must engage
with the world, and of course it needs to have the courage of its
convictions. And I think saying that I'm not ironic about irony itself is
well put, and irony *is* one of those words that has a distractingly
dissipated semantic field. But, at the risk of sounding pretentious I'll say
that not only doe not see irony as superciliousness, I see it as precisely
the remedy for superciliousness. It's that whole Kierkegaardian
'absolute negativity of Socratic irony' thing: the only way of *being* serious
in the modern age. Or another way of putting it might be to invoke
Brecht's Verfremdungseffekt. Contemporary SF needs more

Verfremdungseffekt, not less. Some people will prefer to read the Bible literally; I find it makes a larger and, I would argue, nobler claim to truth when it is read ironically. Kierkegaard and Nietzsche *are* greater philosophers than Kant and Hegel. Jane Austen is a better writer of love stories than Stephanie Myers. Earnestness is a greater danger to art than whimsy. Science Fiction *is* a better mode than that of mimetic fiction.

And this brings me back to reviews. A notional scientist (let's call him Professor Strawman) believes that the relationship between 'science' and reality must be the strictest type of mimesis. This professor likes a bit of Science Fiction, and believes that, informed by science, SF as a mode must embody a mimetic relationship to the real world ('this SFSF book is bad because it misrepresents the precise parameters of Maxwell's equations'). But it is precisely the departures from strict mimesis that make SF worthwhile, that make SF SF. That SF has an ironic relationship to reality is not to say that SF lies about reality – on the contrary, it means that SF has found more eloquent and effective ways of precisely telling the truth about the world we live in.

Replace the salient terms in that last paragraph with 'review' and 'novel'. A review has a duty to accurately represent the novel it discusses, but that doesn't mean that a review needs to be a ploddingly mimetic, neutral reproduction of the novel. On the contrary, a review that ironizes its source text, especially if read in conjunction with that text, can be more expressive and penetrating. Reviews are texts too.

So, here are my reviews and I commend them to you. Topic-wise, they are all twentieth-and 21st-century titles (a collection of essays on older classics of the genre might follow), skewed a little towards the more recent. If that strikes you as unbalancing the whole, then to you I say – hiss. Fff.

Part 1: Science Fiction

Sibilance. My father was always trying to get rid of this in revising his poetry, – 'kicking the geese out of the boat', as he called it – and he thought that he had succeeded.

[Hallam Tennyson, *Alfred Lord Tennyson: A Memoir* (1897)]

Philip K Dick, *Four Novels of the 1960s*

(Library of America 2007)

Some long novels, Martin Amis once noted, are really short novels that happen to go on for a long time (indeed, he thinks 'most long novels are this kind of long novel, where writers routinely devastate acres of woodland for their spy thrillers, space operas, family sagas and so on'). On the other hand *some* long novels are long 'because they have to be, earning their amplitude by the complexity of the demands they make on writer and reader alike.' He doesn't talk about a third type: the short novel that is paradoxically a long novel. I don't mean a condensed book, or a fragment that hints at greatness; I mean that rare item, a book that folds magnitude into hidden dimensions within its narrow one-eighty pages.

Philip Dick wrote those sorts of novels. A sense of something hidden, something underground and flourishing in the interstices, like bluebells growing in the cracks of the pavement (or blooms of *mors ontologica* in amongst the corn) energises his fiction. It's this something that has kept his books alive when better written, better structured and better plotted novels have fallen into obscurity around them. Which is to say that critics can, and do, point to evidence of hasty writing in Dick's works, patches of ragged or inexpressive prose, or occasional addled-head-ness in most of his books (he took a whole bunch of drugs, after all). But even with all that, or conceivably *because of that* there is a quality that PKD's books possess that few other books, in or out of genre, can match. It is a sort of fascinating aesthetic uncleanness, resonant and enduring. More polish would have rubbed that quality away.

Dick's reputation has, of course, followed a strange path: from unconsidered pulp outsider to American Literary Name, or even canonical figure – a rather dispiriting trajectory, actually, that owes much to his popularity with the Big Business of Hollywood production. Dick's acceptance by the establishment has reached a new milestone with his inclusion in the handsome black-liveried Library of America edition, where he can now stand alongside Melville and Whitman, Henry James and Philip Roth. But it is always refreshing to return to

Philip Dick's actual prose and remember how poorly the label 'great American writer' fits him, and how superbly saving that fact is.

So it's nice to hold this volume in my hands; as handsome and compact as any Library of America issue (and as expensive: $35). It contains, as its subtitle says, "four novels of the 1960s," chosen and edited by Jonathan Lethem: *The Man in the High Castle* (1962), *The Three Stigmata of Palmer Eldritch* (1965), *Do Androids Dream of Electric Sheep?* (1968) and *Ubik* (1969). There's no introduction, that not being LoA house style, but there is a detailed timeline of PKD's life, which makes curiously disheartening reading, and there are endnotes that suggest (nine pages of detailed notes for *High Castle*, but only a third of a page – eight notes in total – for the whole of *Palmer Eldritch*) that some novels engaged Lethem more than others. I suppose we might argue that *High Castle* needs more annotation than Eldritch, what with all those references to WW2 history and the like, but in their own ways *Eldritch*, and *Ubik* (covered in a mere fourteen endnotes) are just as baffling to a reader unfamiliar with the 60s. Best of all is the opportunity simply to reread four novels from Dick's great decade. PKD's books go down better when you munch a whole lot of them in a short space. He's a writer to gobble, not to sip and savour.

The Man in the High Castle occupies an unusual place in the PKD oeuvre because it was the only one of his novels to win a major award in his lifetime (it won the Hugo for Best Novel in 1963); or to be more precise, it occupies an unusual place because of what that fact says about the book. It says it's a book liable to find approbation from regular SF fans. It says it works cannily through an ingenious premise, that it's well-written; tightly plotted, that it construes engaging characters via good and eloquent detail from a properly built-world. Which is a long-way-round of saying that it is uncharacteristic for Dick, and rereading it in this new edition (rereading it, I think, for the fourth time) I found that its very polish, its various evidences of craft, alienated me somewhat from the book. Of the four novels collected here it seems to me the least Dickesque, and so the least worthwhile.

High Castle is an example of Hitler-wins alternate history; set in a 1960s in which the USA has been divided east and west between Nazi Germany and Imperial Japan. Frank Frink ekes a living making jewellery and faking antique collectables, an occupation that enables Dick to highlight the slippery problem of 'authenticity', of what Walter

Benjamin called the "aura" (a term that winkles its way into the novel, for instance p. 57), inherent in the whole premise of an alternate history. Frink's ex-wife, Juliana, falls in with an Italian ex-soldier, but like most things in this novel he too is a fake, or more specifically his Italian identity is a disguise: in reality he is a Swiss Nazi assassin. There is a very readable and efficiently-handled thriller plot, to do with microdots and the secret sinister 'Operation Dandelion' to start World War III and nuke Japan. But it's hard to shake a sense of something not there. We don't need Dick to supply us with competent alt-historical thrillers; the writerly world is full of middling writers who can do that, books like Deighton's *SS-GB* (1978) or Harris's *Fatherland* (1992). Dick has precedence on those two authors, of course; but he can't claim to have invented the 'Hitler Wins' sub-genre (Clute and Nicholls list ten antecedents, and that's just with Hitler; which is to say, not counting a mini-masterpiece like Ward Moore's *Bring the Jubilee* from 1953). What Dick can give us is a profound creative *distortion*, and the slightly self-conscious writerly *polish* of *High Castle* doesn't capture this. It is a well-handled short novel that feels like a well-handled short novel. Dick's best books are short novels that feel like they contain enormities.

One feature of the novel that escapes these criticisms, I'd say, is the title character; a marginal figure, plot-wise, but crucial in other ways. The man's name is Hawthorne Abendsen, and his High Castle is a house in Colorado. Guided by the I-Ching, Abendsen has written a novel called *The Grasshopper Lies Heavy*: an alternate-history science fiction tale set in a world in which the Allies, not the Nazis, won the second world war. Dick, in a deft touch, makes plain that this alt-history is not the same as our one (in it the British liberated Berlin and put Hitler on trial, for instance), and the existential uncertainty it entails could, perhaps, have troubled the smooth surface of the rest of the novel a little more. At the end of the book Juliana finally meets Abendsen to ask metaphysical questions about the nature of his novel, and through it of fiction as a whole, but his answers are unilluminating, except in one respect. 'To Juliana [Hawthorne] said: "You have an – unnatural mind. Are you aware of that?"' [p. 226]. It's as if all the naïf-metafictional pre-postmodernism of the bulk of the novel has been a kind of misdirection, so much so that we can almost miss how important this statement is to Dick's aesthetic; how self-contradictory, or monstrous, it would be to say to somebody "you have a *natural* mind" in Dick's cosmos.

The Three Stigmata of Palmer Eldritch is as hectic and ragged a book as any Dick wrote, and is consequently much more dream-haunting and powerful than *High Castle*. It folds a muddle of different ideas together: a dystopic future-world from which people escape into childish games with dolls, illicitly enhanced by drugs; a programme to fast-forward human evolution; a messiah figure returning from Proxima Centauri who might be a malign alien. But its loose ends tangle creatively with its core conceits. (Why is Leo Bulero, supposedly an übermensch "evolved" human, so simple-minded and deliberate? How exactly has Eldritch managed to travel to and from Proxima Centurai so rapidly? Why do the Can-D users need the Barbie-and-Ken-esque "Perky Pat" and "Walt" dolls to orchestrate their fantasy? Dick had been inspired by watching his kids playing with such dolls, noticing how thoroughly absorbed in their play they became, but that was precisely play, and had no need of drugs; drug-addicts on the other hand have no need of toys to enable their highs; that's what the *drugs* are for. Dick's 'Days of Perky Pat' combination conceit falls between the two stools. That's not to say, of course, that it doesn't, somehow, weirdly, *work* ...)

This novel is about many things, not least a sort of consensual-reality accessed via this 'Can-D' drug, or an alternate pharmakon, seemingly alien in provenance, called Chew-Z. There is something sacramental about this, although the symbolism is never heavy-handed. It's possible that the conceit looks ramshackle to modern eyes: we might, for instance, say that we are more likely to be persuaded by an electrocephalic mass-consensual reality, like the Wachowski's *Matrix*, but even then, we recall, entry was effected via a red pill, and food remains a semiological focus throughout the film. Perhaps this bespeaks the oral, rather than anal, bias of SF's imaginative fantasy: we might, for instance, wonder why the SF-loving Comic Book Store Guy in *The Simpsons* is quite so *fat*... 'It's an oral thing,' Dick's Leo Bulero notes [p. 392]. In *VALIS* (1981) Dick made it clear he knew what the German word for *fat* was. He was himself, of course, a fairly slim man.

Indeed, there is something lean and hungry about Dick's fiction. Food is rarely described in his novels; family meals, or feasts, never. (Drinking is a different matter.) It's an intriguing absence, and has to do, I think, with PKD's suspicion about *possession*, something he viewed as equally desirable and unachievable. When we eat something we make it unambiguously *ours*. You and I may bicker over who owns this chocolate biscuit, but once I wolf it down into my belly the debate is over. This is one reason why the pleasures of eating and drinking retain their childish intensity; that portion of our lives when possessing things, and not letting others get their hands on them, can be so vitally important. But it is at the very heart of Dick's vision that things we assume are ours are rarely, if ever, so; not external goods (the material commodities of *Ubik*), but not even the intimate parts of our own bodies, or minds.

Descartes, famously, searching for one thing that he could absolutely and certainly call his own, lighted joyfully on the *cogito ergo sum*. It something he was sure no malicious demon could take away from him. But Dick, famously, is an *anti*-Descartes. He approaches 'I think therefore I am' with the devastating and brilliant *woah*: why do you assume that the thoughts in your head are *yours*? It's an index to the centrality of the Cogito to Western thought as a metaphysical cornerstone, or guarantee, just how unsettling this brilliant, penetrating question can be.

The punch of *Palmer Eldritch* is, in the end, the nightmare of being trapped in somebody else's imaginary world. It reflects upon the nature of literature: the horror of finding oneself a slave to the artist or writer; the sacrament of art that, by entering the body, locks us in. That existential claustrophobia, something he captured as expertly as any 20th-century writer (and which was one of the great themes of 20th-century art) finds particularly resonant expression in *Do Androids Dream*. Rick Deckard, the android-hunter, is surrounded by inauthenticity: his animals are fake; his wife's emotions are decanted into her from a machine; he can't be sure if the people around him are actual or artificial; the god of his religion is nothing more than an elderly actor performing a role.

It's conventional to observe how very different the movie adaptation, *Blade Runner*, is from the original novel, a position that can perhaps be overstated. But as far as this realization of existential claustrophobia goes it holds true. Ridley Scott, trying to find a visual correlative for the novel's sense of claustrophobia, rendered it literally: all those choking streets, crowds, dark, narrow spaces. Dick's instincts were cleverer: his hemmed-in characters exist, counter-intuitively but *rightly*, in the echoing, enormous, empty spaces of a mostly

Adam Roberts

abandoned planet. Scott's replicants, with time's winged chariot hurrying near behind them, are *pressured* to act in the desperate and cruel ways they do. Dick's androids, on the other hand, exist in a weirdly flattened, opened-out world, where vacancy and spaciousness is an externalization of a much more horrifying open-ended moral possibility, a universe in which we can do anything, good or bad, without sanction or support.

Another thing the movie could find no space for is the book's weird and wonderfully dislocating faux-religion Mercerism. It occupies a good deal of the novel, centred on its pointless mystery-that-is-no-mystery, the actor-playing-the-messiah of Mercer himself, set in the stony open-skied wasteland of existential openness. It seems to me that this is why Dick's styling of the androids as essentially children (the scene in which Pris indulges in the peculiarly infantile torture of cutting off a spider's legs has not lost its power to shock) works so well: children, generally speaking, inhabit worlds where authority is close, personal, intimate; parents or guardians never far away, God the Father living in their childish heads as versions of the same principle. Dick's androids are like the children in *Lord of the Flies*, only more so, because they do not have the conventional structures of social morality to lose. The novel as a whole is 170pages that feel, in a good way, like 600.

The fourth novel in this compendium, *Ubik*, is probably the best of the lot, and a superbly controlled piece of work; or rather an expertly *un*controlled tumbling down the mountainside of SF and metaphysics. Joe Chip, a commercial precog, gets caught up in a tangled commercial espionage plot in a world where household appliances have minds of their own, people survive death in denuded cryonic 'half-life' form, and the future – all our futures, death – haunts the present. He survives an attempt on his life, but finds a series of weird things happening in the world. In particular, entropic forces seem to be manifesting in malign and illogical ways: milks curdles unnaturally rapidly; Chip's futuristic car, for instance, changes into a 1939 LaSalle, and then into a 1929 Model-A Ford; an advanced radio becomes a clunky device with valves. Spraying a mystic aerosol called 'Ubik' helps hold off this degeneration, but its effects are not permanent. The titular 'Ubik', indeed, seems to be all commodities: chapter epigraphs wittily ring the ad-copy changes, from 'the best way to ask for a beer is to sing out Ubik' via 'wake up to a hearty, lip-smacking bowlful of nutritious nourishing Ubik' to, finally,

28

the apotheosis of this ubiquitous principle of commercial exchange: 'I am Ubik. Before the universe was, I am. I made the suns. I made the worlds [...] I am. I shall always be.' [p. 797]. In the light of this helter-skelter deconstruction of the props of modern capitalist existence, the snake-biting-its-tail plot of whether Chip survived the bomb blast or whether it killed him trapping him in a half-life nightmare, though perfectly well-handled, doesn't really seem somehow *central*.

Ubik not only feels like a longer novel than its 180pages; it feels like several different novels in superposition. It is, for example, one of the most original spins on the time-travel premise of its era, as Dick's characters uncertainly seem (or perhaps, do) slide backwards through the 20th century. It is, as is most of Dick's fiction, an attempt at a metaphysical novel, in this case interrogating the place of Platonic idealism in a commodified world. It's also fast-paced futuristic spy-thriller, with characters batting between Earth and the moon, getting into fights and explosions and life-or-death chases. Then again it works well as a comic novel, with some superbly funny, satirical sequences. The scene where Chip cannot leave his own apartment until he pays the money his snooty door insists is its fee ('what I pay you,' Chip argues, 'is in the nature of a gratuity; I don't *have* to pay you.' 'I think otherwise,' the door said. 'Look in the purchase contract you signed when you bought this conapt,' p. 629) is famous; but there are lots of similar, underplayed examples. Medical care on the moon is free, we're told, although 'the burden of proof that he is genuinely ill rests on the shoulders of the alleged patient,' [p. 665]. I also liked Dick's sly snook-cocking at some of the conventions of pulp SF, for instance its habit of replacing contemporary profanity with nonsensical supposedly-futuristic ejaculations ('Who cares about the money? Snirt the money!' p. 623).

Re-reading these four novels was a stirring experience. It is a reminder of the fact that for Dick, though not for lesser writers, the point of art is not to represent reality, nor to improve it, but in some salutary sense to *break* it; to work towards some sort of explosive point of spilling-out, or generic transcendence. And the recommendation: the Library of America *Four Novels of the 1960s* is a simply splendid little volume, one of the best ways of accessing four of Dick's best novels. These black covers have swallowed four major novels, but the spine is slender and the meal only expands in the reader's mind. It's a pleasure to note that July 08 will see the publication of a follow-up volume, again edited by Lethem, containing *Martian Time-Slip* (1964), *Dr Bloodmoney* (1965), *Now Wait for Last Year* (1966), *Flow My Tears, the Policeman Said* (1974) and *A Scanner Darkly* (1977). Five of the longest short novels published.

Philip K Dick, *VALIS and Later Novels*

(Library of America , 2009)

You are sitting on the train, or walking in the park, or perhaps you open your front door to an unexpected knock, when a stranger tells you: 'I have had a divine revelation! God spoke to me! I have seen through the veil of illusion to the truth! Let me tell you about it!' What's your reaction?

I daresay for most people it would be negative (a heart sinking, an inward 'oh *no!*'), not primarily from fear of physical harm – although of course there is cultural pressure to regard nutters as actively dangerous – but from fear of *boredom*. This is the great secret of madness, one obscured by the doctrine of 'creative madness': its banality. For every Tasso, Christopher Smart, or William Blake, whose madness generates art of visionary beauty and power, there are countless thousands whose madness generates only screeds of barren verbiage, monotonous regurgitations of leaden 'spiritual' or paranoiac fantasies that lack for us precisely the one thing – the shine of genuine transcendence – that make them so compelling to the sufferer.

To say so is to fly in the face of one of the most persistent of post-Romantic aesthetic notions; not only that true art requires a Rimbaudian derangement of bourgeois sensibilities but more specifically that insanity provides the clearest and most direct mechanism of achieving this derangement. The bald truth, though, is otherwise. Religious mania is a case in point. We are not *frightened* of doorstopping Jehovah's Witnesses, earnest Mormons, or stare-eyed Moonies, so much as we are *wearied* by them. The internet has made this state of affairs more acute. There are so many thousands of websites set up by individuals in the grip of incontinent Biblical hermeneutimania, or giving substance to frothing projection of personal moral crotchets onto the world outside. Of course, SF owns a mansion overlooking this Niagara of hysteria – David Icke's very SFnal alien lizard conspiracy theory is as much a spiritual insanity as it is anything else. There aren't enough bookshelves in the world to accommodate all the books published on Atlantis, UFOs, alien-gods, and other SFnal collages of cod-religious musing. Nor is this necessarily mere harmless eccentricity;

think of Marshall Herff Applewhite and his Heavens Gate UFO cult.

Of course, there is the possibility that you will greet the stranger on the train, or the knocker at the door, with an open heart. Perhaps you share their view that the real world is a trembling skein of illusion. You say to yourself, 'Who knows, maybe they're *not* David Icke; maybe they *actually are* a new Daniel or Isaiah.' Which is to say, perhaps you believe even the crankiest crank deserves the benefit of the doubt. But that phrase doesn't fit this context very well. Doubt is not the currency of pavement prophets and lithium visionaries. Even Philip K. Dick, the God-Emperor of uncertainty, knocked his metaphorical skull against the bullying force of the loony mystic vision. His revelations came into conflict with his art, and this was because his genius as a writer (and genius is not too strong a word) actually depended upon his apprehension of the world as fundamentally *dubitable*. This is not to say that he ever acquired certainty as to the world's precise meaning, even after he became a 'visionary,' but it is to suggest that his visionary period diluted the alienation, *corroded* his dubiety. He was never able to determine what it all meant, but he came to believe, at the end of his career, *that* it all meant.

The something-that-happened to Philip K. Dick that had so profound an impact on him, and his art, began in early 1974. Although religion had played a complex and sometimes hectic role in his imaginative (and actual) life before this, 1974 represented a step-change for his highly strung sensibility. Let's avail ourselves of those wonderfully useful orthographic hooks, scare quotes, and say that 'God' began speaking to him in a beam of pink light, and also out of the Beatles' song 'Strawberry Fields.' Amongst many other things 'God' told him that 1st-century Rome and 20th-century California existed in a supratemporal superposition, that Dick himself was actually the apostle Simon, or perhaps Thomas (a 1st-century Christian, or else a thought-control device implanted by the CIA), or a spirit entity called Firebright, or Buddha; told him his kid had a hernia; and told him that the FBI and the Moscow KGB (the latter via a long-distance telepathic ray) were persecuting him. These messages, he believed, emanated from a 'Vast Active Living Intelligence System' located in outer space. Dick, who before he was anything —even before he was a new messiah – was a *writer*, responded to this circumstance in the first instance precisely by writing. He scribbled half a million words of account, analysis, and interpretation; a document known as the *Exegesis* (only small selections of this have been published, posthumously). He also cast the material in fictional, or autobiographically semi-fictional form, in a late burst of creative writing – most notably the *VALIS* trilogy: *VALIS* (1981), *The Divine Invasion* (1980), *The Transmigration of Timothy Archer* (1982).

Library of America's new edition of this trilogy (together with an earlier but similarly religious-themed novel, 1970's *A Maze of Death*) follows their two very successful previous anthologies of Dickian fiction, both, like this, edited by the estimable Jonathan Lethem. The first (*Four Novels of the 1960s*) appeared in 2007, the second (*Five Novels of the 1960s and 1970s*) in 2008. *VALIS and Later Novels* is as handsome a piece of book-production as the previous two: neatly printed on onionskinny paper (acid-free lightweight opaque) and bound in cloth boards: both durable and readable. It's not flawless, mind. Unusually for LoA the text contains uncorrected typos ('isreally' for 'is really,' p. 188; 'arc' for 'are,' p. 209) and Lethem's annotation is a little eccentrically applied. He gives us hundreds and hundreds of words, and several pages, of gloss on a throwaway reference to 'the T34 tank and the battle of Kursk' [p. 198], but no footnote at all to explain references such as – to pick a few examples from *VALIS* –'Hermes Trismegistus' [p. 451], 'splenolus' [p. 479], 'Bialik' [p. 482], 'amicus curae' [p. 511], or many others. But you might think that such eccentricity suits the volume. Certainly, if you have more than a passing interest in PKD, these are the editions you will want to own.

As with the earlier volumes, LoA house-style means no introduction or preface, although a detailed 15-page chronology fills in some of the necessary biographical background. Here's Lethem's account of the events of 1974:

> In February, after oral surgery for an impacted wisdom tooth, during which he is given sodium pentothal, [PKD] experiences the first of a sequence of overwhelming visions that will last through and intensify during March, then taper intermittently throughout the year. Interpretation of these revelations, which are variously ascribed to benign and malign influences both religious and political (including but not limited to God, Gnostic Christians, the Roman Empire, Bishop Pike [a friend of Dick's who had died in 1969], and the KGB), will preoccupy Dick for much of his remaining life. 'It hasn't spoken a word to me since I wrote *The Divine Invasion*. The voice is identified as Ruah, which is the Old Testament word for the Spirit of

> God. It speaks in a feminine voice and tends to express statements
> regarding the messianic expectation. It guided me for a while. It has
> spoken to me sporadically since I was in high school. I expect that if
> a crisis arises it will say something again...' He begins writing
> speculative commentary on what he comes to call '2-3-74.' [pp. 833-
> 34]

VALIS gives a detailed account of all this, skewed only minimally into
fictional form. The book's deuteragonists are 'Philip Dick' and an alter
ego named, in a piece of rather tiresome etymological whimsy (via the
Greek of PKD's first name, and the *Deutsch* of his surname)
'Horselover Fat.' I suppose we can be thankful it wasn't Equinophile
Thick. This schizoid conceit is leavened by some metafictional play,
such that the details of 'Philip Dick's life (unmarried and childless) do
not map onto those of the actual Philip K. Dick; 'Horselover Fat,' at
one point, ceases to exist. In the novel Fat is the one who has the
revelation from God, and he, together with Dick and a couple of other
friends, try to make sense of it. They finds clues buried in a commercial
motion picture, called *Valis*, made by a rock star 'Eric Lampton', and
his wife Linda – based upon Bowie's *The Man Who Fell to Earth*. In the
novel, though, Fat, Dick and friends visit Lampton and meet a
preternaturally eloquent young girl called 'Sophia' (that is: 'wisdom'). It
seems that the messiah is actually in the world; but then Sophia dies,
and Fat goes off around the world to uncover the 'fifth' saviour.

Some critics think very highly of *VALIS*. I must demur. When I
first read it, last century, I found it sticky and rather baffling. Re-reading
it in this edition I think I've identified what the problem is. It is
massively boring. The reader must become as fascinated with the
scattershot minutiae of Dick's mania or else she will find herself
abandoned in a wilderness of barren assertion and speculation. To be
precise, there *is* an interesting novel struggling somewhere under this
crush of unpalatable horseflesh – a novel that does for 1970s California
religious excess what *A Scanner Darkly* does for 1970s West Coast drug
culture. But its ankles are broken, and its heart gives out trying to
transport Dick's dead-weight 'Exegesis,' undigested chunks of which,
some very lengthy, litter the text. What's so indigestible about this
material is its beady-eyed seriousness: 'The Sybil of Cumae protected
the Roman Republic,' we are told: 'in the first century C.E. she foresaw
the murders of the Kennedy brothers, Dr King and Bishop Pike.' To

which the likeliest response is, 'no, she didn't.' The worst of it is von Däniken-lite:

> The primordial source of all our religions lies with the ancestors of the Dogon tribe, who got their cosmogony directly from the three eyed invaders who visited long ago. The three eyed invaders are mute and deaf and telepathic, could not breathe our atmosphere, had the elongated misshapen skull of Ikhnaton, and emanated from a planet in the star-system Sirius. [pp. 396-7]

But a good deal of it is Dick's own mystic-mumbo-jumbo cosmic narrative; 'Two realms there are, upper and lower. The upper, derived from hyperuniverse I or Yang, Form I of Parmenides, is sentient and volitional. The lower realm, or Yin, Form II of Parmenides, is mechanical, driven by blind, efficient cause' [p. 283]; 'the psyche of hyperuniverse I sent a micro-form of itself into hyperuniverse II to attempt to heal it. The microform was apparent in our universe as Jesus Christ' [p. 255]; 'Real time ceased in 70 C.E. with the fall of the temple at Jerusalem. It began again in 1974 C.E. The intervening period was a perfectly spurious interpolation aping the creation of the Mind' [p. 322]. Archaic syntax ('two realms there are') recurs like a nervous tic; as do liberal sprinklings of Latin (pretentiously, PKD subtitles his 'Exegesis' *Tractates Cryptica Scriptura*), both symptomatic of autodidact unselfconfidence, a kind of overcompensation. It backfires – these things don't actually lend gravitas or a sense of timelessness, they just look nervily pretentious. Quite apart from anything else, timelessness and gravitas are not the currency of Dick's visions: 'He came across a part of the *Book of Daniel* which he believed depicted Nixon. "In the last days of those kingdoms,/When their sin is at its heart,/A king shall appear, harsh and grim, a master of stratagem"' [p. 319]. Little dates so rapidly, and catastrophically, as politically specific interpretations of Biblical prophecy.

It is true that *VALIS* considers multiple possible explanations for 2-3-74, including the idea that Dick (or 'Fat') is simply insane; but the book rejects this on the counter-intuitive grounds that such a diagnosis would be 'reassuring.' The focus here is whether 2-3-74 is a function of one consciousness, or of the nature of reality itself, and we're left in no doubt that Dick considers the latter the right explanation. 'It didn't matter what the explanation was,' says Dick; 'what had now been established was that Fat's March 1974 experience was real' [p. 318]. He qualifies himself immediately ('Okay; it mattered what the explanation was') but refuses to give up the reality: 'at least one thing had been proved: Fat might be clinically crazy but he was locked into reality – a reality of some kind, although certainly not the normal one' [p. 318]. This is demoralizing stuff for any true Dick-head. The sense that what in earlier PKD had been a brilliant, intuitive deconstruction of the conventional model of 'illusion-and-reality' (that, in a nutshell, it really is turtles all the way down) has here been decanted back into old Gnostic bottles. Though our reality is false there *is* a true reality just behind the veil. 'It had now been proved...' is a little startling, too, suggesting as it does not only that Dick has a looser sense of 'proof' than most people, but that he rated 'proof,' in that sense, at all.

In sum, *VALIS* is a novel of prodigious, almost heroic tedium. To say so, actually, is not entirely to dismiss it. On the contrary, we might want to argue that this actually grounds the book's distinctiveness. Istvan Csicsery-Ronay, probably the best critic ever to write on PKD, puts it very well:

> For Dick the connections amongst religious gnosis, ethical double-blinds and mental disturbances were drawn ever tighter as his career progressed. In this he shared one of the cherished beliefs of his beloved German Romantics. But Dick's gods are not remote, magnificent aliens; they work on the most prosaic level conceivable. There is no sublime in Dick's fiction. Nature has all but disappeared. For Dick, banality is as much an aspect of our fallen state as death is. [Csicsery-Ronay, review of *Philip K. Dick: Contemporary Critical Interpretations* by Samuel J. Umland; *Science Fiction Studies*, 22:3 [1995], p. 431]

It's difficult to think of another writer, or theologian, who gives us this insight into precisely the *ordinariness* of religious revelation – a thrilling banality perhaps, but a banality nonetheless. The overwhelming majority of the world's population have religious beliefs of one sort or another, after all. Divine revelation is, in fact, the most ordinary human thing of all. *VALIS*'s scrambled narrative, littered with facts from Dick's free-associative reading, formally embodies a kind of *messiness* of revelation, one that tugs sharply against his putative urge towards oppressive pantheist unity ('One Mind there is... the Immortal One whom we worship without knowing his name'). In the mess, and at the prosaic level, are those portions of the novel it is easier to love: some deft characterization differentiating Dick/Fat's friends; some natty dialogue, some leavening humour. But they are the parts furthest away from the bindweed of 2-3-74 and its elaboration, and the latter chokes the novel.

But a shift of balance of the treatment of exactly the same material only a little, the elevation of contingency to the level of plot and the downplaying of the bullying interpretive instinct, makes *The Divine Invasions* a much more effective novel. Conceived by Dick as a sequel to *VALIS*, it recasts the exegetical material as a more palatably distanced science fictional narrative. Herb Asher, a Dick-figure, lives in an individual dome on the planet CY30 II. In the next dome along is Rybys Ronmey. She, although suffering from cancer and despite being a virgin, is pregnant with the new messiah. The prophet Elija informs the two of them that they must smuggle the child to Earth, but this is no easy task. Earth is governed by a combined Communist party/Christian church organisation, the followers of which mistakenly worship the wicked demiurge instead of the true god. Global governance is effected via 'Big Noodle,' a sort of sentient Internet. Herb and Rybys fly to Earth and get past customs, but their air-taxi crashes, killing Rybys and putting Herb in a coma, in which he relives his former life on CY30 II. The child, though, is transferred to a synthetic womb; it is born, named Emmanuel, and goes to school. The authorities think it suffered brain damage as a result of the accident, although actually it is God who has deliberately forgotten His divinity.

This all works better because it is able to dramatise the ordinariness of its messianic premise: a dramatically compelling sense of divine contingency and precariousness. It's still a fairly ropey novel, mind you: the Marxist-theological world government material is never very believable, and its storyline (conspiracy and plotting) poorly integrated into the plot; and the shape of the story, which shoves the novel into a showdown conclusion, rather undersells the sly comedy and existential slapstick of the first half. But the book's uniquely Dickian associative leaps more often than not redeem its imaginarium from conventionality. The wicked god-of-this-world, Belial, appears conventionally enough as a bestial goat-creature – but then, neatly, Dick reimagines him as an enormous, broken, luminous *kite*. Most of all, it does not bore the reader.

Timothy Archer, a 'mainstream' novel rather than an SF text, is also very far from boring, although it is rather unlike the other two *VALIS* trilogy novels, covering rather different ground in a considerably more rational and controlled tone. Archer is based on Dick's friend, the Episcopalian bishop of California James Pike, who had died in the Middle East in 1969, searching for historical evidence of Christ's life. The novel is narrated by Archer's daughter-in-law Angel, and her voice inoculates the novel against the contagion of the virulent boredom of the 2-3-74 matter. It still informs the book, but in a much less oppressive way than is the case for *VALIS*. It is, like that earlier book, littered with intellectual lumber, orts and scraps of literature, philosophy, and theology picked up by Dick in his omnivorous reading, but here the intellectual superstructure does not overbalance the characters or the story.

The real theme of the book is the effect the dead have upon the lives, and souls, of the living, and the replacement of SF elements with more sociologically observed spiritual components – prayer, séance, ghostly possession—is, whilst not wholly free of the taint of the loonies, much more fictively effective. The low level anguish of Archer's existence – his affair with one of Angel's friends, his alienation from his church, the suicide of his son – comes over as compelling precisely because Dick avoids the grandiose idiom of *VALIS*. By the same token, and unlike *Divine Invasion*, the novel cannot quite stir up the antic, peculiar, creative turbulence that characterizes Dick at his best. It would be nice to call this novel, the last Dick published, his 2-3-74 masterpiece, not least because, in contrast to the consciously or unconsciously poisonous female characters of the other books it has, in Angel, a properly rounded woman. But it fails to come alight.

A Maze of Death is perhaps a strange choice for a fourth text to include in this compendium (*Flow My Tears* or *A Scanner Darkly* would have been a better fit if they hadn't already been included in Lethem's 2008 volume; but wouldn't *Radio Free Albemuth* or *Lies, Inc.* have made more sense here?). Not that its republication is unwelcome. Written and published long before 2-3-74, it is wonderfully ramshackle stuff, with the genuine, animating Dickian tang. Characters living in a universe where God is a scientific fact, accessibly through a real and material 'intercessor', gather on a dead-end planet called Delmak-O; they are supposed to be settlers, but actually spend their time bickering amongst themselves whilst, one by one, members of the group are murdered.

Trying to get to the bottom of this unpleasant turn of events, they journey into the jungle and find a strange motile city which each of them perceives differently. They ask an oracular native form of life various questions about their predicament and get undigested chunks of the I Ching in reply. One character, Seth Morley, comes to believe that Delmak-O is a sham, and that they are actually on Earth. This appears more and more likely, until the moment Dick pulls an ill-judged 'it was all a dream!' twist-ending out of the hat: the characters discover that they are trapped on a marooned spacecraft, passing the time in an immersive virtual reality.

It sounds odd to say it, but the novel's best feature is precisely its clumsiness, or perhaps it would be better to say its *artlessness*. Given that God is a real presence in this cosmos, it's striking how rubbish everything is. The characters exist in a quaintly dated-even-by-1970s-standards future – Seth dissects a miniature robotic device using a microscope and discovers 'resistors, condensers, valves' [75] – full of shonky kit (like disposable spaceships designed for one-way travel), incompetence, and amateurism. Much of the novel has an endearingly fumbling, made-up-on-the-spot vibe, and compared to the post 2-3-74 novels its theology is deceptively simple. Rather sweetly, Dick adds a po-faced preface:

> The theology of this novel is not an analog of any known religion. It stems from an attempt made by William Sarill and myself to develop an abstract, logical system of religious thought based on the arbitrary postulate that God exists.

Since the theology of the novel, as a fictional gloss on Episcopalian Christianity, could hardly be more conventional – between God and Man stands an intercessor motivated by love and ready to offer forgiveness to those who approach him – I take this to be ironic. In point of fact nothing in this novel is 'abstract, logical, and systematic.' It would hardly be so wonderful if it were. (I believe in the Flying Spaghetti monster, but I shall put my belief aside and erect an abstract, logical system of religious thought rigorously derived from the arbitrary postulate that God exists. Well, since there's a God s/he must be fundamental, hence superstrings, hence spaghetti. And since s/he intervenes in the universe s/he must have a means of doing so, hence a noodly appendage. And voilà, purely by disinterested logic I have arrived back where I started.) It may be jerry-built, but at least this novel escapes the curse of 'One Mind there is' 2-3-74ism.

There remains a taboo in Philip K. Dick scholarship about using the 'm' word. Here's Gregg Rickman:

> I do not think Phil Dick was mad, or crazy, or any of those lovely labels some are anxious to apply. *Anxious to apply as then he would be explained away*; and then the power of his visions, the piercing clarity of his writing, at its finest, the way his best works demonstrate that it is *our time* which is out of joint: then he will be dismissible. (*To the High Castle: Philip K. Dick, a life, 1928-1962* [1989], p. xxiii)

The rather awkward sarcasm of 'lovely' aside, this follows Dick's exegetical lead that explaining 2-3-74 in terms of 'madness' would be in some sense 'reassuring' or 'too convenient.' I confess I don't see that it would. 'Mad' has no more dismissive or explanatory power as a word, than does, say, visionary. Besides, 'visionary' (the blurb on the back of this volume calls Dick 'an irreplaceable American visionary') doesn't seem to me to characterize Dick's later books very well. For one thing he is simply not a writer who foregrounds the visual; and for another, his emphasis is rarely on the transcendent moment itself. He is much more interested in the ancillary, belated conversational and discursive attempts to make sense of peculiar experience.

It is a mistake to think that 'madness' has anything in common with 'nonsensical.' On the contrary, a too-strenuous effort precisely to *make sense* is most characteristic of madness. Certainly that intellectually fidgety, remorseless, *tedious* process governs these later books. Calling Dick 'mad' is neither to explain away nor dismiss his work, because the madness, or otherwise, of the author is really beside the point. It is the effectiveness of the art that matters here. My problem with Dick's post 2-3-74 writing is that, irrespective of the state of mind of the author, it lacks the metaphorical clarity of Dick's best 1960s writing. Indeed, the *VALIS* trilogy positively revels in opacity. There are, I daresay, readers who find in these novels' explosion of chaff an eloquent articulation of a genuinely divine cloud of unknowing. I don't.

Blade Runner

(directed by Ridley Scott, 1982)

My favourite line in the whole of cinema: 'Chew: if only you could see
what I have seen with your eyes.' It's because of Rutger Hauer's
overtelegraphed wide-eyed slow paced delivery – he's only a kid, after
all, though in a man's body (and us? the golden age of science fiction is
a kid's age, though the majority of us fans sport adult bodies). But
mostly it is because this line distils the whole film, and the whole *of*
film, into one beautiful image. We watch through Ridley Scott's eyes –
utilising the basic pleasure model that is cinema itself – and wonders are
revealed. It chills us, as Chew is chilled; sends shivers through our
torso. It warms us too. So, I don't mind the plot, although it doesn't
entirely make sense. And I don't mind the premise and the
worldbuilding, all the peculiarly suggestive, though half-digested,
chunks of Dick's original novel (the parades of emus being led through
the crowd scenes; the huge droning advert blimps; 'Methuselah
syndrome' instead of Mercerism; the huge empty building in which J
Sebastian lives – real estate from a deserted world that is situated in the
midst of what, in other portions of the film, is evidently a massively
overcrowded city). I don't at all mind the action sequences, Ford and
Hauer's mannered acting pavane. But I *love* what the film's mechanical
eye lets me see.

In fact, this is what links all the films I love the most: they manifest
what I take to be a new cultural logic in SF. The genre has shifted from
being a literature of ideas (books are good at ideas) to a literature of
enduring, powerful and haunting visual *images* (films are poor at ideas,
but very good at the poetry of beautiful images). This is what *La Jetée*,
2001: A Space Odyssey, *Stalker*, *Alien* and *The Matrix* have in common –
their gobsmacking *visual* aesthetic. But *Blade Runner* beats all of these. It
is the most beautiful, the most haunting, the most visually perfect of all
of them. It is Scott's expert conjuring with near-palpable beams and
shafts of light amongst the cluttered, smoky and misty darkness; the
shadows blocking out a somatically believable city; the gorgeous design;
the *detail*.

And the title. *Blade Runner*, I need hardly remind you, was originally
the name for a completely different film (a Burroughs script based on

an Alan E Nourse novel: smugglers running medical supplies, including scalpels, in a dystopic future America). I won't rehearse the complicated process by which Dick's original *Do Androids Dream of Electric Sheep?* got altered: androids too cheesy and old-fashioned for the go-ahead 80s; *Do Replicants Dream?* liable to baffle rather than intrigue moviegoers. *Blade Runner* imported into the script as a description of what Harrison Ford's Deckard does for a living – don't it sound action-adventure, though? Don't it sound *kinetic* and *chasing-about-y* and *living on the edge?* The irony is this: it turns out the film's title *is* well chosen, although not for those reasons. Indeed, there is at first blush little of the *blade* about Scott's imagined future. On the contrary, it's all very satisfyingly chunky. Those fat guns the cops use; the cars – the cars may fly, but they're too obviously regular cars with lumps of plastic glued onto them to make them look like polygonic versions of themselves – the blocky pyramidic architecture; the very *un*-pared down clutter and thuddiness of the city.

Several critics have explored the extent to which Blade Runner is about eyes: the opening shot of the city reflected in Deckard's eyeball; the Voigt-Kampf test shining its light into subjects eyes; the artificial owl whose eyes gleam red; the machine in Deckard's flat that seems to be able to magnify Leon's photograph (seeing, you see) endlessly without encountering pixels or graininess. Not to mention poor old Chew in his refrigerated eye laboratory. Not to mention the Lear-like moment when Roy squeezes out Tyrell's eyeballs with his thumbs. It's about seeing and the *physicality* of seeing.

Put blades and eyes together and we think: *Un Chien Andalou.* And that's exactly right: what was for Dalí's film precisely a *surreal* logic becomes, under the aegis of science fiction, a kind of Baudrillardian *hyper*real: the same peculiar juxtapositions, the swarms of pygmies dashing through crowded city streets; Gant's gibberish street talk; the generic mash-up of futuristic SF, 30s noir styling, action-adventure and even (Ford's turn as the morality inspector looking for 'little peepholes' in the snake-dancer's dressing room) comedy; the way other sequences from entirely different films (the unicorn from Scott's *Legend*, the road from Kubrick's *The Shining*) keep intruding themselves. All this keeps alive the logic of surrealism; except that SF refreshes that logic, naturalises it and thereby makes it much more invasively deratiocinating and effective. What runs in *Blade Runner* is not Deckard, but *film itself,* hurtling through the gate with its blade-sharp edge. Or spinning (to get modern) even more rapidly in place whilst a blade-sharp laser picks the visuals from its minutely, ornately detailed surface. What runs is the apotheosis of the visual imagination; the sharpness of it. It is what SF can do better than any other form of art.

J G Ballard RHUL Honorary Degree Citation

[*On the 15th July 2009 my college, Royal Holloway University of London, awarded a posthumous honorary degree to J G Ballard. I was asked to write and deliver the citation.*]

Principal, the news of J G Ballard's death on the 19th of April this year, though grievous, was not unexpected. His last published book, the memoir *Miracles of Life: Shanghai to Shepperton* (2008) ends with a dispassionate account of the prostate cancer which, metastasising to his ribs and spine, killed him. The writing is wholly without self-pity, and possesses the unsettling clarity and intensity that is characteristic of all his work.

I present him to you for an Honorary Degree of the University of London. The reason for this honour is, simply, his outstanding contribution to literature.

James Graham Ballard was born in Shanghai in 1930. Whilst still a child he was interned in a Japanese civilian World War II POW camp. He came to the UK in 1946, and from the 1950s onward wrote a unique kind of science fiction, inflected by avant-garde, Surrealist and 1960s pop artistic sensibilities. Rarely concerned with alien monsters or distant worlds, the real theme of Ballard's SF was 'inner space' (he is sometimes credited with coining the term). As he declared in 1962: 'the only truly alien planet is Earth.'

His first four novels were powerful, poetic reimaginings of that old genre standby, the end of the world: *The Drowned World* (1962) and *The Crystal World* (1966) are particularly notable, treating their planet-devouring catastrophes as eerily beautiful processes of unfathomable transformation. A prolific writer with the knack of crafting masterpieces, he had by the late 1970s established a reputation as the laureate of the unnerving. Unnerved readers sometimes reacted with outrage. His collection *The Atrocity Exhibition* (1969) was tried for obscenity in the USA; and his stunning novel *Crash* (1973), with its potent blend of explicit pornography and lovingly-described traffic-accident violence, retains its power to shock even today. But of course a writer as revolutionary as Ballard could never be uncontroversial. From 1960 to his death Ballard lived in Shepperton, and the landscape of Surrey figures largely in his 1970s fiction, transformed either to dystopian grimness in *Concrete Island* (1974) and *High-Rise* (1975); or else, in *The Unlimited Dream Company* (1979), fantastically metamorphosed into an exotic, hyperfertile dream-jungle. *Empire of the Sun* (1984), a fictionalisation of his childhood wartime experiences, was a bestseller, and was filmed by Stephen Spielberg in 1987. Though sometimes seen as a break from Ballard's science fictional mode, this novel is in fact the apotheosis of his SF aesthetic, a fantastical fable of the appalling beauty and persistent estrangement of 20th-century existence. Two masterpieces of late-period Ballard, set amongst the gated-communities and the sterile hedonisms of the super-rich do likewise: *Cocaine Nights* (1996) and *Super-Cannes* (2000), icily potent novels that paint worlds stranger than any interplanetary adventure.

Ballard turned down an MBE in 2006, describing the honours system as 'a Ruritanian charade that helps to prop up our top-heavy monarchy.' But he did not refuse honorary degrees from universities (he was awarded an honorary Dlitt from Loughborough) and he has particular associations with the University of London, where he briefly studied English at Queen Mary's College as a young man. Ballard is the most original and influential science fiction writer of the 20th century, and one of the most important Anglophone writers in any genre.

In recognition, therefore, of his outstanding contribution to Literature, and his association with the University of London, I invite you, Principal, to confer, posthumously, the Degree of Doctor of Literature Honoris Causa of the University of London on J G Ballard.

Ian Watson, *Warhammer 40,000: Inquisitor* (1990)

The Warhammer phenomena, both original and 40,000 flavour, passed me by as a teenager. I certainly knew people who were into it: the gaming, collecting the figurines and painting them by hand, poring over *White Dwarf*, loitering in Games Workshop shops with other teenage boys. Looking back, I'm not sure why it passed me by; I ought, perhaps, to have been prime Warhammer material. As an undergraduate I shared a flat with three guys, one of whom was a heavy-duty *Star Fleet Battles* player, and another of whom had a large collection of hand-painted Warhammer miniatures. This latter gentlemen, towards the end of his third year, took his figurines to job interviews. 'You should see their faces,' he told us, delightedly, 'when I whip them out and put them on the table, halfway through the interview!' As I tried to picture their expressions, he went on, in a more solemn voice, that the figures demonstrated such exemplary indices of employability as 'dedication' and 'excellent hand-eye coordination' ('painting the details is *quite a challenge*,' he pointed out), which I suppose, in a sense, they did. I don't recall him actually getting any jobs, mind you. Although having said that, the individual in question was a medical student, and is now (I believe) a GP, so this strategy must have worked out for him at some point.

Why wasn't I like him? I don't think it was because I wasn't as geeky as he was. Indeed, I'd say something the reverse was true: it was that I was *too* geeky. Whatever else you may say about wargaming, hanging out in Games Workshop shops and the like, it is at least a *social* activity. If I'm honest I was happier without that awkward 'interacting with other human beings' component to my SF nerdery; more comfortable solus in my bedroom reading a book. But the appeal of miniatures is surely core to the appeal of SF more broadly. There's a rather fine Hilaire Belloc passage at the start 'The Inn of the Margeride' (from *The Hills and the Sea*, 1906) that gets to the heart of this, I think:

> Whatever, keeping its proportion and form, is designed upon a scale much greater or much less than that of our general experience, produces upon the mind an effect of phantasy.

A little perfect model of an engine or a ship does not only amuse or surprise; it rather casts over the imagination something of that veil through which the world is transfigured, and which I have called 'the wing of Dalua'; the medium of appreciations beyond experience; the medium of vision, of original passion and of dreams. The principal spell of childhood returns as we bend over the astonishing details. We are giants – or there is no secure standard left in our intelligence.

So it is with the common thing built much larger than the million examples upon which we had based our petty security. It has been always in the nature of worship that heroes, or the gods made manifest, should be men, but larger than men. Not tall men or men grander, but men transcendent: men only in their form; in their dimension so much superior as to be lifted out of our world. An arch as old as Rome but not yet ruined, found on the sands of Africa, arrests the traveller in this fashion. In his modern cities he has seen greater things; but here in Africa, where men build so squat and punily, cowering under the heat upon the parched ground, so noble and so considerable a span, carved as men can carve under sober and temperate skies, catches the mind and clothes it with a sense of the strange. And of these emotions the strongest, perhaps, is that which most of those who travel to-day go seeking; the enchantment of mountains; the air by which we know them for something utterly different from high hills. Accustomed to the contour of downs and tors, or to the valleys and long slopes that introduce a range, we come to some wider horizon and see, far off, a further line of hills. To hills all the mind is attuned: a moderate ecstasy. The clouds are above the hills, lying level in the empty sky; men and their ploughs have visited, it seems, all the land about us; till, suddenly, faint but hard, a cloud less varied, a greyer portion of the infinite sky itself, is seen to be permanent above the world. Then all our grasp of the wide view breaks down. We change. The valleys and the tiny towns, the unseen mites of men, the gleams or thread of roads, are prostrate, covering a little watching space before the shrine of this dominant and towering presence.

It is as though humanity were permitted to break through the vulgar illusion of daily sense, and to learn in a physical experience how unreal are all the absolute standards by which we build. It is as though the vast and the unexpected had a purpose, and that purpose were the showing to mankind in rare glimpses what places are designed for the soul – those ultimate places where things common become shadows and fail, and the divine part in us, which adores and desires, breathes its own air, and is at last alive.

I suppose this appeals to me because my own fiction is, or seems to be (since, believe me, I'm as surprised about this as *you* are), so obsessed with shifts in scale of precisely this sort: from human beings to giants; from giant to microbe-sized beings; models, Big Dumb Objects, detailed sketches and plans of other SF fiction, and the like. But it might be more apropos to relate the passage to the passion some SFF fans feel for miniatures. Perhaps the ground of this love is, precisely, a Bellocish sense of breaking through the vulgar illusion of daily sense (the combination, which wargaming figurines enable, of simultaneous *minute attention to details* and *large scale imaginative transcendence* – 'showing to mankind in rare glimpses what places are designed for the soul – those ultimate places where things common become shadows and fail, and the divine part in us, which adores and desires, breathes its own air, and is at last alive'. Or perhaps that's merely pseudish.

Anyhow, I came to this novel because I've been following up on my 'reading Ian Watson' plan, not because I'd developed any sudden middle-aged interest in Warhammer 40,000. But I must say: I was very pleasantly surprised. The story concerns the titular Inquisitor, one Jaq Draco, a sort of futuristic Witchfinder General in a human-led Galactic Empire, and his search to seek out and destroy 'heretics, mutants, aliens and demons'. These latter are manifestations of the forces of Chaos. They live in the 'warp dimension' through which spacecraft must travel, but are constantly breaking out into normal space to monstrous and destructive effect. The Galactic God-Emperor, in a centuries long coma and only kept alive by machine, in fact uses his prodigious willpower to sort-of-magically hold these forces at bay; but 'he is failing – just as the Imperium is failing, slowly and haphazardly but failing nonetheless.' The novel starts with an assault on a pernicious mutant presence infecting the weapon-factory world of 'Stalinvast.' We then follow Jaq and his three companions (the beautiful female assassin Meh'Lindi, the warp navigator and pilot Vitali Googol, and the Gimli-esque sidekick dwarf Grimm) as they scoot around the cosmos trying to get to the bottom of a conspiracy within a conspiracy, fighting all sorts of nasties, and generally having a great deal of monstrous fun. It's tosh, of course, but tosh of a exceptionally high calibre, and Watson gets the *tone* exactly right. In its own way, melodrama is very hard to write well, and the slightly fruity ponderousness of Watson's prose here (liberally sprinkled with exorcist's Latin) is just right.

Jaq arose at last, staggering slightly. Crossing to her, he extended a palm against her brow. She flinched momentarily. Extending his psychic sense, he spoke words of power in the hieratic ritual language. *In nomine imperatoris hominorum magistris ego te purgo et exorcizo. Apage, Chaos, apage!* [pp. 93-4]

Hmm; I wonder if the vocative of 'Chaos' *is* 'Chaos'? Shouldn't that be *Apage, Chao, apage?* No matter.

The warlock was a bloated, horned hermaphrodite draped in bilious green skin. Oozing sexual orifices puckered his/her sleeping belly. His/her long muscular tongue lashed and probed the air like a sense organ [...]Acrid musk saturated the air. Jewel tipped stalactites hung from the cavern roof, aglow like many little lamps. [p. 125]

So, yes, Watson takes his job here seriously; and the result is wholehearted and often genuinely effective intergalactic Gothic. The grand guignol is evocatively written, the story is engaging, the moral dilemma of the central character – a man who does terrible things, including ordering the destruction of an entire planet, genuinely in the service of what he believes to be the greater good – effective, if one-note. Not least, Watson grapples heroically with the task of suggesting the improbable scales of his preset cosmos within the confines of an 80,000-word tie-in novel. Especially early on, the prose is full of rather artful *Battleship Potemkin*-y touches that sketch-in the populousness and enormousness of everything. As space marines battle through the vast hive-like cities of Stalinvast millions are killed, and millions more flee, 'a river of humanity':

Below, the surge was growing ever denser as if that river had met a dam ahead. Moving walkways must have failed under the weight they bore. Bodies were conglomerating together, asphyxiating. Corpses were carried along, standing upright. The nimblest escapees hopped across the heads of the living and the dead, till a twisted ankle or a grasping angry hand brought them down [...] the very walls of the avenue seemed likely to burst. Upthrusts of men and women forced cones of tangled crushed bodies higher than the rest of the mass. The flood of tormented flesh appeared to be one single myriad-headed entity, which was now compressing itself insanely til eyes started, skin split, til blood vessels sprayed. [p. 35]

There's an E-E-Doc-Smithworthy profusion of modifiers such as 'vast', 'colossal', 'enormous'. Characters bicker over whose provenance is the largest ('You're the hereditary lord of a whole world,' Jaq found himself saying presently; 'whereas I'm the emissary from the lord of the entire galaxy!'). In all this the aesthetic is that of the model miniature: things which are notionally huge described from the point of view of something even huger, such that the detail acquires the feel of intricate, miniature detail:

> The Governor's sanctum was a leviathan suffused with the same dreary red light. Censers burned, further hazing the air. Goggled officials hunched over consoles around tiers of cantilevered wrought-iron galleries. Caged mutants with abnormally large eyes played complicated games on three dimensional boards.

Of *course* they did.

> At the heart of the enormous room an ornate marble building shaped like a pineapple squatted on a disc of steel. That disc must be a lifting platform which could raise and lower the Governor's sanctum sanctorum.

This sort of stuff replicates precisely the gamer's buzz; the Bellocish sense of occupying the minute and the gigantic simultaneously.

My ignorance of the larger Warhammer 40,000 universe means that I can't be sure which of the many very cool details here are Watson's inventions and which are common currency. But, as befits a novel spun-off from a product as much about intricate detail as cool design, this novel is both full of wonderful details and also a very efficient, well-designed piece of narrative space-hokey.

> Veils of sickly pigment draped the void in all directions, lurid, gangrenous, and mesmerizing, as if an insane artist had been set loose to paint, on a canvas, the kaleidoscope of his mad, shapeless nightmare. [p. 165]

This supplants my previous front-runner (the Lawrentian 'Suave Loins of Darkness') as Name of My Next Band: *Veils of Sickly Pigment* goes straight to the top of *that* list.

> Lightning forked across a jaundiced sky as if discharging the tensions between reality and irreality. Some clouds suppurated, dripping sticky ichor rather than rain. [p. 171]

It *has* been a disappointing summer so far, hasn't it?

> Other great buildings were giant mutated solo genitalia. Horned phallic towers arose, wrinkled, ribbed, blistered with window pustules. Cancerous breast domes swelled, fondled by scaly finger-buttresses. Tongue bridges linked these buildings. Scrotum pods swayed. [p. 183]

We recently moved house, and estate agents showed us several Scrotum Pod properties. Prince Charles has spoken out against them, I know, but I personally found them compact *and* affordable. Then there's the clothes! Splendid clothes!

> Weapons and other devices hung within Obsipal's blood-red high-collared cloak; and his belted black robe was appliquéd with glaring white death's heads. [p.19]

I honestly can't think of another Space Opera in which the main villain wears appliqué. Or later on:

> 'Wise Adeptus,' interrupted a beige-clad novice. [p. 226]

This isn't just beige, of course. It's *ironic* beige. Rarely has a novel been as luridly coloured as this one. Decadent excess oozes from every sentence. Our heroes fight bird-footed women: 'her body, clad in a chain-mail leotard trimmed with rosettes and puffs of gauze, was blanched and petite; her hair blonde and bounteous. Yet her feet were ostrich-claws, ornamented with topaz rings, her hands were chitinous, painted pincers' – and Watson knows perfectly well that the most startling thing about her is *the chain-mail leotard*. Evil takes the shape of a vast tentacular hydra composed partly of material ooze and partly of spirit energy from the warp (in a moment of icky quasi-hentai nastiness, Meh-Lindi is mind-raped by one of these tentacles). Beige? Hardly.

At any rate, I rattled through this and thoroughly enjoyed it. By the time Jaq Draco confronts the God Emperor, in a vast cavern hollowed out beneath the Himalayas, I was practically cheering. The Emperor speaks IN LONG STRETCHES OF BLOCK CAPITALS, and we're none the wiser. ('HEAR THIS DRACO! ONLY TINY PORTIONS OF US CAN HEED YOU, OTHERWISE WE NEGLECT OUR IMPERIUM, OF WHICH OUR SCRUTINY MUST NOT FALTER

FOR AN INSTANT. FOR TIME DOES NOT HALT EVERY-
WHERE WITHIN THE REALM OF MAN. INDEED TIME ONLY
HALTS FOR YOU. WE ARE AGONIZINGLY ALONE!') 'How can
a minnow understand a whale?' Jaq cried. Wise words. Wise words
indeed.

Connie Willis, *Doomsday Book* (1992)

This Hugo-winning time-travel novel is much better than Connie Willis's 2011 Hugo-winning time-travel novel, *Blackout/All Clear*, and much much better than her 1998 Hugo-winning time-travel novel *To Say Nothing of the Dog; Or, How We Found the Bishop's Bird Stump at Last*. But although, like those other titles, it is lengthy and quite slow (especially in the first half), and like those other novels the mid 21st-century Oxford Time Travel Institute scenes are less plausible than Jedward's hair, but somehow *this* novel works in a way that those ones don't. If nothing else, it helps explain why so many Worldcon fans keep voting Willis Hugos for mediocre novels: they're still basking in the glory of this one – the medieval world feels real, the characters' deaths (of the plague) earned and actually moving. There's real emotional heft here.

Still: there's no getting away from the question of the anachronisms and historical howlers. Now, I'm not saying these matter terribly much; which is to say, I'm not sure they *do* matter, especially. Shakespeare's historical plays are full of anachronisms – chiming clocks in *Julius Caesar*'s Rome, a character actually called 'Pistol' during the strictly arrows-and-crossbows warfare of *Henry V* – and *those* don't matter. Or we can be more precise, and say: they matter only to pedants. Pedantry is not the best frame of mind in which to enjoy a novel like *Doomsday Book*, because, like Shakespeare, Willis's skill is in capturing the mood of a time, the feel of medieval England, and this she does with impressive vividness. Nonetheless, there is a tiny pedant living in my head, and it could not help itself as I read through *Doomsday Book*. Viz:

- The 14th century was ravaged 'by not only the Black Death and cholera, but also the Hundred Years War' [p. 8]. Cholera? Not such a big killer in the 14th century.
- And here we are in a modern-day NHS hospital: 'the waiting room was in an entirely different wing from the Casualties Ward. It had the same spine-destroying chairs as the waiting room in Casualties.' [p. 63]. A British person would say

'Casualty', not 'Casualties' and never 'the Casualties ward'.

- When the epidemic breaks out in 2054, the UK police instruct people to 'contact the National Health for instructions' [p. 71]. No British person would say this: 'Oh lordy, I appear to have broken my arm. I must immediately hurry along to The National Health.' No. Really. No.

- Kivrin falls sick when she arrives in the 14th century and is put to bed in a manor house as an act of charity. 'There's a rat under my bed,' she notes. [p. 164] Under? Unlikely: tester beds do make their first appearance in the 14th century, but only for the very richest and highest-born. Most people slept on mattresses laid on the floor (perhaps with a wooden rim or lip around them), or on bolts of cloth or on straw, depending on how much money they had.

- Kivrin uses a chamber pot on p.173. 'Chamber pots may have been in use at palaces by the late Middle Ages, although there is little evidence for this practice' [Paul B Newman, *Daily Life in the Middle Ages* (McFarland 2001), 142]. These pots become common later on; if you need a wee in the middle of the mid-medieval night, go piss outside.

- 'It really is 1320. The hearth in the middle of the room glowed dull red with the banked coals' [p. 189] This should be a wood fire. 'Seacoal' was much too expensive to be burned in domestic fires; it was used in industrial processes that required high heat, ironsmiths and lime burners in particular (it was called 'Seacoal' because it was shipped by sea; the wharf where the material arrived in London was known as Seacoal Lane, so identified in a charter of King Henry III granted in 1253. Underground mining of coal was in its infancy in the 14th century).

- "Rosamund is a churl,' Agnes said' [p. 283] I doubt she did: churl means low-born peasant, but more importantly it means 'man'.

- Would a British person of 2054 really say 'I'm afraid I've an important trunk call coming in' [p. 300]? Would a British person of 2012, or 1992, say it? No. No they would not. Not unless they had time-travelled directly from the 1930s.

- 'Inituim sancti Evangelii secundum Luke' Father Roche said... [p. 364] The 'inituim' should be 'initium', though I'm prepared to chalk that up to a typo. But 'Luke' should be 'Lucam' – *that's* just sloppy Latin.

- Kivrin meets 'a clerk' wearing 'a shift and no breeches [...] the shift was yellow silk.' [p. 425]. Silk? Such a shirt would cost more than a clerk made in a decade. The first serous attempt to establish silk production in England was not made until the time of James I, who purchased and planted 100,000 mulberry trees adjacent to Hampton Court Palace (these trees were of a species unsuited to the silk worms, and the attempt failed). Actual silk production in the UK was not successfully begun until the 1730s. Prior to that, the only silk in Britain would have been imported from Lucca or Genoa (Lucca began manufacturing silk only in the late 13th century; Genoa even later), and it would have cost more, weight for weight, than gold.

- 'The Steward came in, carrying his spade [...] His cap and shoulders were covered with snow and the blade of the spade was wet with it. He has been digging another grave, Kivrin thought.' [p. 561]. Not in frozen ground, he hasn't; not unless he has Hulk-like strength. To dig a grave in frozen ground you need first to build a fire to soften the soil, and if he'd done that he wouldn't have snow on his spade.

- '"Mwaa," the cow said from the anteroom.' [p. 605] This isn't an historical error. I just like the idea of an air-kissing cow.

- After heavy snowfall, two more time travellers arrive in 14th-century Oxfordshire. 'A rolling plain lay below them, covered in snow almost too bright to look at. The bare trees and the roads stood out darkly against it, like markings on a map. The Oxford-Bath road was a straight black line, bisecting the snowy plain' [p. 615]. This is lucky for them, since the Oxford-Bath road is the arranged meeting point. But although it looks anachronistic, it isn't, see? There's nothing anachronistic about tarmac-covered roads that have been swept clear of snow by big snow ploughs. Not even in the height of the Black Death when roads were mud, snow ploughs have not been invented and more than 80% of the population are dead or dying. See?

Martin Amis, *Yellow Dog* (2003)

I like the *idea* of Amis. I just can't seem to get my actually-reading-Amis ducks in a row. *Yellow Dog* is a case very much in point. It's a science fictional (strictly: alt-historical) novel, set in a 2003 in which Henry IX sits on the throne of England – his wife is in a coma and his 15-year-old daughter subject to leering, video tabloidesque intrusions into her bathtime frolics. Henry is one character in Amis's tale; another is Clint Smoker, a hack from a sub-*Sun* rag called *Morning Lark*. Another character is the improbable film-star, novelist, rock-star, ideal husband Xan Meo who gets clonked on the bonce and undergoes a change of personality into an obnoxious spoiling-for-a-fight alpha male. Then there's Joseph Andrews, an elderly Brit-gangster even less believable than those delineated by Guy Ritchie. Hard to imagine, I know, but there you go. Amis sets these different storylines running, but seems clueless as to how to bring them back together again: he ends up literally smashing them into one another – very crudely handled. There's also an underpowered conspiracy plotline that's supposed to link them all, but which fails to do so.

It almost goes without saying that *Yellow Dog* is a terrible novel. Tibor Fischer's *Telegraph* review has become one of the most quoted in book review history ('Yellow Dog isn't bad as in not very good or slightly disappointing. It's not-knowing-where-to-look bad [...] It's like your favourite uncle being caught in a school playground, masturbating.'). At least, though, it is terrible in interesting ways, in ways (indeed) that make it a more worthwhile read than any number of much better but deadened-by-competence pieces of fiction. It is, for instance, not a shabby, or ill-considered or hastily put-together piece of work. Indeed it could have done with being rather more hastily rendered: much of it (clogging its heart with the cholesterol of earnestness) is a series of leaden sermons about masculinity, pornography, paedophilia and the relationship between the genders: clearly very long-pondered if essentialist and wrongheaded. Also the prose has clearly been strenuously worked through. There are moments – images, and occasionally whole sentences – where this work has resulted in actual good writing:

> The mist had lifted; out to sea a wildhaired wave collapsed, not all in one piece but laterally, from left to right, like a trail of gunpowder under the torch. [p. 110]

Lovely, that. Amis is good with accounts of the sky, too. During a thunderstorm: 'arthritic feelers of lightning' lancing out 'forming coastlines with many fjords' [p. 299]. But there's something about this sort of writing:

> The bright sky was torn by contrails in various states of dissolution, some, way up, as solid looking as pipecleaners, others like white stockings, discarded, flung in the air [...] others like breakers on an inconceivably distant shore. [p. 289]

The more you read, the more it starts to dawn on you: Amis can write nicely *when he's describing stuff that's far away*. The further away, indeed, the better, as far as Amis is concerned. But when he gets close to people his good writing goes all whiffy and off: congeals into a peculiar ugliness that zooms straight past the human organ of imagination without connecting: 'as he climbed from the car a boobjob of a raindrop gutflopped on his baldspot' [p. 187]. Or else he falls into a polysyllabic verbosity that very markedly falls short of being Nabokovian ("there I am,' he said, with a certain finicky jauntiness embedded in his indignation', p. 272).

That's the problem, right there. Amis has written a novel about people. Novels, after all, are about people. But, in numerous ways (although with a remarkably consistent intensity) Amis despises people. And, you know what? It turns out you can't write neoDickensian social satire – the thing *Yellow Dog* egregiously strives to be – when you're hobbled by such a thoroughly unDickensian contempt for human beings. 'Dickens', as a shorthand, is something like the opposite of contempt for people. But more than that, it turns out you can't write Hogarthian, or even Boschian, phantasmagoria either, not if you're handicapped by that mode of contempt. You might be able to achieve a Waugh-like sharpness, but to do that you'd need to have Waugh's extraordinary prosaic self-control and intensity, and Amis doesn't have it. His objection to the porn industry (and *my*, what a hard-to-hit target Amis has lighted upon with that one) is gender-essentialist. In his world men all love pornography and women all hate it. In a peculiar little riff he speculates that maybe 'women wouldn't mind pornography if reproduction took place by some other means: by sneezing, say, or telepathy.' Then he thinks again. 'But maybe it wasn't that. Maybe women just couldn't bear to see it travestied, the act of love that peopled the world' [p. 335]. So to recap: sex is good if it is about 'love' and 'making babies' and a travesty if it is not. And actually, I doubt even Amis believes his 'maybe' has inoculated him against the infection of loony rightwingnuttery.

Yellow Dog tries, often, to be funny; but it is not funny at all. Its humour is either sneering and hateful, or else – an aristocrat with a servant called Love – feebly Blackadder-derivative. Its play, mostly wordplay, is lumpish and continually reaching for a significance beyond its grasp. Of the inherent sexism of porn's fascination with the money shot: 'they call it the pop-shot. They don't call it the mom-shot.' Yes. Right. I'll go ahead and file that with 'they call it *ma*scara, they don't call it *pa*scara' and 'they call it cargo even though it's carried by lorries and *not by cars at all.*'

Amis wants to say penetrating things about the world we live in. He doesn't. This is a crashing, and an ugly, but worst of all a mute novel. Turns out that even the harshest satire needs a ground in common humanity; that without a sprinkle of the yeast of sentimentality the dough of the Jeremiad will not rise. There are novels that are ugly on account of bald authorial incompetence, although not too many of those get published. Then there are novels that are pretty (even beautiful), or at the least smooth, or airbrushed, or polished, or die cast or neatly plastic-moulded. Lots of those. But it's rare, and rather aesthetically bracing (in a good way), to encounter a novel by a thoroughly competent novelist that is, nevertheless, so gnarlily and outrageously ugly. Valuable, even. Indeed, I would, had I but time and space, dilate extensively upon the merit of this aesthetic of ugliness.

Maybe Amis's cultural prominence has given him enough fishbowl distortion of his sense of *The Way We Live Now* that he genuinely believed *Yellow Dog* to be a razor-sharp caliban's-face-in-the-mirror exercise. But actually one reason the book fails is that it doesn't build a believable world. It manages neither invention nor mimesis. Plus it can't scrub off the sense that Amis satirising Clint Smoker et al is simultaneously thinking that we (you and I, Steven, and everybody else who reads his novel) are indeed *actually wankers*. He has clocked

Nabokov's patrician disdain, but in trying to emulate it he can only manage a sweaty disgust and contempt, and that's not the same thing at all.

Frank Schätzing, *The Swarm* (2004)

I'd heard that Frank Schätzing is one of the biggest names in contemporary German SF, and decided to investigate a little further. His latest, *Limit* (2009), has outsold even Dan Brown, apparently, but it doesn't seem to have been translated into English. So instead I read his previous, *The Swarm*, in Sally-Ann Spencer's Hodder translation.

This very long disaster yarn (881 small-type, close-printed pages in the English) is essentially *The Birds* with marine life instead of birds. At one point Schätzing even has a character say 'it's like a deep-sea version of *The Birds*!', presumably in an attempt to inoculate the book against the reader going 'but this is just a deep-sea version of *The Birds*!' Didn't stop me, though. About halfway through it turns into *The Kraken Wakes*, with the twist that the malign deep sea intelligences waging war on mankind are native rather than alien. Worms chew ocean bed substrate and release enormous quantities of noxious gas; mussels clog ships rudders; lobsters explode in restaurants (no! really!), crabs advance onto the beaches in huge numbers. It takes an awfully long time to get where it's going, and where it's going is neither earth-shattering, nor mind-blowing.

The most striking thing about *The Swarm* is just how prodigiously infodumpy it is. Enormous quantities of regurgitated marine research are artlessly deposited onto the narrative either in gear-grinding descriptive passages ('Eddie switched on the six external floodlights. The four 150-watt quartz halogen bulbs and the two 400watt HMI lights combined to bathe an area twenty-five metres in radius in a pool of glistening light' 323), or else in yawn-provoking dialogue of the 'what do you know about X?' 'I know Y.' 'Very good, but you also need to know Z, A and B' variety.

> 'The worm is methanotrophic. It lives symbiotically with the bacteria that break down methane. [...] You see, depending on the isotope – you do know what an isotope is?'
>
> 'Any two or more atoms of a chemical element with the same atomic number but with differing atomic mass.'
>
> 'Ten out of ten! So, take carbon. It doesn't always have the same

atomic mass. You can have carbon-12 or carbon-13.' [p. 77]

It's a novel of great length but almost no density, a combination that gives it something of the texture of extruded polystyrene. More, the great length works *against* the main function of a thriller (which is to say: thrills) by slowing everything down to a plod. There's one place, though one only, where form and function come together, and where the novel lifts itself out of its nerdily relentless groove... or more precisely, one place where the nerdily relentless groove enhances rather than detracts from the effect: midstory a tsunami is described from inception to devastating passage over densely populated coasts. The unavoidable, irresistible force of this agent of natural destruction is well-rendered. Otherwise the book is very weakly written. It feels like the sort of novel a highly intelligent but shy and geeky thirteen-year-old might perpetrate.

It's possible that the huge length of this novel is, as it were, gratuitous; but I tend to think that there *is* a reason behind Schätzing's laboriousness. This bulk is a kind of chaff, designed to distract the reader from what would, in a shorter story, be revealed as risible: for the central conceit here is beyond stupid, viz that mankind evolved on this planet alongside a second superintelligent tool-using native form of life, amœboid in form, which, despite global reach, a group memory millions of years old, and intimate interaction with the human sphere *nobody has ever noticed before*, and which, after centuries of human pollution of the oceans, *chooses this moment to make itself known in an attempt at speciecide*. *The Swarm* is, I suppose, a better title than *When Superintelligent Oceanic Amœbae Attack*! But the latter would have been more honest.

Vernor Vinge, *Rainbows End* (2006)

No apostrophe in the title, you note: I don't doubt this will be a *Finnegans-Wake*-y trip-up point for sloppy future bibliographers. Well, well, this is an exercise in near-future idea-popping, filled with cool notions as to how contemporary technologies are likely to get extrapolated over the coming decades: internetted contact lenses, augmented reality, belief circles and the like. The novel employs a Wellsian 'Sleeper Wakes' conceit (noted 20th-century poet Bob Wu is cured of the Alzheimers that had put him in a coma and rejuvenated) which enables Vinge to give us an estate agent's tour (or, since this is a US title, a realtor's tour) of his future through Bob's eyes. And it's often interesting, this tour; although not really enough in-and-of-itself to hold our attention. So, alright, Vinge also provides us with a thriller strand: a dastardly plot to exploit ubiquitous Digital Age connectivity and der!-der!-DERR! Control! People's! Minds! – which our hero tackles, helped by his thirteen-year-old granddaughter Miri and a would-be industrial spy/hacker/dude who only appears in the novel in the form of a white rabbit avatar. All fair enough. Although hip 21st-C youngsters are plugged into unimaginable reservoirs of info data, they don't read books, and this is a Bad Thing. I can't argue with that. But, then, I'm 45. Indeed, whilst the novel does have a strenuously forward-looking ethos it can't quite free itself of a certain Dad Dancing at the School Disco ('Vernor Vinge, b. 1944') quality. Vinge dedicates the novel to eBay, for instance, which is a bit wincing. At one point Bob loses his rag because Miri refers to Ezra Pound as 'she' (there's a John Boyd novel – is it *Last Starship from Earth?* – which has a similar moment of outrage at somebody's gender-ignorance re: Rainer Maria Rilke). And whilst lots and lots of cool ideas and moments are, I suppose, a good thing in a novel, the tech stuff *is* frequently a little over-busy, and the thriller plot never picks up enough momentum to compensate for that. This makes the overall reading a bit of a plod. For example, often the prose is cluttered, ashen corporatese of this stripe:

> Even on a slow day, thousands of certificates got revoked every hour. It was a messy process, but a necessary consequence of frauds

detected, court orders executed and credit denied. All but a handful of revocations were short cascades of denied transactions, involving a single individual and his/her immediate certificate authority, or a small company and its CA. [...] no apex certificate authority had ever issued global revocations. And Credit Suisse was one of the ten largest CAs in the world. Most of its business was in Europe, but its certificates bound webs of unmeasured complexity all over the planet, affecting the interactions of people who might speak no European language.

Too much of this (and there *is* too much of this; that passage continues: '[...] failures spread as timeouts on certificates from intermediate CAs and – where time-critical trust was involved – as direct notifications [...] so far there were only small failures as UCSD...') glues-up the machinery of the novel. Much better are the character dynamics, grouchy and real-feeling, with a solid sense of (especially) the emotional complexities of schoolyard interaction. The Hugo voters thought this the best novel published in 2006, and though it's not bad, it's certainly not that.

Ben Bova, *Titan* (2006)

A familiar conceit from time travel SF is *the moment of flabbergasted retro-wisdom*. When 1980s Marty McFly tells 1950s Doc that his President of the USA is Ronald Reagan, Doc's boggled response ('Ronald Reagan? The *movie actor?*')beds in the difference in their respective perspectives as well as wryly suggesting that, you know, it's funny how things work out. In the BBC series *Life on Mars*, noughties copper Sam Tyler warns a hard-drinking 1970s policeman that a third of senior police officers will be alcoholics by the time Margaret Thatcher becomes P.M. His interlocutor replies: 'I'll need something a lot stronger than booze if *she* ever becomes Prime Minister.'

Let's play our own small version of this game. Let's go back a little way and point an innocent-eyed SF fan at the shortlist for the 2006 John Campbell Memorial Award. It was a strong list. The best of its titles is probably the masterful *Nova Swing* by M. John Harrison, but the competition is fierce, from James Morrow's smart, engaging, and wonderful *The Last Witchfinder* to Justina Robson's ambitious and stimulating *Living Next Door to the God of Love*, perhaps her best novel; from Charles Stross's problematic but characteristically effervescent and thought-provoking *Glasshouse* to Vernor Vinge's splendid, satisfyingly complex *Rainbows End*. Even the weaker books on the list have much to recommend them: the nifty and original worldbuilding of Karl Shroeder's *Sun of Suns* compensates for so-so characterisation and narrative; Edelman's *Infoquake*, though patchy, hits the button brilliantly when it's on song. I've read eight of the thirteen shortlisted titles, and of the eight Bova's *Titan* was the weakest by a country mile. By a country *parsec*, in fact. So, wait till I tell you who actually won the award...

Titan is one of the blandest pieces of fiction I have come across in four decades of reading novels. If the Campbell shortlist is a high-class curry restaurant of delicious, spicy and stimulating food, then *Titan* is a single slice of white bread and margarine on a white plate under the neon light of a truck drivers' café. It's a fairly thick slice (502 pages in the paperback), but that only increases the sense of stodge. If I had not been reviewing it, and had been instead captain of my own fate and master of my destiny, I'd have put it down at around page 200 and not picked it up again. As it was I plugged dutifully on to its anticlimactic ending.

The story picks up from Bova's previous wedge, *Saturn* (2003), in which ten thousand exiles, renegades and other folk unwanted by the religious-fundamentalist governments of Earth are sent into space aboard an enormous space habitat called Goddard. It's a cylindrical *Babylon 5*-type place, this, spun to create artificial gravity and luxuriously landscaped on the inside with spacious and beautiful parks, fields, lakes, and towns. Heaven only knows what such a place would cost to build in the post-environmental-collapse world of Bova's hundred-years-hence, but there you go. Anyhow, in *Saturn* there's a revolution aboard the Goddard and the dubious Malcolm Eberly gets elected President. In *Titan*, Goddard arrives in Saturn's orbit and sends a lumbering probe down to the surface of Saturn's moon. The probe refuses to upload its data to Goddard. The habitat experiences a series of minor malfunctions that slightly affect certain things, like the orientation of its solar array. There's a presidential election, in which the incumbent promises that everybody will get rich mining Saturn's rings for water, and his opponent promises to repeal the 'zero growth protocol' that prevents people having babies. One of the two candidates wins the election. The data gets uploaded. The minor malfunctions get sorted. That's your lot; there is no more. 500 pages.

It's hard to overstate, indeed, how underplotted the novel is. The minor malfunctions in the habitat put nobody in immediate peril. The lumbering probe trundles about a Wikipedia entry on Titan. It turns out that it's blocking its own upload protocol because it's been programmed not to contaminate Titan's surface, and it thinks that uploading its data will result in more probes, and concomitant contamination, coming to the surface. This revelation is, after half a thousand pages, a big narrative disappointment. Moreover it makes no sense – if the probe is intelligent enough to think through the implications of uploading its data (they'll send more probes!), then it's surely intelligent enough to think through the implications of not uploading, since that inevitably leads to the habitat sending down not only more probes but (much more contaminating) *actual people* to figure out what has gone wrong. And an actual person is indeed sent down to fix the malfunction. He does this by *promising* the probe that no further probes or people will be sent to Titan if it uploads its data. The astronaut then rashly radios base to inform them that he has just *lied* to the probe. The probe overhears this and *shoots him* in the *arm* with its scientific laser – but uploads its data anyway.

Back on Goddard the election campaign is fought on the gender-essentialist basis that all women want to have babies and that most men want to stop them; a, shall we say, curious perspective on *homo sapiens sapiens*. The plan to mine the rings of Saturn is stymied on the grounds that there are alien microbes living there. Think how many trillions of tonnes of water there are in the rings; and how tiny a dent human mining could make – it's rather as if all oceanic fishing were halted because of the effect on the plankton. But there you go. Then a narrative rabbit is pulled out of one of the presidential candidate's hats, when she reveals that there's no need to mine the rings for water after all, because *comets* are made of water, and several of them come *quite near* to Saturn! This information is greeted with delighted amazement by the occupants of Goddard, as if it has literally only just occurred to them. Try to imagine a population of ten thousand space colonists and scientists setting off towards Saturn with so rudimentary a knowledge of the solar system.

I've read a fair few of the *Grand Tour* novels now, and I have come to the conclusion that Ben Bova is a bad writer. His prose is flaccid, repetitive, and full of cliché. When he is writing exposition he's very dull. When he's writing descriptively he permits no noun to go naked before the reader without slapping on one or more adjectives, and he allows no verb to shed its adverb (from the first page: 'the thick listless wind slithered like an oily beast slowly awakening from a troubled sleep, moaning, lumbering across the frozen land'; from the last: 'On Titan's cold and murky surface Titan Alpha trundled across the spongy mats of dark carbonaceous soil'). Bova perhaps thinks this renders his prose more vivid and immediate, but it has exactly the opposite effect, making it sticky and overegged. Any student who has taken a Creative Writing 101 class, and had their tutor blue-pencil their over-compensating profusion of descriptors, knows better than Bova how to write evocative prose. Indeed, and speaking generally, I can't think of a writer working today with *less* of a feel for the rhythms and expressiveness of the English language.

His dialogue – most of it exposition of one sort or another –

entirely lacks snap, wit, vim. It possesses a uniform greyness such that it would not be possible to tell one character from another by voice alone. Indeed, the characterisation as a whole is wincingly clumsy. His people are like characters drawn by a five-year-old; they have triangular bodies, sticks for arms and legs, splodgy asterisks for hands, and wonky features on their balloon faces. Motivation is treated as a weirdly one-dimensional quantity. Eberly, for instance, wants power 'to have the proof that the people of this habitat still admired him' [p. 157]. There's literally nothing more to him than that. The paucity of this characterisation is then magnified and projected across the big screen of the novel by being repeated ('But they admire me, Eberly told himself' [p. 40]; 'he would bask in their admiration' [p. 41]; 'being admired by everyone – everyone! – that's the really great thing in life [...] I don't need anything or anyone, not as long as I'm chief administrator' [p. 188]) and then repeated some more ('Power is what makes people admire you [...] Power is more important than sex, he repeated to himself. I don't need a woman hanging onto me, not when I have the admiration of everybody in the habitat' [p. 270]) to the point of readerly nausea.

It would be nice to say that some other, SFnal or Campbellian aspect of the novel compensates for all this rubbish – the worldbuilding, say; the politics maybe – but it is not so. There's a problem of suspension of disbelief right at the beginning, where we just have to accept the idea that this luxurious and super-expensive environment was built by authoritarian governments to rid themselves of ten thousand 'dissidents, idealists, troublemakers' ... as if Stalin sent his political opponents to Siberia (an analogy made several times in *Titan*) to live in luxury penthouse apartments, or the 19th-century British shipped their undesirables to Australia and then housed them all in marble palaces at state expense. But even if we swallow that jagged horse pill of a premise, the execution is very poor. Bova wholly lacks the skill to do what (say) Kim Stanley Robinson does so brilliantly in his *Mars* books – to render a whole off-Earth society as a believable, three-dimensional thing.

Technology has notionally made enormous advances by 2096, including charter flights from Earth to the planets, the use of pharmaceutical and industrial nanotechnology, longevity treatments, and the ability to bring deep-frozen corpses back to life. But none of these things have changed the plodding 1950s *feel* of Bova's imagined future. Computing seems to have stalled somewhere around 1988. The Titan probe is so big and clumsy even the Soviets in the 1960s might have thought twice about launching it. Social interaction is slow and old-fashioned. Presidential debates happen via outdoors hustings. Bova's 2096 characters limit their range of reference to things like Eeyore, Stalin, the Gestapo, McDonalds, *Star Trek*, and *Lord of the Rings* – which is rather as if a novel set in 1996 contained characters whose points of cultural reference were exclusively the novels of Edward Bulwer Lytton, *HMS Pinafore*, Napoleon III, the Paris Commune, and Macassar hair oil.

Moreover, in an odd detail – and with the exception of a few thin individuals ('Urbain was a short wiry man, the kind who never worried about his weight' [p. 28]) – the characters all seem to have a weight problem. We're told that there exists nanotechnology to facilitate slimming, but, for some reason, nobody takes it. Instead they fret like senior citizens about what their bathroom scales are telling them: 'Yañez [...] had added nearly ten kilos to his weight since joining this habitat and he worried about that' [p. 62]; 'Wilmot [...] his midsection was thickening' [p. 158]; 'Despite being fairly portly Berkowitz cut a rather dapper figure' [p. 189]; 'A roundish, unhappy looking man standing beside Mrs Yañez' [p. 320]. It's like the novel is populated with the cast of *Star Trek V*.

Then there's Nadia Wunderly, one of the major figures in the book. Anxiety about weight constitutes pretty much the whole of what I suppose I must call her 'characterisation': 'She was a young woman [...] buxom, yes, but also heavyset, thick in the waist and limbs' [p. 25];'a chubby young woman' [p. 46];'Look at me! I'm fat as a pig!' [p. 68];'Wunderly was chubby. Her basic body type was chunky, big-boned. She would never look sylphlike or slinky' [p. 69]; 'I'm going to make a New Year's resolution, she told herself. I'll lose another ten kilos.' [p. 114]; "I've always been kind of dumpy and mousy,' Wunderly confessed' [p. 339]. Did I mention that Bova's version of women was entirely caricatured and essentialised?

But the main impression I took away from this book was of Bova's immense, almost heroic, ineptness as a stylist. This is a book for Thog, not actual readers; a book that repeatedly provokes the response *but what was he thinking?* What sort of author writes a sentence like 'he had none of his miniscule staff with him' [p. 189] without realising that readers are going to picture not a staff of few people, but a staff of midgets? How could any author have a character 'put a finger against his lips' and say 'Wunderly and her frickin' rings' [p. 177] and not see that he's doing an (in the context in which the lines appear) inappropriate impression of Doctor Evil from Austin Powers? What author thinks that describing a layer of clouds as like 'pregnant elephants' [p. 443] is a good idea? Does he not see that writing 'his face went darker than usual. "Now they all think I'm yellow"'[p. 203] will make readers picture the character as coloured like French mustard? Or that describing a woman's skin as being 'like toasted bread' [p. 134] gives the impression that her complexion is *crumby*? And then we read:

> It's like one of those dreams where you are struggling to get away from something horrible but you can't move. Your feet are mired in mud, or sinking into wet concrete. [p. 180]

It's too painfully true.

I shall drive back to June 2007 in my specially adapted DeLorean to meet Doc and tell him who wins the Campbell. His boggle eyes will open wide and his mouth will fall slack. 'Ben Bova's *Titan*?' he will say. 'Are you *crazy*?'

Thomas Pynchon, *Against the Day* (2006)

When I was a student, the rumour was that Thomas Pynchon didn't exist. To be more precise, the rumour was that he was actually a team of anonymous academics from the cream of American universities who spent their summers composing improbably brilliant, densely erudite and fantastically complex fictions which they then, for reasons of their own, published under the Pynchon pseudonym. The evidence for this was (a) Pynchon never appears in public, (b) the only photograph of him is a nondescript young kid in navy uniform from the 1950s (who could, obviously, be *anybody at all*) and, the clincher: (c) the name 'Thomas Pynchon' is lifted from one of the acknowledged masterpieces of American literature: Hawthorne's *House of the Seven Gables*. It would be like two dozen British academics publishing fiction under the pseudonym 'Oliver Twist'.

The reality is less interesting than the rumour, alas, as it often is: of course Pynchon does exist, and is one man. He has given occasional interviews. He has even appeared on *The Simpsons*. But underlying the conspiracy theory was a solid ground of plausible incredulity. How could one man produce such extraordinarily capacious and variegated fictions?

Now that the internet has delivered the global cabinet of wonders direct to everybody's study it'll soon be easy to forget how hard this sort of polymathy used to be, when it involved not a few Google-searches but years in libraries all over the world. Pynchon's reputation depends upon the work of this genuinely polymathic individual, although it also trades on the glamour of his shadowy 'other', the extraordinary and impossible fabulist. Life not so much imitating art as cloning it.

And now we have *Against the Day*, a book as difficult to assess by the criteria of contemporary fiction as it would be to judge Cerberus in with the rest of the Crufts usuals. Sui generis doesn't even begin to describe it. It's not just a question of the novel's great length, or density, or the fact that it orchestrates more than a hundred characters, or that it so deftly traverses half a dozen discourses of science, technology, mysticism, practicality, espionage, adventure, sexual excess and transcendentalism, although it does all these things. It's that it is a book that inhabits its own rumour, as it were. It's a book that contains its own shadow; that generates an alternate novel in the process of generating its own story. It embodies as well as narrates the condition of its own uncertainty.

Summary is expected of reviewers, but it's a tall order as far as this novel is concerned. We start in the 1893 World's Fair at Chicago, and follow scores of characters across most of the globe through the next quarter-century. *Against the Day* is a book about this world in its two guises, how it is now, how it might be; something with which SF fans are well familiar under the rubrics 'alternate reality', 'counterfactual', 'mirror universe' and the like. It demonstrates its author's breathtaking and rather scary command of both the idiom of 'realist' novel, and the idiom of the science fictional; and, indeed, its main point may be the dialectical interchange between these two modes.

To be a little more specific: Pynchon's multistranded narrative weaves itself out of two major nexuses (nexi?) of stories and characters. On the one hand there is the Wild West plotline. Webb Traverse is a dynamite expert much in demand in the mining communities of the American West who treads a dangerous line between following his own Anarchist sympathies (for he'd much rather be using his dynamite to blow-up capitalists and -bosses) and his need to placate the Establishment and ensure the security for his family. He is murdered early in the book, at the behest of evil plutocrat Scarsdale Vibe and his sidekick Foley (a fleshed-out and malign sort-of Mr Burns and Smithers). This act sets in train a complicated revenge plot that overshadows the life of Traverse's children. One of his sons chases the hired goons who actually did the deed through the Midwest and Texas and into Mexico, and afterwards plans to assassinate Vibe himself. Another son, for complicated reasons, accepts sponsorship from Vibes and travels to Europe, where he falls in with a couple of decadent spy organisations, hangs out with mathematicians and beautiful women, joins a quest to locate the mystic Shambala and many other things. When summarised in this manner this story, perhaps, might seem a little random, but the effect of reading Pynchon's dense, often beautiful, almost always sharp-witted (occasionally constipated) prose is that a density of affect accumulates around and gives real heft to the rococo twists and turns of narrative. You *believe* it, even when – or especially when – it slides from the Realist-historical to the fantastical.

The other nexus of story is the one with which the novel starts: the 'Chums of Chance', who are the crew of the high-tech zeppelin *Inconvenience*, and straight out of *The League of Extraordinary Gentlemen*, or Moorcock or some other period steampunk pastiche. Or, more likely (given the precision with which Pynchon evokes this period) they're drawn not second-hand but from the originals. One other rumour about Pynchon, circulating two years ago, was that he had taken up residence in London and was spending long hours at the British library. I like to picture him there ordering up and reading aerial adventure tales from the 1890s and 1900s: Rowland Walker's *The Cruise of the Air Yacht Silver Cloud*, Stephen Partridge's *The Phantom Airman*, Herbert Strang's *A Thousand Miles an Hour*, and J F C Westerman's *A Mystery of the Air*. In *Against the Day* the reader is referred metatextually to a number of titles, amongst them *The Chums of Chance and the Evil Halfwit*, *The Chums of Chance in Old Mexico*, *The Chums of Chance Search for Atlantis*, *The Chums of Chance and the Caged Women of Yokohama*: ghost books, all, but ghosts with a haunting presence in Pynchon's world. My point is that whilst Pynchon is writing a pastiche the thrilling wonder stories idiom he is doing it so expertly that he compels belief.

The Chums and their zeppelin retrieve a mysterious and possibly alien entity from the North Pole. They fly inside the hollow earth and have adventures with the gnomes that live there. The crew journey in a craft that travels beneath the desert sands as a submarine travels beneath the water. They travel in a time machine – indeed, they wander through a whole junk yard of the devices:

> 'Walloping Wellesianism!' cried the Professor, 'its just a whole junkyard full!' UP and down the steeply-pitched sides of a ravine lay the picked-over hulks of failed time machines – Chronoclipses, Asimov Transeculars, Tempomorph Q-98s – broken, defective, scorched by misdirected flares of misrouted energy. [p. 409]

Pynchon's apprehension of SF is nothing if not comprehensive. It wouldn't be far wrong to call it 'comprehensively playful'.

These two starting-points for the novel, the carefully realised 'historical' idiom of Webb Traverse's sons and the lighter-than-air 'scientifiction' idiom of the Chums of Chance suggest a binary; a division between the realist and the fantastical, between mainstream and SF. And this binary is one of the strong structuring principles of the sprawly whole. If I had to put my finger on it I'd say that this is what the novel is 'about'. What is set *against* the day in this book (which is to say, against the *every*day, the ordinary, the quotidian) is precisely the fantastical, the out-of-the-ordinary, an entire 'olio of oddities'. The fantastical-adventure format of the Chums shadows or mirrors the grittier, more down-to-earth sequences with the Traverses; and the delicate touch with which Pynchon interweaves the two of them is one of the joys of the novel. On the one hand the Chums of Chance themselves are precisely borderline figures ('the aeronauts dual citizenship in the realms of the quotidian and the ghostly' 256), who tangle with sideways timelines and bizarre alternate versions of our world, but also with the cast of the other, mainstream-ish story being orchestrated here. On the other hand characters from the quotidian reality ('our' world, we might call it) find themselves slipping, at odd and unpredictable moments, into parallel existences. A door appears in a wall, and through it a character steps to emerge somewhere wholly other and unexpected. In a lovely sequence, Kit Traverse, fleeing America and Scarsdale Vibe for Europe, wanders below decks on his liner, the *Stupendica*. But when he tries to re-ascend he finds he's not on the *Stupendica* anymore; he's on a warship, in a martial alternate reality; pressed to work as a naval rating, he finally absconds at port, makes his way to Amsterdam and finds that he's somehow slipped back into his original reality.

As with the junkyard of time machines, Pynchon plays all the cards in the 'alternate reality' SF-deck. For much of the novel the characters are in search of Iceland Spar, a crystal that (speaking roughly) splits light into two slightly different duplicates of itself; and which can be used either as a lens to shine a light on alternate possible worlds, or perhaps as the key component in a weapon of mass destruction. This medium of doubling refracts, textually, the whole of literature (or near-as-dammit) into the twin discourses of 'realist' and 'science fictional'. We read a doubled and *simultaneous* novel: not 'realist sections followed by SF sections', but somehow, SF and realism continually in superposition with one another.

It's a yin-yang, or day-night dialectic. Against the day, we might say, stands the night. The novel's epigraph is a rather lovely line from Thelonius Monk: 'it's always night, or we wouldn't need light'. Pynchon returns again and again to descriptions of the sky at dawn , or sunset. Characters make elaborate and sometimes startling statements of allegiance to the light. 'I want to know light,' says one. 'I want to reach inside light and find its heart, touch its soul, take some in my hands whatever it turns out to be, and bring it back, like the Gold Rush, only more at stake, maybe' [p. 456]. Or, as the head of a strange London-based religious sect says to private detective Lew Basnet:

> As if imparting a secret Lew could not help thinking he had somehow, without knowing how, become ready to hear, the Cohen said, 'We are light, you see, all of light – we are the light offered the batsmen at the end of the day, the shining eyes of our beloved, the flare of the safety-match at the high city window, the stars and nebulae in full midnight glory [...]' [pp. 687-8]

But the other side never, in Pynchon's book, relinquishes its pull. Another of Webb Traverse's sons, Frank, has a dream of his dead father:

> The sky is always bleak and cloudless, with late-afternoon light draining away. Through the clairvoyance of dreams, Frank is certain– can actually see – his father; just the other side of the closed door; refusing to acknowledge Frank's increasingly desperate pounding. Pleading, even, by the end, crying 'Pa, did you ever think I was good for anything? Don't you want me with you? On your side?' Understanding that 'side' also means the side of the wall Webb is on. [p. 650]

Side means death, then. With a lovely modulation Pynchon leaves a line break after this paragraph, and begins the next section with the seedy, understated yet touching regrowth of: 'It had rained in the night, and some of the ocotillo fences had sprouted some green'. There's a huge amount that is grim, oppressive, painful and ugly in Pynchon's set-against day, but there are also great quantities of brightness, sex, moments of great beauty, and clumsy but rather charming humour. The 'realist' daylight sections depend upon, and in turn determine, the night-time frolics. There is a carefully worked process of doubling at work through the fiction as a whole.

Most of the characters in the novel have phantasmagorical, uncanny or buffoonish doubles. The British thinker Renfrew talks of his German opposite number, the sinister Werfner, although the two men

75

seem, in some sense, to be the same individual. Auberon Halfcourt, spymaster, has a Russian counterpart and enemy, Colonel Yevgeny Prokladka. The Chums of Chance are shadowed by a Russian zeppelin the *Bol'shaia Igra* and its crew the Tovarishchi Slutchainyi (the 'comrades of randomness'). There are, indeed, many dozen similar examples of Pynchon laying out his pattern; but he does it so expertly that it rarely seems forced or over-schematic.

In fact things are a little more complicated than this, since this binary, 'quotidian'/ 'fantastic' actually entails a *four*-fold thematic patterning. This is because, as any matricist will tell you, parsing two terms inevitably generates a fourfold grid (a and b; a and not b; not a and b; neither a nor b). And through the bulk of the novel Pynchon plays myriad changes upon this rule of *four*, not the least of which is a detailed and sometimes baffling investigation into the old theory of quaternions. Then, as the novel moves closer to its end, he seems to lose interest in twos and fours, and instead throws a great number of threes at us. Not least amongst these threes is some three-way sex. Indeed, and despite the fact that up until page 800 or so the sex in the novel has been sporadic and (by Pynchon's standards) quite restrained, the last stretch suddenly explodes with some eye-poppingly explicit couplings. The foresquare, or square-dance, formalism of character interactions – in which key figures very pointedly *don't* meet, or *don't* get it together – gives way to a porn-film excess in which everybody has sex, pretty much, with everybody else.

Against the Day has, of course, been extensively reviewed, and many of the reviews I've read are curiously evasive on the question of whether it's actually any *good*; as if it somehow misses the point of Pynchon to subject him to such petty assessments. It's certainly true to say that *Against the Day* dwarfs other fiction. But then again you might not necessarily find giganticism an attractive quality in itself, or your bedroom walls would be plastered with images of the actor who played 'Jaws' in the old James Bond films, rather than those posters of fine-boned Orlando Bloom or Elijah Wood that you've actually stuck up there. Giganticism can involve coarseness as well as magnitude, and if I tell you that *Against the Day* is a monster you may decide that monstrosity doesn't appeal to you. But monster is also a term of breathless approbation, and that's how I mean to use it here.

There are certainly uneven stretches in amongst the marvellous ones, unsurprisingly so in a novel of this length. Pynchon's American dialogue is almost always excellent, but he isn't as good at capturing a Britishness of tone as he thinks he is ('caught at silly mid on!' and so on); and I don't know many Irishmen who sound like his Wolfe Tone O'Rooney ('what the bloody fuckall would you know about it? [...] and here's hoping that you don't work for the bloody Brits, or I'd be obliged to deal with that somehow'). He has an ungainly habit of ending sentences with prepositions ('[...] due to the money that Ewball's pockets were mysteriously full of.') The hyper-explicit sex is variegated, but does rather exhibit a tendency to fall back onto models of women being made to submit, or being degraded, which makes rather depressing reading after a while.

On the other hand, it would be easy to make a case precisely for this unevenness; like Pynchon's awful jokes, and his refusal to give up the cringeworthy made-up song-lyrics with which he's been interspersing his prose since *V*, an unevenness of tone is actually part of Pynchon's global effect: a refusal to play within the rules of good taste, a sort of heroic and brilliant sprawl. This is also what's going on with the occasional lapses of proper historical verisimilitude. Characters talking of 'antiterrorist security' [p. 25] are being anachronistic in the 1890s; just as RUSH the 'Rapid Unit for Shadowing and Harassment' [p. 708] sacrifices historical accuracy for the progrock joke. In part these occasional moments stand out because, in other respects in this enormous and dense work, the research is so faultless. But 'shadowing' is too crucial a concept in Pynchon's work to go unnoted. And what shadows the book is its own brilliance. Its own sheer excellence.

Gene Wolfe, *An Evil Guest* (2008)

I've now read this novel twice and I'm still not entirely sure what exactly is going on, or whether it's any good or not. Since reviews are largely in the business of giving readers a sense of what a novel is about and whether it is any good, this may prove problematic.

I don't want to overstate matters; on one level Wolfe's new novel is perfectly comprehensible. It's a sort of future-as-1930s-America soldering together of pulpy noir and Lovecraftian horror dusted lightly with some of the props of Golden Age science fiction. The main character is Cassie Casey, a not-very-successful actress in what reads very like Damon Runyon's Depression-era Broadway. There are two other important characters: Gideon Chase, who is a sort of wizard-cum-private investigator, and Bill Reis, a billionaire supervillain (or... *is* he?). The US government does not trust Reis, who has returned from the distant alien world of Woldercan having picked up from aliens there the ability to turn base metal into gold – though lethally radioactive gold, which seems to me of limited usefulness – and possibly the ability to shapeshift, either downwards from humans into wolves, or else upwards from humans into... well, that's more ambiguous.

The US government approaches Gideon Chase to investigate Reis. Chase in turn recruits Cassie Casey, winning her over by promising to make her a megastar. He does this by taking her to a Canadian mountain and using magic to awaken her inner charisma. It's sketchily described, but after the process Casey manifests a glamour previously only latent within her and becomes the starriest of stars, the toast of the town. She is then hired by Reis (who is using the name Wally Rosenquist) to be the female lead in a musical he is putting on called *Dating the Volcano God*. Indeed Reis has fallen in love with Casey, and wants to marry her. Gideon Chase has also fallen in love with her, as she has with both men, and this peculiar love triangle is the main structuring principle of the novel. If she were to marry Chase would she change her name to Cassie Casey-Chasey? What if her middle name were Jessie? Thoughts like these plague the heat-oppressed brain as it attempts to fathom the strange undercurrents of Wolfe's novel.

Because, as we all know, Wolfe's titanic reputation in the genre is mostly due to his novels' complex undercurrents, not to their often diffuse and awkwardly choreographed surfaces. My experience with him is that it is in *re*-reading his novels, and rarely just reading them, that they reveal their excellences. I worked my way dutifully through the *New Sun* books only to feel baffled at the praise lavished upon them. Then, a year or more later, and for reasons I can no longer remember, I picked them up again to reread them. It was a revelatory experience; these novels do indeed deserve their reputation. On the other hand, who has time to reread (and perhaps rereread) in these hectic days of ours? And in the absence of a reread, what sort of surface does *An Evil Guest* present?

The short answer is: a spotty one. There's a lot of stuff about putting on the show *Dating the Volcano God*, all the to-ings and fro-ings of musical theatrical production, that I found rather tedious. There's also a quantity of not very well-handled noir-ish gubbins, mysterious men lurking in corridors with six shooters and the like, which failed to excite me. Fairly late in the novel the action shifts to an actual South Sea Island, and a series of rather puzzling events that seem, after the longueurs of the first 250 pages, to zip by in a rather hectic manner. These events embroider variations upon a Cthulhuesque theme: perhaps star-spawn of Cthulhu/sunken city of R'lyeh-style stuff. I'm not sure. Actually I just wanted to write the word 'Cthulhuesque'; and, having done so, I must say I like the look of it.

From time to time Wolfe attempts humour, something frankly beyond him as a writer. In the South Seas, Casey decides to phone her friend called India. India, in this context, being a person, not the country. Casey has a conversation with a telephone operator.

> 'Calling the States might be a bit costly, though...'
> 'I don't care,' Cassie said. 'I'm going to call India.'
> 'Oh, you've friends in India?' [p. 227]

My aching sides. Or again, here's Cassie crossing the Canadian border, and causing us, the readers, to fall off our chairs with sheer hilarity at her mock-Russian accent:

> The Mountie heaved a sigh. 'Let's see some ID.'
> 'I haf a tattoo.' Looking up at him, she licked her lips. 'Ees var' pretty.Tzum private place, da?' [p. 36]

Presumably Wolfe strains for comic effect because he believes the pulp-noir tradition requires it, but he can't manage it. There are other lapses of tone, too, as for example the (female) assassin who breaks into Cassie's bedroom, puts a gun to her head and utters the snort-worthy line: 'My steel dildo is in your face. One moment more, and its ejaculation will blind an eye' [p. 252]. There are jolting sallies into racist stereotyping: an artificial intelligence with a Japanese accent that says 'arso' and calls itself 'one artificiar interrigence'; or a clutch of South Sea Islanders straight from the Mumbo Jumbo Savages school of central casting. This is how Wolfe thinks somebody educated by the English school system talks: 'Public school, you know. Eaton after and all that rot. Cambridge, only I didn't cop the gown. Pater passed so I did a runner' [p. 239]. As an Englishman I'm here to tell you: not so. Really, for reasons too numerous to list here, not so. Perhaps Wolfe meant to write 'Ceambridge.'

Then there is the central character of Cassie Casey herself. Cassie is a flame-haired, green-eyed, curvaceous beauty (pictured there on the front cover) and is supposed, I guess, to come across as a feisty yet feminine 'strong woman' throughout. I put strong woman in inverted commas there because it strikes me as a phrase now mostly hijacked by the reactionary forces of post-feminism. Casey is not a strong woman. She is a conservative's notion of a strong woman: a woman out of Ruskin's 'Of Queen's Gardens', permitted to explore to the *very edge* of her pedestal but not to step down from it. She is defined almost entirely in terms of her physical appearance and her effect upon men, and she colludes in this objectification. As she sets out for the South Seas, Gideon Chase tells her: 'one day after you get to Kolalahi you'll be wearing a bikini that covers three square inches. And every man who sees you will foam at the mouth.' Her reaction: 'she giggled softly and sat down in front of the best mirror to put on makeup' [p. 217]. The men in her life patronize her shockingly:

> This is one of the things I love about you. You're not at all intellectual – we intellectuals are, for the most part, fools – but every so often you show the most marvelous penetration. [p. 222]

As I say to my wife most days: 'although you are, of course, my intellectual inferior, your pretty little head is sometimes capable of pointing out things that I am too deeply engaged in profound cogitation to have noticed. Well done!' Of course, were I ever to say this to my wife she would beat me violently on a delicate spot with a meat tenderizer, and quite right too. She certainly wouldn't giggle softly and rush to a mirror to adjust her makeup.

Wolfe would of course not be the first significant novelist to have been rubbish at portraying women (we might mention, oh I don't know, Dickens, Melville, Lawrence, Forster...) and I'm not convinced, despite the amount of time she spends centre-stage, that Casey is really the point of Wolfe's novel. Chase and Reis are closer to that: the former an individual everybody thinks of as a fake wizard who is actually a real wizard, the latter an individual everybody thinks is a supervillain who may be a sort of hero. Though the surface of the book often struck me as insipid and even clumsy, beneath that surface are some suggestive and powerful elements, and the intriguing sense of unsolved mysteries. *An Evil Guest* stuck in my head, and worried away at my imagination after I'd finished it, for all that I had so many reservations about it. So I picked it up again.

A reread did not make the problems I mention above disappear, but it did bring out other qualities that may at least be put in the balance. Although the novel has no scenes set upon the alien world of Woldercan, we can intuit some things about it (with its dangerous forests and talking fish I take it to be a form of Fairyland) and it achieves a haunting and effective imaginative quality precisely because of its absence. There are a number of Lovecraftian-variety monsters, and there's one Big Fight between the army and colossal oceanic beasts that happens wholly offstage. Such special effects, by being kept largely in the margins, prey upon the imagination more effectively than they otherwise might.

A lot of the magic in the book boils down to shape-shifting: shifting lead to gold, shape-shifting a man into a wolf ('lycanthropy'), or shape-shifting a woman into a theatrical superstar ('celebranthropy'), and there's a lot of stuff to do with disguises, aliases, doubles and the like. Casey's occupation, acting, is precisely pretending to be somebody she is not: a kind of shapeshifting. Wolfe goes to some length (a) to establish that shapeshifting is limited by a necessary equivalence of mass ('The wolf was as big as he was,' Gideon said, 'because Al is [...] when his cells have repositioned, they make a large wolf. I told you about that, too, once', p. 207), and (b) to detail the weight of key characters ('a picture [of] a younger William Reis than she had ever seen, [standing] next to an older man of about the same height who must have weighed at least three hundred pounds,' p. 301). Readers may enjoy piecing together the clues to make a more coherent whole.

For instance, Reis and Chase never appear in the same room at the same time, possibly, though I'm not sure, in the same way that Don Diego de la Vega never appeared in the same room at the same time as Zorro. Certainly Casey loves both men, and I wondered if the sameness of much of the novel isn't actually a deliberate strategy – whether the novel itself is actually an oblique meditation on Aristotle's venerable distinction between substance and accident, a philosophical position of peculiar importance to the development of Catholic theology (the Council of Trent used Aristotle to explain how Eucharist bread and wine can shift its shape into the body and blood of Christ whilst seeming to remain wholly bready and winey). Catholicism is an important context for most of Wolfe's works, and may be at the core of what's going on in this novel.

I'm still unsure whether it's a good novel or a bad novel, but that fact alone seems to me to point to a distinctive and rather admirable fictional aesthetic. Like most of Wolfe's books, it's unlike anything else being written; and like most of Wolfe's books, it is profoundly suggestive, and persists strangely in the mind after it is read. Not necessarily for the best of reasons. It's a strange novel. Strange isn't necessarily bad, of course, but neither is it necessarily good.

I've decided not to read it a third time.

Greg Egan, *Incandescence* (2008)

Egan's new book is about *finding stuff out*, and that is both its appeal and the ground of its weakness. Finding stuff out, of course, is the bedrock of Science, and has a long and, often, splendid history in the Fiction of Science: epistemological quests, conceptual breakthroughs, 'learning the world'. But finding stuff out is not enough in itself to sustain a 300 page fictional narrative. The imperative of fiction is, in one sense, *not* finding stuff out – which is to say, holding off the revelation, deferring the reader's comprehension, so as to hold her interest and keep her reading. The TV serial *Lost* is fiction, and whilst its endless deferments of explanation are perhaps annoying they are nevertheless, on a narrative level, highly addictive. *Incandescence* is a sort of anti-*Lost*: everything is explained all the time all the way through. It is, in other words, a sort of *Found*, and as fiction it suffers accordingly.

This is what we find: a society set a million years into the future whose basic circumstances are explained straight away; a galaxy saturated with life, divided between, on the one hand, the spiral arms, home to the diverse high-tech but recognizable lifeforms to which Egan gives the rather dental name 'the Amalgam'; and on the other, the inaccessible, mysterious, seemingly indifferent inhabitants of the galactic core known as the Aloof. The story concentrates on two citizens of the amalgam, Rakesh, whom we are told straight away is descended distantly from actual fleshly DNA beings, and Parantham, whose ancestors were embodied by an AI. They accept a challenge indirectly laid down by the beings of the Aloof: a meteor that has been circling the core for fifty million years carries the remnants of radiation-scarred DNA. Parantham and Rakesh's mission, should they choose to accept it (and they do) is to find out where the meteor originated, and to decipher its significance. To do this they must travel into the realm of the Aloof. There's a whiff of glamour about this, since all previous incursions from the Amalgam, though benign, have been equally benignly but firmly rebuffed, and so their mission is also about uncovering something of the mystery of the core. We're not immediately told the results of their enquiries, because those enquiries constitute the novel, but nor are we told why their enquiries matter, because the novel's real interest is *the process of enquiry itself.* Which is to say, Science.

Then we find a second narrative, braided in alternate chapters with the first. It concerns lifeforms that are physiologically insectoid, though psychologically rather human, inhabiting the tunnels of a worldlet called Splinter. Roi starts the novel as part of a work team tending the vegetation upon which their society depends (we're immediately filled-in on the physical and social set-up of the worldlet and its hexapodic inhabitants). Meeting an elderly male called Zak, Roi becomes interested in aiding his scientific experiments. Together, and despite the fact they live in a wholly pre-Industrial society ignorant of the most basic physics, where children learn addition and subtraction but not multiplication, where time is calculated only in heartbeats, and where calculations have to be written on plant leaves, they discover Newtonian physics, algebra, a quasi-Einsteinian understanding of space-time as curved, and various other things, which in turn lead them realize that the strange physics of their world bespeaks imminent tidal-gravitational disaster. For three quarters of the novel I boggled more than a little at the improbable genius of these insects. The novel's ending (I eschew spoilers) explains the extreme rapidity of their Age of Enlightenment, although I retained a portion of bogglement – it didn't seem to me to add up. In fact the Splinter-bugs come across as ciphers through which Egan rehearses the process by which scientists undertake experiment after experiment in order to move closer to the truth. At the weightless centre of the Splinter, Roi and Zak fire pebbles using a spring-loaded tube and watch them orbit around the Null Line, whilst having conversations like this:

> Roi said: 'its orbit was smaller than ours, so it was racing ahead of us?'
>
> 'Yes.'
>
> 'And the way it moved away from the Null Line and then back again, that's because the orbit wasn't a perfect circle?'
>
> 'Right,' said Zak. 'We remain a constant distance from the Hub, but there are orbits like this that draw closer to the Hub and then move away again.'
>
> Roi contemplated this. 'What if we could put a stone into an orbit that wasn't a perfect circle, but was still the same size as ours overall? With the same period?'
>
> 'That could be very useful,' [Zak] said eventually. 'We ought to

see it execute a fixed, cyclic motion instead of running away across the chamber.' [p. 89]

Yes, their exchanges really are as dry and unengaging as that, pretty much all the way through. Parantham and Rakesh are not much better. 'Before Rakesh could invoke any kind of high-powered statistical analysis, Parantham said "that can't be right." The chemistry-based ranking was not at all what might have been expected [...] the chemical profile of the region's stars placed the rock's origins in a completely different direction than that from which it seemed to have come. "It must have undergone a sharp course change," Rakesh suggested, "maybe even passing through another planetary system on its way.""Either that, or its chemistry's distorted for some reason," Parantham said' pp. 75]. And so on.

It is not that the book wholly lacks interest. I was mildly intrigued by the DNA-riddled meteor, not so much for its own sake but because it seemed to promise insights into the Aloof – insights which were not, ultimately, forthcoming. I was less intrigued by Zak and Roi's interminable toing and froing with stones and springs inside the Splinter, to which adheres the odour of fourth-form school physics labs. On the other hand there are some witty touches too. I like the idea that space travel in the distant future will involve selecting a star on a map, whereupon a menu pops up asking, 'are you sure you really want to travel to this star?'

Eventually, by the book's end, the stuff we have cumulatively found out about Splinter and the DNA-meteor adds up a bunch of stuff. And when the two narratives come together, as we know they must, the story is over, apart from a rather leaden Prime Directive dilemma. That's it, there is no more. I was left thinking that the worldbuilding specifics of the Splinter are *sort* of cool, although only sort of, and that the novel as a whole feels like a neat-oh short-story idea that has been stretched and stretched beyond the capacity of its elastic to snapback.

Which is to say *Incandescence* is not Egan's best novel. Oddly for an author of his stature, there are various evidences of a clumsiness of execution—clumsiness on the level of the fiction, I mean; for the Science, once we get past throwing pebbles in zero-g, is as gosh-wow as we might expect. Prose style has never been Egan's *forte*, and to some extent that's fair enough, since his fans will not be buying this novel for Updikean excursi capturing the vivid intensities of perception. That said, it's a shame that Egan seems innocent of the proper use of the subjunctive mood ('if this world was a bacterial graveyard [...]' p. 102) or the inelegance of ending sentences with prepositions ('[...] the abundance that she was used to.' p. 40). More, the *framing* of the tale throws up awkwardnesses. On the one hand, Egan flourishes various super-high-tech features of his future life. On the other, characters from a million years in the future send down avatars that are called, by narrator and characters both, 'jelly babies' [p. 105]. Are we to suppose that *jelly babies* of all things have survived so lengthy a span of time? Will our descendents in a million years *really* still be pushing grains of rice around a plate with a fork?

Then again, can one talk of 'a whirlwind tour of history' [p. 80] or say of a character that he is 'armed with the map of weights' [p. 82] in a world like Splinter that has neither whirlwinds nor armies? Of course, one way of addressing this would be to make the tacit assumption that Egan has translated not just words but concepts into something accessible to 21st-century Anglophone readers. Which is fair enough, although it makes me wonder why directions on Splinter are rendered not 'north,' 'south,' 'west' and 'east,' but 'Shomal,' 'Junub,' 'Garm' and 'Sard,' a strategy that leads to much stylistic indigestibility, for instance: "'If I'm garm of the Null line," Roi mused, "but not shomal or junub, the Splinter will still carry me in a circle'" [p. 63]. That's likely to make my list of 2008's top-ten flat ugliest sentences. And when, later, one of Egan's characters declares 'we can understand the direction "three spans garm for every one span rarb"' [p. 114], it starts to look like he's just taking the piss.

Which brings me to the subject of infodumping. Here's one dump from the very first time we meet Roi, at the end of her work shift:

> A group of wretched males clung to the rock, begging to be relieved of their ripeness. Roi approached to inspect their offerings. Each male had separated the two hard plates that met along the side of his body, to expose a long, soft cavity where five or six swollen globes sat dangling from heavy cords [...] she used her mating claw to reach into the males' bodies, snip the globes free and deposit them inside her. [...] The ripe seed packets secreted a substance that the males found extremely unpleasant, and whilst unplucked globes did shrivel up and die eventually, waiting for that to happen could be an ordeal. There were tools available for severing and discarding them, but that method was notoriously prone to spilling an agonizing dose of

irritant. Something about a female's mating claw [...] sealed the broken cord far more effectively than any tool. (p. 14)

You'll remember a similar scene from Henry James's *The Golden Bowl*:

> Prince Amerigo removed his clothes. His male generative organ, known technically as a 'penis' (although it had a wide range of other, slang and informal names) was no long flaccid and had become stiff, acquiring the consistency of wood or bone. It had also become slightly larger. The Prince achieved this transformation by subconsciously – autonomously – diverting a small proportion of his blood flow into the organ, where a spongy tissue became engorged with the additional fluid. This bodily alteration in the Prince's organ was accompanied by an emotional and psychological desire, that he experienced as a sense of urgency, to insert the 'penis' into Charlotte's vaginal cavity, using friction to stimulate the release of spermatic fluid. This urgency would eventually dissipate if the penis were not inserted, but the Prince experienced it in the moment as a form of pain, not physical but none the less aggravating for being psychological, and his preference was for full mating with Charlotte.

Of course not. Of course, we might say, James doesn't *need* to write that, because we all know what is involved in the human sex act, while Egan does need to introduce his dumpy little chunk of info because we don't know what is involved in his insectoid creatures' mating. Of course we don't know: Egan has just made the species up. But I don't think this is actually what is at issue here. (Imagine *The Golden Bowl* being read by an inexperienced teenager vague on the precise details of the sex act, or by somebody unaware of the precise mechanism by which a penis becomes erect: would spelling these details out enhance their reading experience? Of course not.) Egan's paragraph is in part a way of marking the difference between human-ness and alien-ness. But it is more than that. It is a desire to communicate a large quantity of information in as *efficient* a manner as possible. There's nothing more *efficient* than an infodump. What is any scientific paper if not a dump of info? But efficiency is an inadequate aesthetic, particularly for the novel. The appendices to *The Lord of the Rings* convey much more data in a much more efficient manner than *The Lord of the Rings* does itself. That does not mean that they are to be preferred as a reading experience. There are many better fictive methods for marking estrangement from the ordinary than this.

Naturally, a scientist does not desire to toy with her audience, or play peek-a-boo with her data: she wants to uncover things, not to cover them over with artful narrative suspensefulness. Nor do scientists lay out data so that we can *intuit* its significance (as it might be: 'the door dilated'): the scientific model is that they spell this significance out clearly and fully. That is what this particular scientist (Gregory Egan BSc) does in this novel. He does it all the way through. It is deadening. Science is the enemy of mystery. Fiction, however, requires a degree of negative capability immiscible with the scientific method. The best SF authors – and that includes Egan himself, in *Diaspora*, or *Schild's Ladder* – find a way of holding these two elements in an effective emulsion. *Incandescence* doesn't emulsify in that aesthetically satisfying manner; lumps of fact-based and extrapolative ideation float in a weak fluid of narrativised character. I find the result to be not very good.

Neal Stephenson, *Anathem* (2008)

Considerably better formed and more enjoyable than Stephenson's prodigiously clotted *Baroque* books, *Anathem* is a pudding baked of equal parts Harry Potter, *A Canticle of Leibowitz*, Tolkien, Heinlein's juveniles (or some of them) and Bertrand Russell's *History of Philosophy*. A thousand pages of Fatasy, give or take. The first third is set inside the scientific convent (a 'concent' in the vocabulary of the tale) in which Erasmus, the narrator, lives. The second third moves our core characters around the larger world at great length and in great detail, and the last third reveals the working of the Big MacG, which has been slowly digesting inside the stomach of the tekst throughout. This Big-MacG (a Newfo, and the implications of same) is tastier than many, although as empty of vitamins and minerals as any I've tasted, but the main point of Stephenson's tekst is the worldbling, which is *very* expensive and showy. For people who like worldbling this is presumably almost a perfect book, but those who prefer something a little less flashy, a little more substantial in aesthetic and novelistic terms, may find it tiresome.

Continuing with the downside, the narrator is unusually bland, the other characters almost nonexistent and often interchangeable, and the author's application of his styless has resulted in a great wasteland expanse of grey prose through which the ridder must trudge if s/he is to untie the spoilbinding. I found ridding an effortful process. The dialogue is prolic, clumsy and built on the principle of redundancy ('"Do you remember the total eclipse of when we made a camera oscura so that we could see it without burning our eyes?"'"A box," I recalled, "with a pinhole at one end and a sheet of white paper at the other."' [p. 281]. Try, I beg you, to imagine *anybody talking like that in the real world:* 'Do you remember reading a book in which the prose is flavoured, evocative, sharp and effective? Do you remember such a book?' 'A binding,' I recalled, 'of many sheets of printed paper into a single artifact, upon which are printed the consecutive sequences of words that, when taken together, tell a story.') But it is surely beside the point to object to the tell-don't-show styless, or to the myriad annoylogisms, which are amongst the showiest elements in S's worldbling. My problem with the tekst can be boiled down to one focus: its monstrous and inflated infodumping. Of course I appreciate that for some ridders, and perhaps for many ridders, this 'problem' will be the whole *point* of the book. The entirety of the tekst is one gigantic Infodump, and that's that.

I didn't believe the 'concent' notion – either in larger sense, that such bastions of a particular sort of privilege could survive millennia against the context of international secular politics, or in terms of their internal logic (confining populations of young people of both sexes together, with the added spice of there being no risk of pregnancy, would surely result in *enormous* amounts of shagging. Now there's *some* shagging hinted at in the novel, but it's kept within YA bounds of propriety). My own progress through this treaclestorm of a narrative was slow, and my main emotion upon completion was relief. But for all that I can understand, and had some faint inkling of why, some readers have fallen wholly in love with this book.

Review Glossary

ANNOYLOGISMS: Words invented or new-coined specifically for the purpose of delaying a ridder's passage through a spoilbinder, thereby making the process much more burdensome than it need be. In some communities this term has lost its negative connotations and is used to refer to any defamiliarising or worldbuilding use of invented terminology.

BIG-MACG: A triple layered MacGuffin product, containing a higher proportion of cholesterol than a regular MacGuffin. The consumption of too many Big-MacGs may lead to fanbesity.

BLOCKBLOCKER: A word coined in opposition to 'blockbuster': a tekst that assembles massy boulder-like obstacles in the way of a ridder's passage.

CRITIASS: Named for the Platonic dialogue in which Plato gives his eponymous speaker the opportunity to discourse upon Atlantis. Modern day Critiasses devote themselves to deprecating the inferiority of modern imaginary worlds (particularly those in contemporary Fatasy) when compared to the achievements of the classics.

DULLKEEN: An apparent oxymoron. Originally this term was used to criticize writers who imitated certain features of the ancient author 'Tolkien' – specifically his great length, his fondness for coining new words and his simple quest-narrative structures – without imitating his sublimity, profound moral and imaginative engagement or mastery of tone and mood. In later use, when dullness itself became increasingly prized as an aesthetic virtue (cf. yawngasm), Dullkeen was taken not as oxymoronic at all, but as something closer to tautology. Eventually all new imitations of Tolkienian fatasy were dullkeen.

FANBESITY: A variant of Fatasy, which may be descriptive of (a) a Fatasy novel itself, (b) the individual whose diet consists wholly of such teksts, irrespective of their individual body-type, or (c) the state of the genre as a whole.

FATASY: Originally a contraction of the Amglish phrase 'Fat-ass Fantasy novel', the term in present use carries no negative associations and is merely descriptive of a genre in which the very notion of a 'thin fantasy' has become something of a contradiction in terms.

HARI-PARTER: Committing a form of tekstual suicide by increasingly expanding the parts of an ongoing tale until they reach such size that the guts of the story split open and spill all over the ground (see Rowmbling).Painful and grisly.

MacGUFFIN'S: Extremely successful company that provides standardized plot-devices, especially those whose exact composition is a mystery but which are appealing enough to encourage ridders to consume product.

NARRACTOR: A character who narrates. More specifically, a character whose sole focus of characterization is that s/he narrates the story in which they appear. There is usually nothing more to such a figure than a blandly generic niceness and a lot of day-to-day details that contribute to the worldbling of the story.

NEW-FO: A new form of UFO. The particulars of the Newfo vary from place to place, but may include twists such that the pilots of the unidentified spacecraft turn out to be us, or that such craft travel not so much from star to star as from Platonic reality to Platonic reality.

RIDDER: An individual who reads a book in order to rid themselves of an onerous spoilbinding. In most recent usage, a person in thrall to a narrative, and usually somebody doomed to the disappointments of anticlimax.

ROWMBLING: Going interminably *on and on* after the manner of J K Rowling. Particularly applied to tekst that get longer and longer the more famous an author becomes. See also Hari-parter.

SPOILBINDING:.A tekst that binds its ridder to its unfolding narrative by withholding 'spoilers'.

STYLESS: Originally this word, a variant spelling of 'stylus', referred to the instrument of writing. In later usage, and in keeping with a general valorisation of the 'neutral' or 'ordinary Joe' stylistic preferences of most readers, this became a term of praise for the writer who downplayed 'literary' or 'purple' prose.

TE DIUM: Quasi-religious song in praise of the dullness of enormously elongated narrative faldapiffle.

TEKST:.A text (such as a novel) with a high 'technological' quotient that tests – as it might be – the patience, the endurance or the imagination of a ridder.

WORLDBLING: A variety of worldbuilding in which a great many details of an imaginary world are put on rather showy and vulgar display in order to impress upon the ridder the prodigious imaginative wealth of the author. The imaginative wealth of the author, it can be added, is not usually in doubt, although some critiasses, especially those that value restraint, subtlety and inflection, question the judgment of authors who indulge too blatantly in worldbling.

YAWNGASM: A strange circumstance whereby prolonged boredom leads to a state of near ecstasy. Not as unusual as you might think, actually.

Ian R. McLeod, *Song of Time* (2008)

MacLeod's Arthur C Clarke award-winning *Song of Time* is, notwith-standing its various near-future aspects (its virtuality crystals and genetically engineered plagues, its nuclear war and ecological catastrophes) a backward-, not forward-, looking book. It is concerned with the ways memory shapes our life, and this Proustian theme keeps the novel's focus always on the past as a function of the present. It doesn't quite work, either as a novel or as a meditation, but it's an ambitious piece of writing for all that.

Roushana Maitland is an old woman living in a plush Cornish house called Morryn. She recalls her life as a girl growing up in Birmingham, the death of her beloved brother to a terrorist-created disease, her rise to worldwide fame as a brilliant violinist, her bohemian life amongst the artists, musicians, decadents, faux-messiahs and gender-benders of future-Paris (a notionally mid-21st century but actually very 1920s-flavoured city), and her life married to a brilliant, slightly unhinged conductor. We're in, I suppose, the 2050s, but the music is all Bach, Mozart, Chopin, Stravinsky and, in a *Desert-Islands-Disc*-style sop to popular taste, one reference to Thin-White-Duke-era Bowie. There's a rather touching assumption that mid-21st-century cultural life will revolve around classical music concerts and performances, even as the world's ecosystems implode and nuclear war rages ('people had grown sick of big beats and clever virtualities, and they liked the idea of dressing up and going out for the evening to watch living people performing music which somehow sounded fresh and new despite its age' p. 269). It's MacLeod's world, and he can do what he likes with it of course, but I can't say this rang true for me.

The hook upon which all this garrulous reminiscing suspends is the appearance in Roushana's life of a beautiful young man – washed up, injured, naked and nameless, on the shore near her house. She carries him inside, dresses him in her husband's old clothes and calls him – since his Bournean amnesia has wiped his own name – Adam. We can all agree, I'm sure, that this is an excellent and auspicious name for anybody to have. The mystery of this figure's actual identity is one of the things that moves the story on, along with the question of whether

Roushana is going to upload herself into a post-mortem virtual existence as many of her friends have done. Scenes of aged Roushana with Adam are interwoven with gobbets of reminiscence of her earlier life, to uneven but heartfelt aesthetic and emotional effect.

Part of the problem is that too much of the autobiographical stuff is what Salinger called 'all that David Copperfield crap': I was born in such-and-such a year in such-and-such place; I went to school at X. I went to the University of Y and got a job doing Z. I married; I had a number of kids; my parents died; something remarkable happened (as it might be: war; misadventure; disease; tragedy), but afterwards my life fell into its regular rhythm. For all its fascination with the trappings of Modernist Paris ('here were the precious glasses which the myopic Joyce had supposedly used to write *Ulysses*,' p. 235) *Song of Time* is all very pre-Modernist in its aesthetic project: life conceived as a series of notional high points, rather than the more oblique but much more emotionally compelling epiphanies that trace out (say) Stephen Dedalus's existence in *Portrait of the Artist as a Young Man*. In Roushana's account there's a good deal of detail, but much of it is inert and some of it is tell-don't-show polystyrene ('It was Hindu against Muslim. It was black against white. It was tribe against tribe. As a long-festering war broke out here in Birmingham as well, bodies were dangling from streetlamps,' p. 93). You don't quite believe it.

Another problem is that this is a novel centrally about music, which necessitates a great deal of dancing about the architecture. There's something tiresome in being repeatedly told about 'Karl Nordinger, and his magnificent *Fourth Symphony*' when the prose gives us no sense of how this alleged master-piece *is* or *sounds*. MacLeod perhaps wants to suggest that his musicians are pushing the sonic envelope, but he doesn't pull this off: 'it had,' he says at one point, 'a complex beat, shifting from 4/5 to 4/4, but flowing in a way which felt entirely right to the heart and the hips' [p. 130]. Hmm. He's talking about a piece of music that carries through a consistent 4 beats per bar (that's the first part of the slash) but shifts the note-value of each beat from one-and-a-quarter to one. This wouldn't be a complex beat; it'd be a squeezebox rhythmic of alternate *slightly* slower and faster. You'd find more jolting-but-right rhythms in Squarepusher, or Tool. Maybe MacLeod is thinking of the opening of Mussorgsky's *Pictures at an Exhibition*, which starts 5/4 and then shifts to 6/8, a more complex, though more comprehensible, rhythmic progression. Or maybe he's thinking of Dave Brubeck's 'Take Five,' which is also in 5/4 time (not, though, in 4/5 time). But maybe he's not thinking of anything of the sort, because in other places his sense of what makes great music is McCartneyesque tunefulness ('coming up quite spontaneously with that tune which everyone in Paris was soon humming,' p. 135), and the examples of actual music he includes are things like the pretty but harmonically unexceptional Irish folksong *She Moves Through the Fair* (he calls it 'an English folksong', p. 141). We are supposed to take on trust that Roushana's memories are soaked through with gorgeous, brilliant, new music, but I never did. Similarly the Parisian scenes make the suspension of disbelief harder than it otherwise might be: the Route Périphérique is called the '*Periphique*' [p. 143], MacLeod thinks the French for truffle is '*truffe*' [p. 188; it's not] and he writes 'de monde' instead of 'du monde' [p. 194]. Moreover he thinks Beckett's *Waiting for Godot* is 'a Dadaesque tragedy' [p. 187]. I'd say it's hard to think of two words that apply less to *Godot* than those two; and putting them together like that, oxymoronically, just looks odd.

Enough nitpicking. Not every reader is a pedant, after all. There are broader pleasures to be had here, and some of them derive from MacLeod's often-praised prose itself—although I have to say that stylistically this is an only *intermittently* impressive book. There are many sentences that are simply beautiful, and MacLeod clearly has a good ear for a striking image or comparison: 'Car and house alarms were squalling, buses lay overturned, and the pavements were already glittery from looting' [p. 92]. 'The vast mote of some leviathan is floating across the sky as it mouths and digests whatever poisons have been cast here from other, less fortunate lands' [p. 102]. I loved the description of the steps up to Morryn blurring 'in Escher angles of light and shadow' [p. 211]. He's very good at the Sturm-und-Drang stuff:

> Then they are down beside the raging waves and the boathouse, part hewn-stone, part cliff, part cavern, Morryn's last outreach, at which the sea tongues and mauls, lies ahead. Blinding white froth rolls out of the blackness, draws back, rolls in again. Shingle slides. [p. 288]

Some of it (a grand piano's lid being called a sail; lemon-coloured light – Craig Raine and Derek Walcott, there) is second-hand, but that doesn't stop it being striking.

The style, though, is terribly uneven. For every well-turned sentence there's a sentence that is just horrible: 'I noticed again the view through the window when Blythe and I returned to the charming virtual room she had first greeted me in' [p. 159]; 'Comets can approach enough to give us the apocalyptic willies' [p. 241]. MacLeod has a fatal affection for 'resolutely,' a word he uses indiscriminately as adverb and adjective: 'resolutely Anglo-Saxon enclaves,' 'resolutely fully dressed,' 'resolutely asleep,' 'my resolutely English ears,' 'resolutely male,' 'resolutely granite-grey' (Bodmin, this), 'I stroked his resolutely flaccid penis,' 'a resolutely self-contained package,' 'resolutely doing the American thing' [pp. 19, 30, 46, 80, 101, 151, 196, 197, 218]. We can appreciate that certain words tend to stick in a writer's ear; that's one reason why revising one's first drafts is a needful activity. The problem here is not just the repetition but the sense that MacLeod evidently thinks 'resolutely' a nonspecific intensifier rather than an inflection of the word 'resolve' (does he really mean to say that Claude's penis was flaccid because Claude had *resolved to keep it so*? I have to say that's not my experience of how the organ works). Sometimes the writing seemed to contradict itself, as with the improbably silent rainstorm ('Silence fell. So did the rain' 125), or the physiological improbability of 'his nose was both Negroid and aquiline' [p. 127].

In other words, though the prose is sometimes good, the overall impression is one of unevenness. The first-person voice, throughout, is slacker and more prolix than it needs to be; the dialogue isn't particularly deftly or expressively handled, and the details often clog rather than illuminate. All of this collaborated to make my experience of reading *Song of Time* frustrating rather than pleasurable. That said, as the novel draws to its conclusion it accumulates a genuine, and affecting, emotional heft. Perhaps it is in part a consequence of the momentum of a fairly long novel (which in turn perhaps justifies the sometimes stodgy build-up): certainly as it closes the fate of Roushana, the identity of 'Adam' and the sheer pressure of memory acting upon the present become properly involving and even a little moving. On this emotional level, then – which I take to be the level for which the novel aims – the novel works, at least in the final stretches. This is not to say that it achieves its implicit Proustian ambition (one of Nordinger's pieces is called 'Swann in Love') of articulating the strangeness and depth of memory's action on the present. It does manage some striking effects, although it also reads as often mis- as well-judged. As far as this review goes Roushana, on memory, gets the final word: 'I can't remember if I ever noticed before that penises could float.'[p.211] Well. Quite.

Iron Man

(directed by Jon Favreau, 2008)

It's fun. More, for much of its length, this almost lives up to the ideal; the ideal being that the title is short for *Irony Man*. There's some movement in this direction, with Downey Junior's wisecracking screen persona, but only some. In fact the heart of the film (the gleaming, metallic, circular heart) is clumsily, even painfully unironic. It's the dream narrative of US military involvement in the Middle East: one American is able to go to Afghanistan, kill only the bad Afghans, leave all the virtuous Afghani men women and children alive, and then leap clean away into the sky having Done Good.

Iron Man's suit, classically, is a wish-fulfilment dream of *invulnerability*, in medieval-knight or Ned Kelley mode. What this film adds is a two-petal garnish to that ancient human fantasy: first, the magic-carpet dream of jet-flight mobility and second, the equally potent dream of *perfect moral choice*. For Stark's magic suit comes fitted with software that allows him not only to see everything (from the kid's ice cream blob falling from his cone, to the wicked Taliban fellah hiding behind the wall) but also to lock-on and, assisted by his silky-voiced computer advisor, discriminate good from bad. That's the film's major mendacity: that accurate moral judgement and effective ethical action are predicated upon an ontology of perfect, mechanical invulnerability. The exact opposite is the truth: our ethical potential is grounded in our vulnerability.

The next stage in the analysis would be to trace this misprison, the belief that ethical behaviour must be grounded in invulnerability, deeper into the US psyche: the obsession with guns, the catastrophic foreign policy. But that would be a large and complex task, and beyond me at the moment. Intuitively, though, I wonder if there's something in it.

China Miéville, *The City and the City* (2009)

I read this novel.

It's worth reiterating what a superb writer CM is. I wonder if there's a danger, when any creative artist reaches a certain threshold of celebrity, that commentators no longer feel obliged to note *how great they are*. It's assumed, unspokenly, but in a passive-aggressive-let-me-list-only-the-faults-in-the-new-Dylan-album sort of way that overlooks why the new Dylan is required listening in the first place. Miéville may be entering the stage in his career where a tendency to niggle blots out the core fact that he is, and remains, a major contemporary novelist.

More, *The City and the City* is, I would say, the best written of all Miéville's novels: his prose has never been so deftly, evocatively or expertly handled. His dialogue – within the parameters of the crime idiom in which he is working – is better than it's ever been. It is all powerfully atmospheric; tightly constructed; very readable.

The novel's central conceit (apologies for the spoiler: although it's something made apparent in the book from very early on) is the superposition of two cities in the same location: run-down Besźel and on-the-up Ul Qoma, both occupying the same bay in an vaguely Eastern Mediterranean location. There are places, 'crosshatchings' where it is possible to pass from one city to the other; but the only legal access is through 'copula hall' and the suitably Byzantine bureaucracy that governs it. To pass at any other place – or even, technically, to *notice* the other city – is to perpetrate a terribly serious infraction, punishable by a shadowy group of secret enforcers known as 'Breach'. There's also a tertium quid in the topographic mix: a third interurb known as 'Orciny', in which some people believe and some do not, and which may or may not actually exist (there's never any doubt that Besźel and Ul Qoma exist). Orciny. The 'or' in that name gets to the heart of it; the novel's studied imaginative elaboration of the excluded middle, its fucking around with the either/or logic of Western thought – or as one character puts it, 'the pissing little neither/nor' [p. 284] – (hence the book's edging-out-of-the-West, borderline-near-eastern setting: it wouldn't work if set in Bristol/Weston Super Mare). 'We're all philosophers here,' Tyador Borlú, the policeman-protagonist, claims at the end.

Borlú also carries that 'or' in his name. But if his first syllable suggests he's *tied* (his base, and ours, is Besźel) his second and third syllables hint at the possibility of a portal for him. There's a wealth of punning in the book, much of it ingenious. But it's not mere garnish: Miéville layers his core conceit all the way through. He dwells on liminal states, grey areas, halfway houses (the Besźel police can put someone under 'half arrest' for instance), and overlapping categories – academia is a rich seam for this: 'archaeology [...] folklore, anthropology, Comp Lit' [p. 87] are all zealously guarded distinct entities, despite clearly all being pretty much the same thing. Archaeology, indeed, is an important part of the whole ('digs are constant in Ul Qoma', 61), presumably because archaeology is all about the simultaneous topographic existence of cities... of – as it might be – Constantinople and Istanbul. Because, you see, if you've a date in Constantinople she'll be waiting in Istanbul.

The novel is a Fantasy, and a compellingly realized piece of worldbuilding. A core trope which could in less skilled hands have been fey or risible is rendered concrete and compelling. Sights, smells, sounds.

It works brilliantly.

It doesn't really work.

The novel is a crime story, and the lineaments of murder, clues, suspects, chases, gunfights and revelation are all dutifully copied across from other sources, but it reads flatly, overly-familiar, especially compared with the ormolu precision and evocativeness of the fantasy. A young woman is found murdered, and the novel-as-narrative is the story of Borlú's investigation into this crime. But it's not this investigation that propels us through the book. It is not that the crime story is poorly handled per se, but rather that it sets up an interference pattern with the fantasy that defuses the effectiveness of either. I argued this place and want neither to repeat myself nor not to repeat myself, but I finished the book thinking that the epistemology of Miéville's crime narrative doesn't parse the ontology of his worldbuilding in other than superficial ways.

Superposition threatens to overwhelm the narrative. Miéville is no stranger to neologism, of course, and some of it works here. But some of it is pretty strained (khat is called 'feld' in Besźel because feld is the Besź word for the English *cat*. Um...) and some of it flat awkward. To describe buildings that exist in both cities, 'topographic' and 'doppelganger' get portmanteaued into 'topolganger': a word I couldn't read without thinking of a large group of people simultaneously having sex with the celebrated Israeli star of *Fiddler on the Roof*.

More jarringly, structurally speaking, this self-conscious fiction is artfully draped in real-world reference (Pahlaniuk's written a novel about Beszel; Van Morrison's toured there) as if to intimate that *fiction and real life* coexist in the same way that Beszel and Ul Qoma do. But this isn't right: in the case of Beszel and Ul Qoma one doesn't have precedence over the other. Life, however, trumps fiction; only delusionals and schizophrenics think otherwise. The danger the trope of superposition continually risks is of falling *between* the two worlds, into the nullity of Orciny, rather than of properly representing the proper both-wave-and-particle thang. And in the final analysis (sorry: more spoilers) Borlú cannot rest in either Beszel or Ul Qoma, but must vanish into the nebulous and ultimately not-as-believably-rendered realm of the organization known as Breach. Which has seemingly magical powers of surveillance, apprehension and punishment. Although these are revealed as being actually just exactly the same powers that the other police have.

That *The City and the City* is the best written of all Miéville's novels becomes, almost, a problem, although it sounds like an odd thing to assert. But Miéville's reputation is based upon books that achieved their greatness not despite but *because* of a gnarliness of articulation, a sculpted rawness that did sometimes veer into the purple, or clumsy, or clotted writing, *but not in a bad way*. Here things are a little too clipped, too polished, to achieve the imaginative overhang – the gorgeous, ungainly excess – that is the glory of Miéville's earlier major achievements. More, Miéville's Chandleresque tone can't manage the leavening wit that makes the best noir more than just a pose in black-and-white and fedoras. There are moments of attempted humour here – or there are lines that have the form but not the content of wit: a woman has 'skunk-stripe hair like a film-studies academic' [p. 58] and a security guard 'a mid-period David Beckham mohican' [p. 154]. But their effect is to pinpoint a kind of hollowness at the heart of the rendering.

I don't need to tell you how good a writer CM is.

I didn't read this novel.

Star Trek

(directed by J J Abrams, 2009)

I'll concede one thing, only: this film is jolly enough. The time passed. It's kinetic, apparently fashioned according to the current blockbuster logic: 'imagine a 13 year old boy at your shoulder at all times; if, for any reason, that boy goes 'boooring' at any character, sequence or shot – *cut it out*.' Certainly the special effects are visually very nice. It is full of lovely little details. But actually, it's more than full of details: it is *nothing but* details. Its contempt for the larger architectonic requirements of filmmaking and storytelling amounts to a slap in the fangirl/fanboy face.

There are two parts to my dislike of this movie, and I'll start at the level of most obvious: [*item*] that the plot holes are more than holes. Red matter has been injected into the script, leaving vast distorting black holes of unlogic, anticontinuity, nonsense and bollocks everywhere.

Here's the plot: the Romulan villain, Nero, in charge of a vast spaceship shaped like Don King's hair, is dragged through a black hole back in time. (Elderly Spock is also dragged through, although, for reasons unexplained, he arrives back in time 25 years later). Nero pops out and chances upon a fully armed Federation battleship. Now: the Romulan craft is a commercial ship, for the extraction and portage of raw materials – hence its enormous size. This is as if to say the Exxon Valdez slipped back in time and chanced upon the HMS Ark Royal. Who do you think might win if two such vessels fell to fighting?

Anyway Nero blames Spock for the destruction of his whole world, and has his mind set on vengeance (which is to say: on '*V*ENgeance!'), so he immediately wastes the Federation ship, and Kirk's father, and then *completely vanishes for 25 years*. Whither goeth he? Not to pursue his *V*ENgeance!, certainly, or we'd hear about it. Somehow he manages to hide a vast, futuristic Edward-Scissorhands-Hairstyle-In-Space from all comers. Then he returns 25 years later because he knows (how?) that the space-time anomaly is about to open again. (Presumably it hasn't been open the whole time, like a barn door, or surely somebody would have gotten around to investigating it). Through pops Spock with the Red Goo that destroys worlds. Good! Now Nero can destroy *Spock's* world, and *make him watch as he does so*, just to learn him. Does Nero make Spock watch from the bridge of the Romulan spacecraft? No: he deposits him, unguarded, on a planet adjacent to Vulcan.[2] Judging by how big Vulcan is in the sky of this ice world it must be about as far away as Earth is from our own moon – although it is entirely uninhabited by Vulcans, and is regarded as a fantastically remote and faraway place on which to dump unwanted Star Fleet officers by the Federation.

The next stage in Nero's plan is to dangle a big laser-platform at the end of a very long chain into the atmosphere of Vulcan, in order to dig a hole right down to the core and deposit therein a small phial of the Magic Red Goo. Stop for a moment: it's worth dwelling on this, because this Terror Weapon, Shatterer of Worlds is the main menace around which the plot of the film orients itself. It's dangled on a long chain. Why? Well, in order to provide the filmmaker with a Very High-Up Platform on which to stage swordfights and fistfights, adding the spice that our hero might fall off the edge to his certain death to the conventional thrills of punching and slicing. Similarly, Nero vanishes mysteriously for twenty-five years only to allow Kirk enough time to grow up. No other reason. Nice of him, really.

But wait: let's think about this chain, on which the laser platform depends. Is it super strong? By no means. At the end of the movie Spock, flying a spaceship no bigger than a shuttle, cuts it neatly with a quick phaser blast. Now: Captain Pike, in charge of Starfleet's hideously beweaponed flagship, comes upon this Weapon of Terror in mid-blast. What does he do? (Never mind that the Vulcans haven't destroyed it with their own planetary defences. The Vulcan science council can manufacture Planet-Blasting Red Goo, but have nothing in their cupboard that could chop through an anchor chain). Now admittedly, Pike stumbles into the middle of a battle, because Star Fleet doesn't have long range sensors, and their ability to broadcast communications

---

[2] I like to imagine the following exchange, after the event – NERO: how did you feel as you *watched your world being destroyed? Muahaha!* ELDER SPOCK: the who did the what now? NERO: wait... didn't you see the destruction? E.S.: I've been inside my cave. All I've seen is the, eh, inside of my cave. To be honest, this planet isn't a place where you want to be *wandering around outside* too much, especially not with your attention fixed *upwards* – there's enormous ravening red beasts under the snow, you know, will eat you quick as mustard.NERO: You were supposed to be *watching!* My revenge depends upon you actually *watching!* E.S: Well excuse-use *me.* Would it have killed you to say something beforehand? Let me know a *time?*

breaks down entirely if somebody fires a Big Laser, and their ships lack the sorts of warning systems that would prevent them from coming out of warp into the middle of a debris field (something that must result in a lot of collateral damage to the fleet, you'd think). So Pike's caught on the hop. But nevertheless, could he not direct one single phaser blast to cut that cable? One photon torpedo? Could he not send out a shuttle to shoot it? Could he not – if these other options were denied him – direct a shuttle on autopilot to fly into and *smash* into the cable? No, his plan is better: send three members of his crew skydiving down on the platform to wrestle mano-a-mano with the Romulans guarding it.

Fuck. *Off.*

There's a much bigger, much more damaging problem here, though. Plot holes are one thing, but this is something far more serious. It is that this movie cannot, no matter how much it strains and heaves, *think systematically.* The individual is the entire horizon of its universe. Now, when you're 15 (say), and particularly when you're 15 and male, your own hormone-saturated individuality – its ego, its randiness, its stroppiness – can look like a whole universe unto itself. But it's not. Society (community) is the necessary context of individuality.

What was so great about Trek – and particularly *TNG* and *DS9* (less so *Voyager* and *Enterprise*) – is that it *got this.* What's cool about *TNG* is not Picard, or Riker, or Worf: it's the representation, on primetime TV, of a whole and properly functioning organization. Properly functioning in the sense that it *works*; it is efficient and adaptive and coherent without being too rigidly hierarchical or oppressive. It wasn't just a number of individuals going through the motions of relating to one another, but a network in which individuals had their place. It's a model rather than an actual society (of course it is: the representational logics of the medium dictate that). But it is a model with surprising quantities of nuance and believability.

This is why *Deadwood* (which is more than just swearin' Al Swearengen: it's the representation of a whole believably interconnected and functioning town) and *The Wire* (a whole, and rather larger, town) are so sublime, and why those two titles are better than the third member of the Holy Trinity of Great Contemporary Telly, *The Sopranos*: which did become, increasingly, too much 'Tony Soprano (plus support)', especially in its later series.

Now, the representation of *TNG*'s Enterprise was coloured

Utopian, of course: and of course it can't duck the accusation of nerdiness. Nerdiness, clearly, is The Worst Thing in the World. If there's one thing we learned from George W. Bush's presidency, it's that it's *much* better to have the allegedly reformed, onetime drunk hellrake with no knowledge of the details but *a strong gut-sense that he can make the right decision* in charge, than the policy-wonk guy with the high IQ and the good grasp of the inherent complexity of national and international relations. Jesus. Imagine if we had one of *those* in the White House.

Nevertheless, the representation of *TNG*'s Enterprise was a believable and rounded piece of collective realization. The latest Trek? Not so much. Not, indeed, at all.

*Trek*09 is a text so absolutely incapable of representing a collective – a functioning group, a society – that it strays into rank idiocy. It is teenage wish-fulfilment bang-zap-frot fantasy all the way through. But (and this, I'd say, is what people celebrating the Star Warsification of the Trek franchise in this film, are missing) precisely what made Trek so notable in the first place was its creation of a communitarian world. Not an ensemble cast all vying for screen time; a knit-together group of people. The Star Wars universe is an open-ended, malleable space for individual adventure. The Trek universe is about having a place. It is, really, about belonging.

So *Trek*09 grandly misses the point. My problem was not that Kirk, in this film, is a tool at the start and a tool at the end. He is, but that's not the problem. The problem is that *Star Fleet* is so toolish, so completely, dysfunctionally unbelievable *as* an organisation. Kirk is a cadet and an arsehole, who is under suspension. Nevertheless, Pike promotes him to First Officer on the strength of (a) I admired your father and (b) I liked the way you burst into the bridge and yelled at me that we needed to raise shields and ready phasers. When Spock takes charge and Kirk argues with him Spock *ejects him from the ship* (because the Enterprise lacks a brig? Because the brig isn't fitted out with a huge scarlet hairless icebeast? Who knows?). When Kirk gets back on board, he goads Spock into attacking him and then seizes the captain's chair. This is presented as a necessary and saving action, but it all speaks to an *organization* in its death throes. Hiring Some Guy You Met along the Way as chief engineer (in effect: 'you're real smart about engines and shit… you do the job') is part and parcel of this dysfunction. The

Enterprise, as a group of individuals functioning together to crew a space ship, is, in this film, and for the first time in the Trek franchise, Not Fit For Purpose. It's a wholly unprofessional bunch of people squabbling and vying. It's dysfunctional. And I've now used 'dysfunctional' three times in this one paragraph. Which is stylistically clumsy, but at least stresses the *main* feature of Star Fleet, as an organisation, as presented in this film. Dysfunctional.

The opening sequence – the best portion – doesn't suffer from this. The evacuation of the USS Kelvin looks like a coordinated, effective group performing a difficult task. People follow orders even though they're not happy about it, because the orders are in the best interests of everybody. This isn't the world of Star Fleet 25 years later, which is all contempt and testosterone, staff yelling and throwing punches at one another; senior officers have sex with their subordinates; those in charge making random seat-of-pant decisions about staffing, strategy and everything else, or else abandoning their posts to rush off and rescue their mum and dad. Rather than, you know, *doing their duty.* All very much unGood.

The larger function of this myopia is a complete inability to even begin to deal defensibly with the representation of genocide. The mass-murder of all the universe's Romulans *and* almost all the cosmos's Vulcans is not just here offensively stupid plot-pointing. Although it is that. It is something that the film cannot comprehend on any level except the personal. What is the murder of an entire people? What it really boils down to is, like, Spock losing his mother. It is really, the film is saying, just an individual tragedy. That's so enormously and profoundly mendacious it's breathtaking. It is summed up, for me, in Old Spock's volte face about meeting Young Spock. First of all he refuses to do so, even though it would be a very useful and helpful thing to do, and even though the fate of entire planets hang in the balance, for reasons to do with the sanctity of the time lines, and the potential for disaster. Later he happily chats with his younger self, and reveals that the actual reason he didn't pop up earlier is that he didn't want to get in the way of Young Spock's bonding with Kirk. Vital that their friendship be cemented, you see.

Imagine a world in which genocide really mattered less than whether you and your best friend were getting on swell. The world of *Trek*09, ladies and gentlemen.

Charles Yu, *How to Live Safely in a Science Fictional Universe* (2009)

Charles Yu's novel is pretty superb: involving, clever, perky, properly science fictional and above all funny. The narrator-protagonist, coincidentally also called Charles Yu, is a time-machine repair man pootling around the titular cosmos of 'Universe 31', an unfinished minor universe full of familiar odds and ends from 20th-century SF.

The novel is not plotted in a linear manner. Indeed, it's not really plotted at all. Charles spends most of the book lurking in his machine, bunking off work, interacting with various synthetic personalities and dwelling on his childhood relationship with his dad. All this happens within a sort of möbius narrative framework: for Yu has shot a future version of himself dead, trapping himself in a temporal loop. More, he's not writing his own narrative so much as transcribing it from a copy given to him by his future self: 'A man brings a book with him back in time, giving it to himself and instructing himself to reproduce the book as faithfully as he can. The book is then published, and after its publication the man buys the book, gets in a time machine and starts the cycle all over again. The book is a perfectly stable physical object that actually exists, despite the fact that it seems to come from nowhere.'

Yu's great skill lies in translating this intriguing but abstract notion into genuinely affecting emotional terms. The short-circuit of time travel, a familiar SF conceit from Heinlein's 'By His Bootstraps' to the *Terminator* movies, becomes an eloquent metaphor for the action of memory in our lives.

Appropriately, pages are busy with the tricks of self-referential game-playing: diagrams; footnotes; pages left blank; excursions into 'the interstitial matrix' that 'fills up the space between stories' and the like. All this could easily have been up-own-fundament annoying, and is sometimes a touch too cute for its own good. But it is all redeemed in the telling by the charm and skill of Yu's voice, pitched somewhere in that interDouglas space between Coupland and Adams.

Because it is a novel fundamentally about a young man's

relationship with his father, its frame of cultural reference is biased towards such SF as the original *Star Wars* trilogy or Philip K Dick. It also understands that levity is the best way to get at some of life's most serious truths. Han Solo, the narrator notes, was 'a hero because he was funny'; Yu's 'phone booth sized' time machine is as much Bill & Ted as Tardis. The thing is: the novel's brilliant stylistic and formal larking about grounds rather than contradicts its emotional truth. Yu's möbius loop doesn't spin free of the pains of living, and we never lose sight of the vertiginous truth Yu memorably articulates (in theorem form) as 'at some point in your life, this statement will be true: Tomorrow you will lose everything for ever.'

Now SF comes in all flavours; and many fans take their genre very seriously indeed. But I sometimes wonder if the default mode of SF isn't comic. After all, there's something inherently playful about the genre, predicated as it is upon mucking about with the premises of reality. SF is an ironic, not a mimetic, mode of art. The best SF is extravagant, prone to creative incongruities and hyperspatial jumps of comprehension, just as jokes are. And like a really good joke, the best SF works because it touches on something that matters to us. In all these ways, *How to Live Safely* is a most excellent debut.

District 9

(directed by Neill Blomkamp, 2009)

In lieu of a proper review of this film, below is the result of me ('@arrroberts') live-tweeting as I watched it on the TV, a little while ago.

> Watching District 9. Much better than District 8 – the best District since 3.
>
> *—about 23 hours ago via Twitter for iPhone*

In reply @Paul_Cornell tweeted: 'Skip ahead to 13. It changes a lot.'

> The aliens are called Prawns. I'd say they look more like Bishops.
>
> *– about 23 hours ago via Twitter for iPhone*

They don't look like Bishops, of course. If anything they look like Queens. But that wouldn't work, gag-wise, so well. Ho hum.

> The main alien is called Christopher Prawn. Coincidentally that was A A Milne's original preferred title.
>
> *– about 22 hours ago via Twitter for iPhone*
>
> Several close-up shots of running people's faces reminding me rather of Sir Digby Chicken Caesar.
>
> *– about 22 hours ago via Twitter for iPhone*

My wife was watching with me; it was she who noted the resemblance between this recurrent camera p.o.v. trick and the Mitchell and Webb sketch. She expressed eloquent and forceful annoyance that I was tweet-passing-off her observation as my own. But, you know: that's marriage.

> Ooh, I say!
>
> *– about 22 hours ago via Twitter for iPhone*

Can't remember what that one was about. Probably some of the loud bang-bang gunplay and exploding-bags-of-blood special effects.

After the end of the film, I articulated my overview of it in the following few tweets:

Good film. Though I get the feeling somebody from the Studio saw an early cut & said: 'hmm, needs another half hour of mindless shooting at the end.'

– about 22 hours ago via Twitter for iPhone.

District 9: some plotholes. There are supposedly 1.8 million prawns, when the film clearly shows there are only 25 or so.

– about 22 hours ago via Twitter for iPhone.

Given that they're all CGI, presumably it wasn't a casting/budget issue.

– about 22 hours ago via Twitter for iPhone

Also, I didn't understand why the prawns didn't just take their superguns and steal all the catfood in the world.

– about 22 hours ago via Twitter for iPhone.

That last tweet was about District 9. If you didn't realise that, or haven't seen the film, it might confuse you.

– about 22 hours ago via Twitter for iPhone

I think that about sums it up, except for my sister, who @'d me halfway through with: 'great film!! fakkin prahns!!', which has a certain laconic precision arguably missing from this review.

The Book of Eli

(directed by The Hughes Brothers, 2010)

HUGHES A1: You know what's cool? *The Road.* Did you see that film? That's a cool film.

HUGHES A2: You're not wrong, my brother. Kind of a downer, though.

HUGHES A1: All the way down.

HUGHES A2: You know what it was missing?

HUGHES A1: What?

HUGHES A2: Ninja swordplay.

HUGHES A1: Well – what film *isn't* improved by Ninja swordplay?

HUGHES A2: Ninja swordplay is *cool.*

HUGHES A1: Way cool!

HUGHES A2: Tell you what, though. You know what's cooler than a Ninja swordsman?

HUGHES A1: What?

HUGHES A2: A *blind* Ninja swordsman!

HUGHES A1: Wowz! Like Rutger Hauer in *Blind Fury*?

HUGHES A2: Rutger Hauer *is* cool. Who's cooler? – except, maybe…

HUGHES A1: …a black Rutger Hauer?

HUGHES A2: You read my mind!

HUGHES A1: Obviously a black Rutger Hauer is going to be cooler than some pasty-faced white Rutger Hauer.

HUGHES A2: That's nothing but the truth. There's something missing though. What? What's missing?

HUGHES A1: Cannibalism?

HUGHES A2: Obviously we'll include the cannibalism.

HUGHES A1: Scenes from *Deadwood*?

HUGHES A2: Yeah, yeah. But…

HUGHES A1: *Mad Max 2*?

HUGHES A2: You think I'm an idiot? Of course *Mad Max 2*! No… something else…

HUGHES A1: Distinguished elderly British character actors making fools of themselves in rags with fake US accents?

HUGHES A2: Goes without saying. No, I'm thinking something else is needful.

HUGHES A1: [*Pulling the name from thin air*] Truffaut's *Farenheit 451*?

HUGHES A2: What?

HUGHES A1: Not all of it. Just the last scenes.

HUGHES A2: That's it! That's the perfect combination of cinematic influence for the greatest film ever made in the history of mankind! *The Road* meets *Blind Fury* meets *Mad Max 2* meets *Farenheit 451* with a dash of *Deadwood* and *Rising Damp*, just for good measure.

HUGHES A1: Let's do it!

HUGHES A2: Yeah! [*Pause*]

HUGHES A1: You don't think...

HUGHES A2: What, my brother?

HUGHES A1: You don't think... that people might think... it's a bit silly?

HUGHES A2: Did they call *The Road* silly? Is a *Utah Film Critics Association Award* silly? Is it?

HUGHES A1: You're right! Let's do it!

Lost (2004-2010)

1.

A transfer is 'lossy' if the amount of information encoded in an original becomes markedly depleted in the process of copying it. This might happen for many reasons. So, for example: transferring a six-season, 120-hour TV drama (including dozens of main and scores of minor characters, a welter of interlacing plotlines, complex internal mythology, and huge fan paranarrative) into a short review article for an online venue. That's going to be lossy.

That said, now that the show is over this process has become markedly less lossy. That's because whilst *Lost* was ongoing, there was no way of knowing which of the blizzard of details, plotlines, characters, and so on had a bearing on the central mystery of the show. Now the finale has aired, a lot of those earlier data – all of which was earnestly pawed over by fans at the time, held up to the light, microscopically interpreted for possible meanings – have simply dropped out of the picture. Was it all about the numbers? About the Dharma Initiative? About time travel? About polar bears? Well, now, we know the answer.

This review, like Caesar's Gaul, is divided into four parts. Part 2 attempts to summarise the show's tangled storylines; part 3 offers some general observations; and in part 4, I discuss the show's finale. At that point I spoil without compunction. Be warned.

But perhaps there is a danger in attempting to respond to a series like *Lost* after the end. The main motor of the show, the hook upon which were painfully suspended so many millions of fans, myself included, was 'What's it all about?' (alloyed with a little 'What's going to happen next?'). The last few episodes of season 6 provided the definitive answer to the first of these questions, and that answer will now inevitably colour memories of the show. More: that answer will tend to *diminish* the show – as we all knew it would, even before we had an inkling of what it was – not only in the sense that it closes down the other avenues of possible interpretation, but because it involves a kind of optical illusion of coherence. We need to hold in mind just how wonderfully streaked, freaked, spattered, and dribbled this show used to be. How superbly it resisted the stare-eyed hermeneutic obsessions of its fanbase (myself included), not with mere opacity but by a sort of glorious promiscuity of more 'meaning' than even we could stomach.

A point of comparison might be *The X-Files*, a similarly multiseason show about the search for meaning in a world in which conventional, scientific reality is interpenetrated in various dramatic ways by the supernatural and superscientific. But to make the comparison is straight away to be struck by the tonal difference between the two shows: *The X-Files* was low-lit, nocturne-coloured, over-focussed, earnest to the point of po-facedness. *Lost*, on the other hand, lives in the memory as luminous, inventive, effortlessly surprising and compelling; stupid but in a creative, engaging sense.

The X-Files started out with a neat conceptual reversal: a man and a woman investigate strange goings-on, but it's the *man* who's all intuitive and emotional and credulous, and the *woman* who's all sceptical and scientific and rigorous. But *The X-Files* couldn't sustain its integrity, perhaps because it was focussed too tightly on just two main characters – but more probably, I think, because the longer it went on the more fatally diffuse its mythology became. In individual episodes, *The X-Files* treated many various aspects of supernatural folklore, but as the series went on these aggregated to a point where the show was committed to a view of the world in which *everything* was true, no matter how absurdly boneheaded: UFOs, ghosts, Bigfoot, ESP, government conspiracy, anything and everything.

Lost has worked the other way, turning and turning in a tightening gyre as the aggregating revelations channelled viewers along towards a conclusion rather than simply an ending. But it also managed to be an inclusive text, welcoming and beguiling where *The X-Files* became increasingly rebarbative. It was, at its best, less a show about finding answers to puzzling questions and more about coping with extraordinary, supernatural circumstances – coping as a group, being-in-the-world with friends. Although it seems a strange thing to say, given how violent and extreme much of the drama was, it was this friendliness that underpinned the show's enormous commercial success.

2.

We start with the crash of a passenger airplane (Oceanic Airlines Flight 815 from Sydney – a nice in-joke about-turn one-upping of one of Tintin's better adventures, *Vol. 714 pour Sydney*) upon a tropical Pacific island. This island is a place with some very unusual features: a strange poltergeist force that kills people; apparitions of the dead; polar bears. There are, we discover, others on the island, a secretive and dangerous bunch. There is a radio transmitter broadcasting a sequence of numbers – 4, 8, 15, 16, 23, and 42 – that as the series progresses appear in various guises, possessing (it is implied) a mystic significance.

The show has a large ensemble cast, but certain characters came quickly to the fore: Jack Shephard (Matthew Fox), a spinal surgeon; Sawyer (Josh Holloway; we later learn this character's real name is 'James Ford'), a louche con-artist; Kate Austen (Evangeline Lilly), a prisoner wanted for murder; and wheelchair-bound John Locke (Terry O'Quinn). Other characters include Charlie Pace (played by hobbit-actor Dominic Monaghan) a drug-addicted British rock star; Claire (Emilie de Ravin), a heavily pregnant Australian with whom Charlie falls in love; Michael Dawson (Harold Perrineau), an American separated from his wife – their young son Walt (Malcolm David Kelley) is with Michael on the island; Sayid Jarrah (Naveen Andrews), a former Iraqi National Guard torturer; Sun-Hwa Kwon (Yunjin Kim), a wealthy Korean woman and her husband Jin-Soo (Daniel Dae Kim), who speaks no English; and Hugo 'Hurley' Reyes (Jorge Garcia), a laid-back dude from California. We learn about these characters, and others, in great detail, in part through their interactions with one another on the island, but more because the show is built upon a lamination of on-island narrative interspersed with flashbacks to characters' pre-island lives.

Much of the first season is given over to the day-to-day business of surviving – building shelters, hunting and gathering food and so on – with the flashbacks, though sometimes crudely handled, on balance adding impressive roundedness to the ensemble. Folded into this are various inexplicable developments. John Locke's incurable spinal injury is miraculously cured. The survivors spot an incongruous polar bear. Jack Shephard sees the ghost of his father. A terrifying worm-shaped cloud of black smoke occasionally flies out of the jungle and kills people. Locke discovers a strange hatch-door embedded in the ground, and becomes convinced not only that the island is magical (and he and the other survivors 'special') but that if he can only open the hatch, all his questions will be answered. The hatch, however, resists his efforts.

Indeed, the 'hatch' storyline was drawn out to the point where it became actively annoying. It was the writers' way of parsing what they evidently took to be a core theme of the show: faith. Locke's groundless belief that the hatch would provide him with answers, and his faith in the island more generally, functioned as a figure for 'religious faith' more generally, and was opposed to Jack's empirical scepticism. Jack, the de facto leader of the survivors, doesn't think the island is special; he just wants to get everybody away and home. Rescue, though, doesn't arrive, and the writers' thumbs were in the balance from the get-go. Locke's 'faith,' though without rational basis, gifts him a luminous surety and existential focus; Jack's faithless practical goal only emphasises how hollow and miserable his existence is – unsatisfied in his job, separated from his wife, bereft at the loss of his remote father.

Once the premise was established, watching *Lost* became mostly a matter of attending to the narrative moves made by the writers, each of which took us closer to or further away from the 'solution' to the island's mystery, which viewers in effect marked, as with a kind of mental chess notation, '?'or'!', or occasionally as '?!' The slow revelation that there were others living on the island, called, logically enough, 'The Others,' merited '!' The decision to draw out the Locke/hatch storyline for so long, on the other hand, was '?' – although the final opening of the hatch, which turns out to be marked with the mystic 4, 8, 15, 16, 23, and 42 numbers, was one of the highlights of the series. (In Hurley's flashback we discovered that he had been propelled from happy poverty to a miserable, indeed cursed wealth by winning the lottery with these exact numbers. 'The numbers are bad!' is his succinct judgment upon them.) At the bottom of the hatch is a 1980s bunker, furnished with supplies by its builders, the mysterious 'Dharma Initiative,' and inside is Desmond (played by Henry Ian Cusick). Desmond must type 'the numbers' (that is, 4, 8, 15, 16, 23, and 42) into an antique computer terminal every 108 minutes. If he doesn't, he has been told that the island will explode. Will it? Who knows? The excellence of this narrative conceit is in its neat embodiment of ontological arbitrariness: that point where unfounded faith and unfounded doubt bite hard into life – having to adjust the whole of one's existence to adapt to an inflexible 108-minute cycle, all the time wondering whether you are simply wasting your time. At any rate the Flight 815 survivors move into this bunker and take shifts at the button. This has the unfortunate consequence that Desmond's character can be moved into a much less dramatically fruitful star-crossed lovers' storyline.

After a sluggish, '?'-heavy second season – which, it seems, helped shed quite a proportion of the show's audience – *Lost* picked up again for the third. There were further mysteries, and the Dharma Initiative's extensive spread of now-mysteriously-abandoned hatches and buildings contained further clues, not least an 'orientation film' for new members of the Initiative (!). A second set of survivors, who were in the tail section of the plane when it crashed, are discovered, rather needlessly complicating the ensemble (?). Amongst the survivors, a love triangle is clunkingly elaborated throughout the second and third series: Jack and bad-boy conman Sawyer both fall for pert Kate, despite (or perhaps because of) her murderously dark past. She in turn loves one, or other, or both; the writers spin it out. I found this all very '??', but I know fans for whom the whole Jack/Sawyer/Kate thing was thoroughly '!!'. It is revealed that Yemi, the brother of Flight 815 passenger and Nigerian drug-lord 'Mr Eko' (Adewale Akinnuoye-Agbaje), crashed on the island (in a short-range propeller aircraft that has somehow made it all the way from Africa to the mid-Pacific) and died. Mr Eko's flashbacks make it clear that, like many characters, he has done very bad things in his life. Now that he's on the island he builds a chapel, to point up the writers' interest in religious faith and atonement, and then is randomly killed by the black-smoke monster (??). Indeed, throughout all six seasons the writers demonstrate an almost psychotically cavalier attitude to killing off characters, something undertaken in the first instance in the interest of dramatic intensity and what Aristotle called *peripeteia*.

The 'Others' send an individual called Ben Linus (played by the excellent Michael Emerson) to infiltrate the survivors' camp, but they rumble him, lock him in a cell, and torture him. There's a good deal of torture in the show, actually, and it is handled with pretty much the same moral idiocy found in – say – *24*: ethical scruples are simply overridden by a spurious urgency that is actually only the formal motor of serial TV entertainment (that *the plot move on*, that *viewers not be bored*).

Nevertheless, the introduction of Ben was a '!!!' move by the writers. For we discover that Ben is actually the leader of the Others, and his ruthless yet queerly heartbroken Machiavellian manoeuvrings, which range from manipulating people and emotional blackmail all the way up the scale to murder and indeed mass-murder, illuminate not only the rationale of the 'Dharma Initiative' (of which he used to be a part, but which he himself brought to an end via the expedience of murdering all the staff with poison gas) and the island itself. Everything Ben does, he does 'for' the island, about which he has a faith even more fundamentalist than John Locke.

Ben, though, describes himself as only a deputy. He works for the guy really in charge: a mysterious individual nobody has met called 'Jacob' ('a great man,' according to Ben). In one splendidly oddball scene, Ben takes various people to Jacob's house, a ramshackle hut ringed by a trail of grey dust on the ground. When they go inside the place seems empty, but then the furniture starts flying about, a shadowy figure is very fleetingly glimpsed moaning (was it?) 'Help me,' and everything goes quiet. The 'Who is Jacob?' question was a perfectly pitched narrative chess move.

We discover at the end of series 2 what happens if the numbers are not entered in the Dharma Initiative's machine – a huge explosion and bright light in the sky that wreaks some kind of nonspecific havoc. Jack is still focussed on getting the survivors off the island, and Ben is focussed on keeping them there. An obstetrics-themed plot is introduced: the island has magical healing powers, but by the same token it rebuts birth, and pregnant women spontaneously abort. Ben's 'people' – the 'Others' – have attempted to overcome this in various ways, not least by shipping in a pregnancy specialist called Juliet Burke (played by Elizabeth Mitchell). But two of the survivors – Australian Claire and Korean Sun-Hwa Kwon – give birth to babies (?!). An Australian billionaire called Charles Widmore, played by Alan Dale ('Jim from *Neighbours*' to millions of Oz and UK fans) is looking for the island, for his own reasons, and sends in a team of mercenaries, one of whom kills Ben's daughter. As the series of the show piled up the plotlines began to become impacted, like a bad tooth. At the end of series 4 the writers played one of their intermittently brilliant moves. Against a creakily melodramatic plotline of bombs in freighters, fights and flights, and the culmination of Jack's efforts to get his people home, Ben *moves the island*. He does this by descending into an icy subterranean chamber and turning a giant wheel set horizontally into the wall. This makes the island vanish; and incidentally ejects Ben Linus through space/time into the Sahara desert. For sheer bravura unexpectedness, I annotate this '!!!'.

My reproduction of the series in review-summary form is growing lossier and lossier, I'm afraid. Season 4, broadly, concerned the fates of those Losties who followed Jack off the island. In a nutshell, they were not happy. A bizarre-even-for-*Lost* conspiracy by Charles Widmore's people sunk a fake Flight 815 at sea (??), from which the returned Losties are presented to the world's media as the only survivors – a fiction they acceded in to keep the island secret and their friends still there safe. But Jack is miserable, despite living an outwardly happy L.A. life with Kate raising Claire's baby as their own. He becomes convinced they must all return to the island. John Locke has similar ambitions, and has been travelling around trying to persuade the returnees to reband and go back. Suicidally demoralised by his failure to do so, he decides to hang himself. Ben Linus turns up, talks him out of self-murder, extracts some information from him, and then *throttles him with the cord* (!!!). Not for the first time waning viewer interest in a too-messy tangle of plotlines is redeemed by a strikingly pitched surprise development. At any rate, with an improbable series of contrivances, the off-island Losties are returned to the island, John Locke's corpse included. Once there the dead Locke apparently comes back to life.

Season 5, broadly, manoeuvred the show in an explicitly SFnal direction with a dose of time travel. A handful of key characters, including Sawyer, Juliet, Sayyid, Hurley, and a new guy with the ability to commune, spirit-medium like, with dead people (Miles Straume, played by Ken Leung), are all thrown back in time to the 1970s, and the height of the Dharma Initiative's presence on the island. They assume false identities and become, improbably enough, key members of the initiative; Sawyer and Juliet fall in love and live idyllically together for several years. But their true identities are eventually revealed. The season ends with a farrago of nonsensical plotting about schlepping a 1950s atomic bomb (miraculously portable) to an energy rift in the island that the Dharma Initiative is excavating. Jack believes that detonating the former in the latter would cancel out the initial crash of Flight 815 and permit everybody to get on with their lives. Narrative obstacles are placed in the way of this move, but in a fairly desultory way, since we never doubt the Chekhovian dramatic principle by which an atom bomb, once introduced into the narrative, must be used. And so it goes: the bomb goes off; Juliet is killed; Sawyer is heartbroken; and the Losties are blown back to the present day, although not (as Jack believed they would be) into a timeline in which the plane never crashed.

Like the unopened hatch in the first two seasons, the time-travel storyline in season 5 feels in retrospect like a massive piece of narrative padding. But – to repeat myself – that probably says more about the problem of hindsight than anything else. In the moment, and despite myriad cheesinesses, it was superbly absorbing stuff. More, the writers announced that season 6 would be the last, winning over at least some of those fans who had become disillusioned with the thought that a solution to the show's core mysteries would be endlessly deferred. On the other hand, season 6 made plain a shift away from the basically science fictional narrative logic of season 5. We moved into rather self-consciously mythic, supernatural imaginative topographies; and the 'Big Themes' of 'faith' and 'atonement' with which the writers had flirted in the earlier seasons came galumphing back in to stamp all over the finale with hobnailed boots. Discussing these will entail spoilers, so before I get to that let me put down a few more general observations.

3.

Any potted account of *Lost*'s main storylines, such as the above, must tend to make one thing clear: that it was at root *a ludicrous show*. Daft, implausible, hyperactive, given to lurching shifts of focus and scale of positively Van Vogtian proportions. To say so is not to dismiss it, of course. Ludicrous is not the same thing as risible. The show's genius was in the way it fully inhabited its ludicrousness, the way it turned the clunky paraphernalia of TV melodrama into a near-perfect simulacrum-fable of profundity. It did this by playing *with* the grain of its daftness; always ingenuously in tune with its own absurdity, neither too archly knowing nor embarrassed by it. Narrative contrivances a first-year screenwriting student would dismiss as too hokey were deployed not once but many times – the literal ticking bomb, for instance; the Mexican standoff; the run-and-chase. The scriptwriters enjoyed the metaphorical narrative sugar-rush of killing off major characters (or in

121

one variant of this: of introducing a new character in such a way as to make it plain s/he will be a new major player, only to kill him/her before they even get going). In small doses this can be joltingly effective, textually speaking; but it became so totally a feature of the *Lost* universe that it ended up creating a weirdly parodic version of humanity. *Everybody* on the island, it seemed – no matter what other traits their characters displayed – *everybody* was only ever a moment away from punching somebody, torturing somebody for information, or shooting somebody else dead. I think only Hurley and Charlie, amongst the major characters, abstained from the social performance of murderous violence. For everybody else it was a mundane business; the pistol whipping, the rifle shot to the chest, the thrown knife into somebody's back. Cumulatively this created the vibe that pretty much all the people on the island were *terrible terrible people*. Picture a world as a tropical island paradise wholly populated by conscience-free, violently disposed supermodels. Et – *voilà*.

Nor was the show helped by its codes of representation. The opening episode (in its day the most expensive TV pilot ever made) set the bar high: a wham-bam launch with properly cinematic production values. But as the show went on, the cracks increasingly began to show. A half-dozen Hawaiian locations had to serve for the whole island, and several of these became debilitatingly over-familiar with reuse, however cleverly the set-dressers attempted to disguise them as new. Budgets were pared as the overall viewing figures declined. The plane in the first episode looked like (because it was) a real smashed-up airliner; the plane in the last episode looked like (because it was) CGI, and cheap CGI at that.

Then there's the acting. With only two exceptions, the acting was awful throughout. This was, I think, because most of the players were cast for their looks rather than their acting chops. Matthew Fox, for instance, is a very handsome if slightly squirrel-eyed man, but as Jack his performance was staggeringly one-note – a sort of strangulated, doe-eyed miserable intensity *all the time*, regardless of situation. Evangeline Lilly is very comely, but her 'Kate' completely failed to communicate the conflicted depths of an abuse-survivor and murderer, achieving instead only a sort of simpering tangle-haired prettiness. Josh Holloway is also very comely – better looking than Jack, actually – but his performance as Sawyer consisted wholly of scowling. No matter what his character was supposed to be feeling or doing, Holloway buckled his handsome brow in to a scowl and bit off his dialogue. One need not be Stanislavski to see that 'acting' and 'scowling' are not the same thing.

Yunjin Kim's comeliness is of a more soulful sort, although her role, especially her scenes off-island, required much more than she could give, acting-wise. Daniel Dae Kim, another good looking man, may or may not be a proper actor; his role didn't give him the chance to show us. Naveen Andrews' Sayyid was little more than a fake 'foreign' accent and a lot of moody positioning of his handsome mug and sculpted body. And worst of all was Claire. Her part needed an actress who could convincingly portray a young woman robbed of her child passing through murderous insanity and back into the light. Emilie de Ravin could do nothing more than stand there angling her undeniably pretty face at the camera and blinking slowly. The principle at work was that of US daytime soaps, viz: 'When you look as good as I do, who needs acting?' There will be fans who disagree with this assessment, and champion the acting ability evident in the portrayal of one or other of the characters. This is because they fancy the actor in question.

There were two exceptions, but even they struggled with the scripts they were given. First off, Michael Emerson did something very memorable with Ben Linus: a wonderfully nuanced balance of needy weediness and a steel-tough resilience. When, as he often did, he resorted to murderous violence, we believed it completely, but Emerson's acting was such that even the most brutal behaviour did not alienate us from him. And this was a problem in the long run, because the writers didn't know what to do with him, whether to spin him as hateable or loveable. They plumped for the latter, and it tangled foolishly with the fact that Ben was responsible for more murder on the island than anybody else.

And secondly, in Terry O'Quinn's John Locke the show found an actor with a remarkable screen-presence. That said, Locke only really came into his own in the final season, where he played not Locke but the evil alt-Locke. Here O'Quinn's effortlessly carried, slightly sinister charisma, his ability to combine charm and menace, worked superbly. But this in turn brought out the problem in the earlier seasons. In life Locke was fundamentally a pitiable character – a loser – and O'Quinn struggled to fit his larger-than-loser presence into the role.

Putting all these beautiful people (Ben, Charlie, and Hurley excepted) through the over-caffeinated bounceabout contortions of plot also meant that the show as a whole kept losing its focus. It toyed with *Robinson Crusoe*, or *Tempest*, allusions, but they sputtered into nothing. It picked up the notion that everything might be an SFnal material novum, and then entirely *Lost* interest in that. It seemed to be saying something obliquely about 9-11 – from the world being changed by a catastrophic plane-crash at the start of season 1, to the sight in season 6 of Iraqi Sayyid's death by suicide-bombing (he grabs an about-to-explode bomb and runs off down a corridor, blowing himself up for the greater good of his friends). But no ideological coherence emerges from that sort of reading. Characters are named after famous philosophers (Locke, Bentham, Rousseau, Hume) but without any actual philosophical content behind the gesture.

A fan who even dipped a toe into the para-material generated by fans could see that part of the appeal of the show was in its tantalising detail, any one of which could be the key that explained everything. In an important sense, the point of the show was the elevation of this kind of detail to a new aesthetic prominence. When its big reveal finally came, as it must, part of it would be to dissolve much of this beautiful tracery. And so it was. Bye-bye mystic numbers, Dharma Initiative, polar bears, big-wheel-for-moving-the-island and wholly-unresolved-why-can't-people-give-birth-on-the-island storyline. Hello Jacob, smoke monster, and mystical fable of faith and atonement. Boo.

4.

This review has been lossy, but the series' finale was lossier still. Almost everything that made the show compelling was filtered away. Instead we were left to chew on the ship's biscuit of one dry, stodgy fabulation: Jacob brought the Flight 815 survivors to the islands as 'candidates.' He had been surveilling their lives remotely for decades so as to select them. The revivified John Locke is revealed as the smoke monster in human form. The monster has a murderous animus against Jacob, and a desire to get off the island; but an unspecified rule or charm prevents him killing Jacob directly. So he persuades Ben Linus to kill him instead. There's a weird narrative cul-de-sac concerning a temple staffed by various quasi-religious types, hitherto unmentioned in the series; but Smoke Monster Locke, unfettered now that Jacob is dead, kills most of the occupants of this, and persuades most of the Losties that they must all leave together.

It's a ruse, though. Smoke Monster Locke actually wants to destroy the island and everybody on it. There are vague but dire warnings that if he escapes from the island it will be the end of the world. Meanwhile, interspersed in almost every episode, are what the scriptwriters rather wincingly call 'flash-sideways,' glimpses of a timeline in which Flight 815 never crashed, and all the main characters, living notably improved lives, interact with one another in LA.

The antepenultimate episode, 'Across the Sea,' finally and rather disappointingly revealed the kernel of the series mythology. We go back to the island, in AD 44. A Latin-speaking unnamed character (played by The West Wing's Allison Janney) rescues a heavily pregnant shipwrecked woman, delivers her twin baby boys, and kills her. She raises the children as her own: one – Jacob – dressed in a conveniently allegorical white tunic, the other, unnamed, in a black one. Her business is guarding the island, or more specifically guarding a particular magical cave full of magical light. This, we're told, is 'the source, the heart of the island.' Her intention is for the son-in-black to take over her guardianship when the time comes; but he instead becomes obsessed with leaving the island, and collaborates with the tribe that inhabits the place to that end. For some reason, though we're not told what, he must not leave the island. So mother knocks him out, kills the entire tribe (yet another unremarked, casual, small-scale genocide) and instead gives the job of guarding the source to a reluctant Jacob. Angry, the son-in-black stabs his mother to death, and in retaliation Jacob throws him into the magic cave, killing him but transforming his spirit into the smoke monster.

We are asked to believe that all the shenanigans of the previous seasons have actually been the circuitous process by which Jacob chooses to recruit his replacement – after two thousand years, and for unstated reasons. He has narrowed this down to six: Kate, Hugo, Sawyer, Jack, and the Kwons. He manages to explain the state of affairs to these six, despite being dead. After hearing his explanation, Jack volunteers to replace him. In the final episode the characters all converge on the heart of the island; Desmond descends into the cave of light to discover an antique temple, a pool of glowing water, and in the middle a large stone bung. Removing this makes all the magic water drain down the plughole, causing the island to start to sink into the sea. It also robs Smoke Monster Locke of his invulnerability, which means that Jack is able to kill him, although he himself suffers a fatal wound in the process. Jack drags himself back to the magic cave, reinserts the bung, and restores the island's magic before finally expiring. Hurley, it seems, must take over Jacob's role. The startled viewer mentally pencils in a '??' to annotate this plot-move before the nature of the flash-sideways is revealed – it is a timeless space created by all the characters, who are all dead, so that they can 'find themselves' before moving on – and '??' becomes '???'

The initial objection to this denouement is that it's shit. A more nuanced response is that it is anticlimactic, underpowered, and doesn't make sense. Purgatory here is all the main characters flying into an early 21st-century LA. knowing neither that they are dead, nor that they ever knew one another or ever went to the island in life. They *did* go to the island; the narrative conceit is the island was 'real' and this flash-sideways not. But they must 'find one another' by coincidentally bumping into the others until some significant contact triggers a memory of their time on the island, and with it the knowledge that they are dead. As to why some characters are present in this purgatory and some not, or why some are present but (like Locke's father) in a vegetative state, or why dying entails temporary amnesia of life until you meet some, but not other, dead people, or why Desmond has been given the job of orchestrating a final grand get-together at a church – which job he undertakes in part by running Locke down in his car – none of this is clear. At the church, Jack is the last to understand the true state of affairs. Only when he discovers his father's coffin to be empty, and has a chinwag with his old man's revivified person, does he realise. He comes into the main body of the church where, teary-eyed and grinning, the entire main cast is assembled. The series then ends on a gag-reflex-tickling group hug. Indeed, as a couple of reviewers noted, the final scene looks much more like a Hollywood wrap party than anything that belonged in the show itself.

The point of this ending is not religious, actually; or not specifically doctrinally religious. That is to say, the show went out of its way to present its notionally purgatorial afterlife as inclusively non-denominational. Jack's Dad may be called 'Christian Shephard' ('Really?' Kate asks, with a knowing smirk), but when he appears to his son he stands before a stained glass window devoted upon which we see the Muslim Crescent, Jewish Star and Hindu Wheel, as well as the Christian cross. The same rather superstitious ecumenicalism was presumably behind the decision to set the death/rebirth/atonement 'Across the Sea' episode not in A.D. 33 but in A.D. 44.

This is important, actually. The show's lurch into the post-mortem existences of its cast was not so much a religious move as it was a laying the writers' cards on the table. Whilst the show ran, I, like many fans, believed the ultimate resolution would be science-fictional – material, pseudo-scientific. I was wrong. The finale makes plain that the idiom of the show all along was magic.

This, in the absence of any more specific explanations, covers the 'answer' to the many unexplained loose ends. Why was Miles able to commune with dead people? It was magic. How could it be that the numbers 4, 8, 15, 16, 23, and 42 cropped up so significantly, coincidentally and ubiquitously? It was magic. How was Ben Linus able to spin a wheel and make an entire Pacific island (all the stuff below the waterline, we assume, as well as all the stuff above) vanish and reappear somewhere else? Magic. How were the brothers' lives (and the lives of some other characters) so lengthily extended? Magic. What, in the final analysis, was *Lost* about? The finale makes the answer to this question plain: it was about magical thinking.

Perhaps that looks dismissive, but I don't mean it to be. 'Magic' here is not a catch-all or non-specific term. In fact, understanding that the show is about magical thinking enables us to be more specific about the emotional focus of the show. *Lost* was about magic in a general sense, but more specifically it was about *bereavement as magical thinking*.

I'll conclude this review by expanding upon this last point a little, and I'll do that by quoting from an essay by Roger Luckhurst: 'Reflections on Joan Didion's The Year of Magical Thinking' [New Formations 67 (2009)]. 'Magical thinking,' Luckhurst points out, 'is in fact an incredibly hot topic in empirical psychological research.' However rationally scientific and material we might think our lives to be, 'magical thinking' is a palpable and very significant socialcultural fact. Research into this aspect of our lives retains much of the intellectual framework set up by J. G. Frazer's The Golden Bough (1890), in which sympathetic magic works through the laws of similarity and contiguity ('things which have been in contact with each other continue to act on each other at a distance after the physical contact has been severed'). Beliefs about who can and cannot catch AIDS and from what objects, for instance, differ around the world but consistently privilege magical and moral pollutions over the facts of viral transmission… Research has also targeted how stressful situations reduce the ability to control cognitive operations and thus amplify magical thinking, a process in which 'individuals may generate solutions that increase their control over the sources of stress.'

Luckhurst notes that 'Modernity' (we might particularly include 'science fiction' here) 'has defined its rationality through the suppression of magical thought.'

This is what Weberian rationality means: 'the world is disenchanted. One need no longer have recourse to magical means.' Belief in magical agencies becomes aligned to the primitive and the child. Edward Tylor, one of the first professional anthropologists in England, argued in 1871 that the function of anthropology was to seek out and eliminate 'survivals' of primitive thought, the 'pernicious delusions' such as magic that could only be associated with 'the lowest known stages of civilisation.' Frazer's study of magic was conceived within the same evolutionary framework. Magic was the most primitive set of human beliefs, 'a spurious system of natural law' that hadn't yet advanced to the more conceptually sophisticated delusion of religious belief, which was in turn finally overthrown by a rational understanding of causation. Freud propped himself on Tylor and Frazer's model for his discussion of animism, magic and the omnipotence of thought in Totem and Taboo.

Luckhurst goes on to note that 'every one of these theorists, however, was perplexed by the brute *persistence* of magical thinking into the heart of modernity.' He cites a number of subsequent writers who have addressed this. Simon During, for instance, has examined the rise of 'secular magic' in modernity, the imperfect stamping out of superstition creating instead 'a fuzzy and variegated vernacular modern magic' that is a strange mix of superstition, religious sentiment, and a knowing suspension of disbelief. This describes the milieu of *Lost* pretty well; and I'd say it makes more sense to read the show's fascination with 'belief' as being about 'enchantment' rather than adumbrating a specifically religious agenda.

The key context for all this, as Luckhurst notes, is bereavement.

Confronting death's radical discontinuity 'prompts all kinds of magical evasion and beliefs in forms of posthumous survival.' Grief plays 'magic tricks' on our subjectivity and cognition. 'In Charles Taylor's terms, the modern self is 'buffered, 'yet traumatic events puncture that protective sphere and return us instantly to the pre-modern self which is 'porous', and thus open to all kinds of belief in occult transmissions and sympathetic magic... the psychoanalyst Sandor Ferenczi believed the same thing. 'In the moment of trauma,' Ferenczi said in the early 1930s, 'some sort of omniscience about the world [...] makes the person [...] more or less clairvoyant.'

Lost, as a show, begins with a massive dramatic externalisation of the traumatic event – the plane crash – which is in turn the symbolic articulation of a specific bereavement: Jack is on Flight 815 carrying back the dead body of his father. The key players have similar paternal bereavement experiences: Sawyer became a con-man himself because of a traumatic childhood experience in which a con-man (whose name Sawyer adopts) resulted in the death of his father. Kate is herself responsible for the traumatic death of her abusive father. This triad is at the emotional heart of the show, flanked by Locke – whose own abusive father abandoned him, tricked him into giving up his organs, and tried to kill him – and Ben Linus, whose father was a sadsack alcoholic whom he eventually killed. All these father-oriented storylines find their nexus in the symbolic father of the island, the man with the Biblically patriarchal name 'Jacob' (who himself, significantly enough, is revealed to be fatherless). The murder of this father-figure, and his replacement, is where the show reveals itself as having been going all along.

Lost is not about 'fathers' in a general sense, then. It is more specifically about the death of fathers; about how we live when our father has passed away. Fathers are what is *Lost* in *Lost*; and negotiating the process of bereavement is what orchestrates the various sorts of magical thinking on display in the narratives. The nice irony is that the show, by staging its own finale, has enacted its theme. What's *Lost* for fans of the show now is precisely *Lost*; we are bereaved of our weekly fix of island magic. That's how this deeply addictive, daft, yet sadly missed show worked.

Hannu Rajaniemi, *The Quantum Thief* (2010)

Well, this is very good indeed. It's set in a far-future, post-disaster, high-tech, suavely elegant solar system – more specifically, most of the novel takes place in 'the oubliette', a sort of Howl's-Moving-Castle city on Mars. The mix is something like 40% *Dancers at the End of Time* and 60% Charlie Stross – though judging by his author photo, Rajaniemi would look a smidgeon less incongruous in an *A-Ha* tribute act than would Stross. But the book has Stross's inventiveness, and deep intelligence, and farseeing imagination, alongside Moorcock's stylish feel and flow.

At the heart it's a heist story: Jean le Flambeur is sprung from a deep space prison by the enigmatic warrior Mieli and her Banksish sentient spaceship *Perhonen*, in order to pull-off a complicated crime upon Mars. Meili is in the service of a mysterious, capricious goddess-like being, and the plot unwraps its several mysteries in a very satisfying manner. The Oubliette in particular is a splendid creation; not so much in terms of its far-future hardware as its social codes of privacy, guarded by information-exchange veils called 'guevelots', policed by 'tzaddicks' – and its currency, *time*, to be lavishly spent or carefully hoarded as citizens countdown towards a 'death' that reprocesses their consciousnesses into 'Quiet' machines that do all the hard areoforming and city maintenance work. There's also a quick-witted Holmes-like youth, with a genius for solving crimes. I didn't entirely see what, in a world of unimaginable quantum computational power, he *had* that made his data analysis so special or so superior to machinic AI deductive powers, but perhaps it makes more sense to see him more as a function of the genre (crime and detection) than the worldbuilding.

If the first quarter is an occasionally thorny read, it's because Rajaniemi launches straight in with a commendable density of unexplained description and without the condescension of infodumping. But every detail has its place in the larger whole; everything hangs together by the lights of not only scientific but social plausibility, and a critical mass of readerly understanding is reached by about page 100 when everything clicks into place. There is a lot of drinking... almost a *Finnish* quantity of drinking in fact. There's a bit of sex. There's chocolate. The ending is very solid, too, although, since I'm contractually obliged to niggle, I was a touch underwhelmed by the swarming monsters that attack at the showdown: the 'phoboi'. They are (this is a mild spoiler, I suppose) the reason why the moving city has to move, but they struck me as under-realised. Plus: they were called 'phoboi' because that the Greek for 'fears', but the naming clashes a little with the fact that Phobos is, of course, a Martian moon.

Still, this is the most striking SF debut for ages and ages. If you have any interest at all in contemporary hard SF you will read it.

One thing I particularly liked about it was how nicely it was written. I need to qualify that statement, mind you. The prose is positively clogged with neologisms, and the risk is that some, perhaps many, readers will simply butt their heads against prose of this sort:

> The spinescape view is seething with detail, a newtork of q-dots under the skin, proteomic computers in every cell, dense computronium in the bones. Something like that could only be made in the *guberniya* worlds close to the Sun. It seems my rescuers are working for the Sobornost.

But for all its vocabulary density the *rhythms* of Rajaniemi are just lovely – he has a real feel for language, remarkable for a non-native speaker. Paragraphs are threaded along a pulse of iambic or anapestic pacing, tweaked and garnished with enough metrical variety to stop it becoming monotonous. This sort of thing:

> I roll the thought around my head. It seems too *simple*, somehow, too inelegant, too fragile. Would the old me have done that? Stored secrets in the exomemory of an Oubliette identity? It chills me to realise that I have no idea.

Which is to say:

> I roll the thought around my head. It seems Too *simple*, somehow, Too inelegant, Too fragile. Would the old me have done that? Stored secrets in the exomemory of An Oubliette identity? It chills me to realise that I have no idea.

It's not Shakespeare; but it's certainly a cut above the run-of-the-mill tech-saturated prose of this sort of tale. Recommended.

On the other hand, I don't believe 'Rajaniemi' is actually a Raja.

He's not even from India. (He's Finnish, I believe). I assume this is a courtesy title, like 'Duke' Ellington, 'Sir Mixalot' or 'Shahkira'.

Hannu Rajaniemi, *The Fractal Prince* (2012)

The Quantum Thief, Rajaniemi's first novel, caused quite a stir in SF circles. Legendary thief Jean le Flambeur is sprung from a deep space prison by enigmatic Oort-cloud warrior Mieli and her Iain-M-Banksy sentient spaceship *Perhonen* to mastermind a seemingly impossible heist. But it wasn't the story so much as the *flavour* of the book that was so impressive: an SF narrative so hard you'd need a sclerometer to measure it, but written with a sinuous, fin-de-siècle intensity.

Now we have its sequel, *The Fractal Prince*, a direct continuation of *The Quantum Thief* in both story and tone. Once again we start with the hero in a literalised version of a classic thought-experiment (in the first book it was the prisoner's dilemma; in this one Schrödinger's cat). Again le Flambeur must use his wits against hostile artificial intelligences, competing posthuman clans and virus-infected virtual realities. And again the reader must work through prose as stuffed with neologisms as a chocolate chip cookie is with chocolate chips: Zoku jewels, pellagrinis, soborhost bodies, utility fogs, qutlinks, spimescapes and guberniyas. None of it is glossed; you work out their meanings from the contexts of their use. Or you don't.

When setting out their worlds, some SF writers fall back on the 'As you know, Bob...' manoeuvre: having one character explain to another something they both already know about their world. It's a clumsy business (you don't find it in contemporary-set novels, after all: 'As you know, Bob, a car is a four-wheeled engine-powered vehicle used to transport people from place to place...'). But it happens because SF writers need somehow to get the reader up to speed with a world which is, by definition, unfamiliar. To his credit, and the reader's occasional bafflement, Rajaniemi's repudiates this strategy altogether. Despite writing about a far-future considerably stranger than most, he simply throws his reader in at the deep-(space)-end. It can be hard going.

That's not to deny that Rajaniemi's prose *can* be unpacked, with a little effort. Here's the narrator examining a robotic assassin: 'I wonder at the intricacies of its synthbio cells in a diamonoid frame, the fusion power source at the base of the spine and the nifty q-dot transmitters' – comprehensible enough, even if we've no idea what q-dot transmitters actually look like, nifty or otherwise. But at its worst the prose becomes positively indigestible. 'The q-bubble struggles to keep up with the barrage it is taking across the electromagnetic spectrum and switches to neutrino tomography around the Bekenstein epicentre.' That brings, I confess it, no images at all to my mind.

Not that any of this is mere technobabble. Rajaniemi has more degrees in higher mathematics and quantum physics than you could shake a stick at, and the consensus from people who know about these things is that all the elements of his world are scientifically spot-on. But they still sit oddly in a book written less like conventional Hard SF and much more like *art nouveau* (and isn't that two word French phrase a splendid epitome of what SF ought to be?) Here, for example, is le Flambeur in a virtual reality: 'I am standing in the middle of a white forest. There are straight trees with pale, birch-like bark and impossibly symmetrical foliage shaped like crowns or hands in prayer.' As writing that's striking, evocative and, frankly, more like it.

The bottom line is that Rajaniemi is a baroque writer. By 'baroque' I mean not just that his work is characterised by elaborate details and conceptual curlicues – although it is. I mean he writes by *folding* abstruse science and mannered artistry in architecturally intriguing ways. Now 'baroque' can do many things really well, but it can't really do the Sublime, that sense-of-wonder splendour evoked by the vastness of space or the dizzying perspectives of deep time. The stuff that makes the hairs prickle at the back of the neck. When Rajaniemi describes 'an artificial sphere the size of old Earth, made from sunlifted carbon, thinking thoughts bigger than the sum of humanity', his description simply lacks the heft, the mind-wow, that a writer like Steve Baxter so powerfully creates. It's 'a distant amber bubble in the sky, like a snowglobe': more like a model of something than a colossal actuality. And that's true of the whole novel, I think. *The Fractal Prince* addresses some of the largest issues – immortality and death, love and betrayal, the power of the story – but it feels more like an intricate, bejewelled device than a deathstar. Often beautiful it's also, often, rather stiff: a complex but inert piece of art, a mannequin rather than a real boy. But that's as much a strength as a weakness. Thoughtful, hard, densely realised and highly patterned, there's nothing quite like it in contemporary SF.

Robert Browning's 'A Toccata of Bacigalupi'
[Paolo Bacigalupi, *The Windup Girl*, 2010]

I
Oh, Paolo Bacigalupi, this is very strange to find!
I can hardly misconceive you; it would prove me deaf and blind;
For at last I've read your novel, clocked the 'up' it seeks to wind.

II
Your genetic engineering makes a tasty premise; Thai
's rarely heard in science fiction (something we should modify)
And your world-building is nifty, when the oil has gone bye-bye.

III
Ay, because the setting's vivid, teeming and believable
...Varied characters and tensions, a corrupted carnival:
I was never east of Europe – it's as if I saw it all.

IV
But the Geisha is a problem: cheeks so round and lips so red,–
Sexbot who cannot avoid enjoyment whilst abused in bed:
As critique of exploitation, this, I'd say, is underfed.

VI
All the violence she endures is *sexualised* – a racist blend
(Read what Said says in *Orientalism* on that) and
Contradicts the (quote) 'redemptive violence' of her story's end.

VII
Still, five hundred pages finished. Oh, they praised you, it is true!
'Bravo Paolo! *That* was SF! Worthy of hullaballoo!
'Here's the Nebula, the Campbell, Locus – half a Hugo too!'

VIII
As for Thailand and her people, merely born to bloom and drop,
Here on Earth they bore their fruitage, mirth and folly were the crop:
How much clockwork's left, I wonder, when the winding has to stop?

Jean-Christophe Valtat's *Aurorarama* (2010)

Valtat's *Aurorarama* is a steampunk novel. I have some problems with steampunk as a genre, and discuss them below (there's a part two to this review, you see),but I want to start out by noting that *Aurorarama* is very good indeed, considerably steamier than the standard punky moist air, even though set in a brilliantly chilly alt-historical North Pole. I recommend it.

We're in New Venice, 'The Pearl of the Arctic,' and the era is sometime around the turn of the 20th century, or one version of that turn refracted through Valtat's 'pluriverse.' New Venice itself is a generically familiar but still very handsomely mounted location. Ruled by a secretive and authoritarian 'Council of Seven,' and policed by an elegant but ruthless secret police force, 'the Gentlemen of the Night,' it is nevertheless a stylish location:

> Brentford, leaving the bridge and its sculpted bears, reached the Arctic Administration Building and headed toward the Botanical Building, further on the right. Its lights were turned down, and the glass-and-metal structure loomed large and mysterious. One could sense the life inside, the silent but stubborn relentless growth. [p. 96]

The plot follows two main characters: Brentford Orsini (that's him, on the bridge), a city administrator from a good family with dark secrets in his past; and Gabriel d'Allier, a foppish dandy and academic with a decadent, druggy lifestyle. The two are friends caught up in the secret movement opposing the oppressive Council of Seven, who run the city, and accordingly pursued by the state. Matters seem to be coming to a head: a strange, ominous black airship is hovering mysteriously overhead; Eskimo bandits are circling the city; and a sled without a driver has arrived out of the north 'where nobody lives,' pulled by a dog-team, and drawing after it the body of a woman.

It would be folly to try and summarize the rest of the serpentine, dreamlike plot, for this is a restlessly inventive and sweetly surreal novel. We get the usual steampunk technological artefacts mingled with strange Vurt-like drugs and supernatural goings on to boot. Indeed, *Aurorarama* explicitly blends conventional narrative pleasures with the logic of dreaming: a girl tattooed all over with a starmap; moonlight lovemaking on the ice; Polar Kangaroos; Zeppelins powered by 'Vapouric Ether' [sic] and navigated by anarchists. Aurorarama mixes in scenes from 1960s hipster jazzland and figures from a Bosch painting ('three men, clad in the traditional black overcoats, white bird masks and wide-brimmed hats of their plague doctors' outfits' [p. 12] – these are the Scavengers, a kind of untouchable caste who handle the city's garbage). All that sort of thing. The dream logic that structures the novel has a lot in common with stage magic ('Stella came down and bowed to the audience, but as she stood up, her head remained stuck in mid-air, while the rest of her body faded out', p. 191). Quite a lot of the novel has to do with music, bands playing frying pans strung like guitars and other, steam-powered instruments (in Pynchon mode, Valtat supplied us with terrible lyrics as well as descriptions of the bands). Some of the novel consists of, to appropriate one character's phrase, 'hypnagogic sequences of related and slightly absurd events he had little control over' [p. 233]. But counterbalancing the dreaminess, and ensuring the novel hangs together as a novel, is a muscular command of the ripping yarns narrative idiom, including chapter titles like the exclamatory 'Eskimos to the Rescue!' or indeed the triple exclamatory 'Hypnotized!!!' and 'Terrorists!!!' The titular machine is a particularly splendid invention, a device that turns the aurora borealis into a gigantic visualization medium, like 'a slightly damaged hand-colorized fantascope movie' [p. 346].

Better yet, the novel is as well-written as it is well-imagined: full of nice phrases – 'the vandalized Bibi Eybat oil wells burned non-stop in the night, in true Zoroastrian fashion' [p. 153]; a blizzard 'whirls madly like a trapped wolf' (p. 174) – and Valtat handles his cod-19th-century tone sweetly: 'he beheld, almost miragenous through the whirling snowflakes, four hooded shapes hurrying away down the back alley'[p. 197]. North Pole politics are 'poletics'; people travel around not in taxis but 'taxsleighs', and the prose approaches the business of swearing with a degree of propriety ('[…] they were against the Council then, and now those *phoque-in-iceholes* work hand in hand' p. 69). Although, at the same time, the writing *sometimes* falls into the uncanny valley between the formal idiom of Victorian prose and the unidiomatic stiffness of a non-native speaker ('"This is very kind of you. But it happens that one likes to hunt for oneself, even if one is a bad hunter," he said' [p. 41]). I don't mean to be a *neat-piquer*. That Valtat, a French national, wrote this long, accomplished novel in his second language represents an almost Conradian achievement. So if I gracelessly note that sometimes the style doesn't quite hit the bull – 'It would, Gabriel thought, enlighten his return home [...] provided he would not go alone' [p. 68]('provided he didn't go home alone' would be more idiomatic); or 'as he hurried he could perceive rooms whose open doors revealed the strangest scenes' [p. 160]; 'perceive' isn't the right word there, I think – then I must also declare that Valtat's command of English is better than many published Anglophone authors I could mention. Overall, this is a very good novel indeed.

2

So, steampunk. We might want to ask whether this novel, with its manifold excellences, is a symptom of a subgenre in rude health; or whether it is a late bloomer in an exhausted imaginative idiom. I'm not sure how we might want to answer such a question.

What is steampunk? It is a studied dismantling of the consecutiveness of history in the service of a particular set of styles and fashions. As such, it is part of a larger phenomenon; what Fredric Jameson's famous 1984 essay 'Cultural Logic of Late Capitalism' identified as a 'mesmerizing new aesthetic mode' that has recently 'emerged as an elaborated symptom of the waning of our historicity, of our lived possibility of experiencing history in some active way.' It may be less useful than otherwise to invoke this phenomenon's brand name ('postmodernism'), because that term has become so scratched and scrabbled, so contested and overused as to approach uselessness. But Jameson is on to something, I think, when he describes the last half century or so as characterized by 'a strange occultation of the present', a situation in which a kind of formalized nostalgia symptomatically reveals 'the enormity of a situation in which we seem increasingly incapable of fashioning representations of our own current experience.'

Ours is, in other words, a situation in which our sense of history is exhausted; overwritten by an inventively but debilitating aesthetic nostalgia that functions as a deliberate simplification of the past – Jameson calls it a 'sterilized' and 'fetishized' version of the past: 'our own pop images and simulacra of that history, which itself remains forever out of reach.'

Steampunk is precisely this mode of Jamesonian pastiche, driven by a nostalgia for the styles and manners of Victorian English combined with a sense that the convenience of contemporary technological advances – or, perhaps, more: the exhilaration of the technological sublime itself, upon which so much SF is predicated – can be disengaged from the actual circumstances of their historical production and retrofitted, as it were, into the past. The problem with this is its mendacity: I mean both its ideological untruthfulness, but also its radical misprision of history as such. Things like technological advance are not random events; they are determined by their historical circumstances. The reason the Victorians did not invent computing and space travel is not that they happened not to get around to it, and not that mere chance got in the way; it is that the entire social and cultural ground of their collective lives was not productive of such advances. Had circumstances been trivially different to the way they actually were, Babbage might have actually manufactured his difference engine, but even if he had done so, the computer revolution would not have followed, as the night follows the day, the way the side-whiskered granddaddy Gibsonian-Sterlingesque *The Difference Engine* suggests. The actual computer revolution, from the 1980s to the present, is not a chance event, or even a chance series of events; it is the superstructure of a particular complex economic, social, and cultural base. It required not just a few clever people making clever designs to produce personal computing and the internet; much more importantly it required an entire human economy and culture receptive, or productive, of the million elements that fit together into the whole. It takes more than a Babbage to make this happen. A similar case could be made for the more commonly appearing tropes of so many steampunk novels: flying machines long before the Wright brothers, robots before Toyota, and so on. The fantasy of steampunk, in fact, is the old bourgeois one: that one talented individual matters more than the whole weight of history. It is the fantasy of being freed from the larger context of historical necessity.

And actually, steampunk is not really a matter of this or that technological gadget; the appeal of the genre is in the way it finesses the past into the present. This is an aesthetic strategy it shares with Heroic Fantasy (or much of it) as a mode: a disinclination to encounter the past as past. Most 21st-century representations of a notional 'past' are based on the idea that people in the 19th century (or, in post-Tolkienian

Fantasy, the middle ages) were basically people exactly like us, and therefore people with whom it requires no effort from the reader to identify. The differences the works do register are superficial ones – the relative deficiency of cool technology – that can be supplied, in the case of steampunk, by retrofitting modern technology into stylish pseudo-Victorian garb (or in the case of Fantasy, by supplying the deficiency with 'magic'). Not concrete deserts but neo-Gothic prettiness ('Brentford's apartment was located in another wing of the Botanical Building, accessible through an exquisitely crafted wrought iron spiral staircase. This led to a flat decorated in the finest Art Nouveau style, as if the iron girders had melded with the hothouse plants' p. 100).

At its worst, then, steampunk is just an exercise in escapism, history as fancy dress: the brutalist aesthetic of modern-day big-scale technological artefacts is softened with a little elegant 19th-century design panache – instead of the black, slug-shaped enormousness of a modern nuclear submarine we have Captain Nemo's vessel; similarly large but *beautiful*: silver and art-deco-silhouetted, ornamented with attractive curlicues and stylish lines. Real-life London's Millennium Dome is an ugly, functional affair; the domes in Valtat's *Aurorarama* have more je ne sais quoi ('the dome itself, supported by white pillars, was of jet-black jasper encrusted with diamond stars and silver filigree work' p. 159). In place of today's Pacino-in-*Scarface* vulgarity of vocabulary and manners, we have characters who speak in mannered Johnsonian or Dickensian phrases, who dress not in shell suits and jogging pants but in exquisitely tailored suits. Or, to cut to the argumentative chase: steampunk gives us not the grinding desolation of post-Darwinian existential insignificance, but a golden ticket back to the pre-Darwinian cosmos (or, a little more precisely, to a Cosmos trembling on the brink of falling into the angst of Modernity) where the universe is *fitted* more comfortingly to the individual's hopes and importance. Civilization, but with more profound ontological discontent replaced with the diverting transitory discomforts of adventure narrative.

To use steampunk diagnostically, in other words, is to suggest the ground of its appeal is a sense that the modern world is lacking in *refinement*. What steampunk tells us is that there's nothing to prevent the marriage of contemporary technological convenience with the elegance and the good manners of the 19th century. Shorthand for this, of course, is *breeding*, and to think of it like that is to understand the extent to which steampunk is embroiled in reactionary ideologies of class superiority.

Having said all that, one of the things that lifts *Aurorarama* out of the standard steampunk rut is its awareness of its own mode precisely as a recirculation of styles ('Once again fashion had completed its meaningless but pleasant cycle and come back to its starting point' p. 67). Valtat's novel does understand, I think, that steampunk is a kind of dream of the Victorian age, and dreams are simultaneously beguiling and semiotically fluid. Dreams in *Aurorarama* are actual codes, to be deciphered by those in the know to reveal detailed messages. Here is Brentford trying to make sense of one of his dreams (excuse me if I don't gloss every reference here):

> Let us be more precise, he thought. He had wanted to speak to Helen or for Helen to speak to him – the woman (and a lot more than that) whose dead body he had left on the ice field a few years before, after her magic had saved the city. Vomiting ectoplasm on the ice field may have been merely a consequence of his desire to communicate with the dead Helen. And so must have been the Ghost Lady, for a spectre was more or less the form he would have expected Helen to take if she appeared. 'Mr. Osiris' was another clue. After Helen had saved the city from Delwit Faber's coup with the Lobster Girls and the House of Hellequin, Brentford had found crumpled in her hand the formula Isis had used to stop the Chariot of the Sun in order to help the diseased Osiris. The very name Osiris could be vaguely construed as a play on his name, Orsini, which in Italian was itself a pun on bear (a bear even appeared on his coat of arms). It would be only logical to find a bear on the arctic ice field, all the more since arctos also meant 'bear.' Being on the ice, then, like the references to Ross, meant only that he was simply dreaming of himself waiting for a vision of Helen, not to mention that ice is the best backdrop for the kind of clear and sustained mental images he'd been hoping to see. The Ghost Lady calling him Mr. Osiris signified that, if she was not Helen herself, she was conscious of Brentford's history with Helen, and was perhaps some sort of messenger. 'Did you fly?' was more difficult to decipher, but Brentford remembered now that when Helen had made him join her on a kind of shamanic trip, he had found himself flying over an unknown city. So, as he summed it up, the dream was just a rather simple image of his own longing for Helen, and the message he had got was, after all, pointing to her

more clearly than he had first thought. [pp. 76-77]

The point is that after all this pre-Freudian Freudianism, all this squirreling around in the dream-matter to pull out nuggets of significance, Brentford concludes: 'Of course, there was still the tiresome hypothesis that it was a simple circular circuit of wish fulfilment and that he had only received under a different form what he had first put into the dream.' That, I'd say, gets to the point of it. What we get out of steampunk is what we put in. 'After all,' we're told a little later; 'the place is nothing if not nondescript. The North Pole and four hundred miles off it are just the same endless expanse of dreary faceless desert... Or to put it otherwise, the North Pole is Nothing' [p. 84].

Aurorarama's first section ('Qarrtsiluni') begins with this intriguing epigraph:

> The form familiar to our stage of culture, which aims at weaving together and combining motifs into a whole, while gradually shaping itself toward a climax and tending to an explosive conclusion, viz. the dramatic construction, has no place in the intellectual life of the Eskimos. [C. W. Schultz-Lorentzen, Intellectual Culture of the Greenlanders, 1928]

It's bold of Valtat to adhere, more or less, to this off-kilter Eskimo logic in his larger narrative. The nothingness is doing interesting things in this novel. What I mean is that this is a novel that replaces the nuts-and-bolts techno-fetish of the mode with a pataphysical or surreal dream-fetish, that works its oxymoronic white-heat white-(arctic)-cold dynamic out into all the corners and limbs of its sprawling text. Highly recommended.

Scarlett Thomas, *Our Tragic Universe* (2010)

After a great deal of contemplation I've boiled it all down to these two points.

One: people aren't wearing enough hats.

Two: ever since there have been stories, people have understood that *life is not like stories* and, consequently, that stories are not really like life. Narrative compresses, elides, focalises and above all gifts *structure* to its events in ways life doesn't; or to be more precise, in ways life only does in our heads. Fictional representation of life is always misrepresentation, and our recognition of ourselves in the mirror of text (that girl is *just like me!* Hey, the story's set in Dartmouth – I know Dartmouth really well! I completely grok her messy relationship situation!) is always misrecognition. This, if you like, is Deconstruction 101; the realisation that, in this context, there really is no such thing as representation. Lacan noted that 'the mirror stage,' the moment when a child sees herself in the mirror and recognises that it's her, is a misrecognition (it's not her; it's an image of her) with profound consequences for the development of subjectivity – that, indeed, misrecognition is constitutive of our subjectivity.

This stuff is really neither new nor *particularly* profound. It goes back at least as far as Aristophanes, whose great plays *Frogs* and *Thesmaphoriazusae* are amongst other things expert interrogations of the relative merits and functions of heroically idealising versus deflatingly 'realistic' art. Thomas makes quite a play with Aristophanes' Aeschylean-Euripidean standoff in *Our Tragic Universe* ('tragic,' you see). I'll come back to that. But this theme, of the cleavage between the shape 'art' gives experiences and the messy contiguity and shapelessness of life, has been behind some of the greatest literature in the European tradition. It's what *Don Quixote* is about; it's the ground of all the playful shenanigans in *Tristram Shandy* (I was often put in mind of this novel when reading *Our Tragic Universe*, actually); *Northanger Abbey* plays it for laughs, sort of; Proust made it his great theme; so did David Foster Wallace.

Wait – what was that about *hats?*

143

Our Tragic Universe centres on Meg, Thomas's narrator-heroine, living in a damp cottage in Dartmouth, scraping a living from freelance writing (pulp novels and reviews) whilst fretting that she has made no progress on her 'proper' novel. Meg's boyfriend is Christopher, a man who, in trying to live a life without negative environmental consequences, actually manifests a rather monstrous self-absorption and blindness to the low-level misery he causes to those around him. Meg, stuck in this relationship, has kind-of fallen in love with Rowan, an older and married man.

Our Tragic Universe is good on the people. Thomas is a very talented novelist, and one of her talents is a knack for believable, graceful and likeable characterisation – and that, given the pettiness, self-indulgence and venal annoyingness of many of her players, is quite some achievement. Meg's voice is superbly handled; the dialogue is supple, even in its infodumping mode; the prose is fluent, splendidly observed, very nicely done: a significant advance on the lively but sophomoric prose of Thomas's breakthrough title *The End of Mr Y* (2006).Indeed, this novel contains all that book's fizz, its beguiling emotional honesty and its cleverness, whilst managing to rein in its more garishly extended-adolescent aspects. This is a very good novel indeed.

However, and though it *is* good on the people, *Our Tragic Universe* isn't really *about* the people. It's about the metaphorical millinery. Which is to say: it's about the stories people tell and to which they attend, both in the sense that these creatively misrepresenting stories structure our experience of life, and in the meta sense: for this is a novel about a novelist writing a novel that plays games that involve, in a nutshell, colliding what we expect of stories into what we know of life.

Accordingly it is not really a criticism of *Our Tragic Universe* to say that it is not a great story. That is its point. It is a novel that sets out purposefully to deconstruct the premises of narrative. What saves it from mere up-fundament-vanishing annoyingness is the enormous charm with which its deliberately inconsequential non-story is told. This, indeed, is the main point I'd want to make in this review. Thomas is a superbly *charming* writer: warmly witty, genuine, smart, funny, well-observed and cool.

And, actually, 'non-story' isn't quite right. Thomas's book reflects the truth that the world is full of stories; that they proliferate endlessly.

What the world doesn't provide is *neat* stories, or stories that fit our lives, or – above all – stories that come to loose-thread-tied *endings*. The paradigm is something like this Meg childhood reminiscence:

> One time I saw a spider catch a wasp. I hated wasps, and I was quite pleased when this one flew drowsily away from me and got stuck in the web. In an instant, the fat spider came and started wrapping up the wasp in its white silk. The wasp struggled at first, and I felt sorry for it. But then it stopped moving. The spider worked away, turning it around, cocooning it, its thin, jagged legs moving this way and that, each one as precise as a needle on a sewing machine. Then it picked up the wasp in its front legs and took it carefully up to the centre of the web the way a human would carry a newborn baby. I watched for ages, but nothing else happened, and when I came back the next day the whole web had gone. Another day I found some string in the damp, creaky holiday house and made a shoulder-strap for my flask. [pp. 68-9]

This is very nice: an absorbing little narrative that deftly magnifies something mundane and trivial into something existentially resonant. The detail is spot-on, too – that 'needle on a sewing machine' simile not only precisely evocative, but connecting with a larger thematic in the novel about 'textile' (from, as Thomas knows very well, the Latin *textus*, which also gives us *text*), weaving, knitting, sewing. But most of all, the set-up leads us to expect a narrative resolution that Thomas's elegant sidestepping at the close neatly frustrates. The whole novel is not only full of this sort of thing, it is structured on a larger level according to this principle.

So, when she was a girl Meg met a magic man who put the Cutty Sark in a bottle and who told her fortune: '[...]you will never finish what you start[...] you will not overcome the monster. And in the end, you will come to nothing' [p. 76]. We can't accuse Thomas of not playing fair in her writing, because this is exactly what happens, to Meg, as to all of us. We none of us finish what we start, and we all come to nothing. This is what it means to be mortal. And if we don't overcome the monster, that may be because the monster doesn't exist. What this magic man is saying, in a nutshell, is that it is not in the nature of life, even a varied, interesting, satisfying life, *to offer closure*. Life discloses, it doesn't enclose. We can take such advice in the rather melancholy self-accusing way Meg initially does, or we could take it as liberating. That's up to us.

Thomas plays games with the sorts of expectations narrative conventions generate for the reader. In Meg's adult life that same ship-in-a-bottle washes ashore at Dartmouth. Is this coincidence, or something more structured and connected? There's a good deal of laying the ground for something significant to do with the 'Beast of Dartmoor' which may, or may not exist, and may, or may not, have eaten a key character. It is hardly a spoiler to suggest that this storyline does not pay out, like a narrative one-armed-bandit.

One framing device for all this is a big science fictional idea with which the book flirts: that we might all be living in a simulacrum. *Our Tragic Universe* starts with Meg writing a review of a book called *The Science of Living* by 'Kelsey Newman.' This is a Tipleresque Omega-point confection that argues the end of time will involve the concentration of unlimited powers of information manipulation which in turn will result in the creation of an infinite simulation of reality in which everybody who has ever lived will be recreated. Thomas mentions Tipler specifically, but I assume she shifts this notion onto her fictional 'Newman' so as to go in non-Tiplerian ways with it. So, Newman thinks we are massively more likely to be already living in this simulation than otherwise, and he has written a follow-up title called *Second World* which offers 'a blueprint for living' based on the assumption that the Omega point is real and now. When Meg submits her review the editor of the journal denies ever having sent her the book in the first place. Is this significant? Is there a cosmic conspiracy at work? Or is it purely coincidental? Or is it some third thing, some excluded middle of coincidental-conspiracy reminiscent of *Foucault's Pendulum* or *Crying of Lot 49*?

There used to be a publishing category called 'the novel of ideas.' It's fallen from favour, although we can read *Our Tragic Universe* as a late entry in the mode, I think. And by that token, I'm not convinced Thomas is *sure* enough of her ideas – or to be more precise, not sure enough that ideas alone will entertain its readers. When Thomas Hardy met readers, and those readers told him that they had read one of his novels, his question was always the same: *'and did it hold your attention?'* This is, obviously, a core writerly anxiety. It takes a brave author to ignore the suspicion that they are boring their readers.

How does Thomas set out to hold her reader's attention? She

indulges, as have others, in what we might call the _QI_-ification of contemporary publishing. _QI_, for those ~~SH readers~~ not familiar with it, is a BBC game show chaired by Stephen Fry in which panels of celebrities strive to be 'quite interesting.' Like Thomas's novel, the vibe of the show is non-combative and unnarrative, and like the novel it trades on a pleasing combination of likeability and wit. But most of all, it tickles our mental Trivial Pursuit glands. Books by writers as diverse as Bill Bryson to Neal Stephenson to Dan Brown are crammed with _interesting facts_. Other books, books perhaps that refuse to play this game, may find themselves judged and found wanting by the criterion of _quantity and accuracy of interesting facts delivered_.

And in _Our Tragic Universe_, a crate-load of quite interesting facts is unpacked and parcelled out to the reader. A lot of it _is_ interesting, too, though some of it acts a little gummily upon the progress of the whole, and some of it is wrong. Thomas makes an extended play with '[...] lost his bottle of oil,' a phrase Aeschylus inserts deflatingly into Euripides' dramatic speeches. She takes it to be 'a formula' and about the way 'in tragedy if somebody loses a bottle of oil it's a really important bottle of oil and they end up dead' [p. 48]. But this isn't right; Aeschylus's point is bathetic, not tragic – comically deflating Euripides' too-regular metrical speechifying. There are other bum notes: 'a TV satellite had come down in the Pacific and caused a tidal wave that had a devastating effect on one of the Japanese islands' [p. 62]. Not unless it was the size of Phobos, it didn't. Not that the bum-notes really matter. This novel contains a wealth of enjoyment, and a banquet of food for thought. You won't be bored.

If I end my review, though, with a qualification, I do not do so in an attempt to be off-putting. Because, really, you should read this novel: you'll enjoy it. My niggle was that the non-ending was not non enough for my tastes; that, to be particular, there's too much soap-opera of Meg's relationship with her noisome boyfriend. But I must add a rider, to the effect that my tastes are not the same as most people's. I might have preferred a more modishly alienated and oblique story, but Thomas has instead given us a remarkably engaging, multifaceted emotional trajectory. I was drawn into Meg's affective life; I understood why she was with horrible Christopher, though I also wanted her to ditch the loser. All this is integrated seamlessly with the larger questions the book raises. Hmm – how can I put it?

In 'Picture This', one of Blondie's better songs, the female narrator begs the listener to imagine certain things:

> Picture this, a sky full of thunder.
> Picture this, my telephone number.

Now that I'm in my crusty middle-age, I tend to take that couplet as an ironic juxtaposition, for, after all, the cosmos – its vastness, its sublimity – has no interest whatsoever in individual human dating troubles or crushes. But when that song came out, and I was young and easy beneath the apple boughs, I suppose I took it differently. It seemed to me then to embody a straightforward truth: that the turmoil in my heart at asking a girl out and the turmoil in the sky as the thunderheads clashed and storm possessed the heavens – these were, somehow, the same thing. Because they were both iterations of a kind of intensity. Except, of course, *they weren't*. Except of course, my crusty middle-aged perspective, being less illusioned, is also less mendacious.

And that's my point. *Our Tragic Universe* juxtaposes the celestial significance and the small-scale emotional bumps in non-ironic and wholehearted fashion. That means that readers smart enough to appreciate its intelligence and young enough not yet to have developed calluses on their organs of feeling will find this novel to be one of the best of the year. Besides, who listens to Blondie nowadays? You're more likely to be into Lady Gaga. Now *there's* a person who knows how to wear a hat.

Battle: Los Angeles

(directed by Jonathan Leibesman 2010)

Aliens invade coastal cities worldwide. In Los Angeles the US Marines mobilize to fight them – and fight them they do. At length. There's your movie, in a nutshell: it's *Black Hawk Down* with aliens. There are many explosions, and many thousands of rounds are fired. It's a grunt's-eye-view of *Independence Day* rendered with some of *Cloverfield*'s shaky visual flourish. It's the glacial visual poetry of Tarkovski's *Nostalghia* combined with the aching psychological insight of *Wild Strawberries*-era Bergman.

Well, not that last one, obviously.

But what an earnest, dusty, sweaty, muscular, *strenuously* macho movie this is; the script marinated in testosterone, the production actively supported by the Marine Corps (for whom, as several reviewers have noted, it in effect functions as a recruitment tool). War is good guys versus bad, full-on, *bang bang bang*. Men are men and aliens are toast. There are only two female characters in the entire film: one a tough and ballsy solider (Michelle Rodriguez); the other a civilian veterinarian (Bridget Moynahan) who contributes nothing to the ensemble apart from looking pretty in a dishevelled sort of way. No, that's not true; she also uses her veterinarian skills to enable Staff Sergeant Shouty McRock PatriotAct (Aaron Eckhart) find the aliens' weak point ('I need to know how *to kill them*, goddammit!') by vivisecting one of them. Otherwise it's all men, all the time; manly men doing manly things in a manly way.

Our team of heroes fights its way across Santa Monica to rescue some civilians from a police station, then it fights its way back again, moving cumbrously from fire-fight to fire-fight, killing many aliens. Having rescued the civilians, the Marines singlehandedly locate the alien command and control paraphernalia and blow it up.

The director, Jonathan Liebesman, occasionally leavens the monotony of all this with some slightly less frantic interludes. These give characters the chance to whoop and punch the air, by way of expressing their satisfaction at having killed large numbers of aliens (indeed there was in the film as a whole, it seemed to me, rather more whooping than was entirely necessary). On other occasions characters' jaws harden and the soldiers' eyes get a little teary, but this emotion is always a manly choked-back emotion. Indeed is actually always the same emotion – the bruised heart inside the rock-hard chest – and the eventual outcome of the film is never in doubt.

In sum, *Battle: Los Angeles* is less a film and more the experience of sitting inside an oil drum for two hours whilst people hit the outside with metal rods and drop firecrackers in at the top. Of course, it doesn't pretend to be anything other than what it is: a gung ho actioner that takes no prisoners, least of all prisoners with names like 'nuance,' 'complexity,' or 'depth.' I'm happy to concede that I (preening, effete European liberal that I am) probably don't represent the *target* audience of such a film. Had I watched it in a movie theatre in Texas filled with red-blooded patriotic fans, my sense of its potential *qua* entertainment might have been different. As it was, in a four-fifths empty cinema in Staines, it seemed to me a fatally monotonous example of the 'more *must be* more!' school of filmmaking – if one explosion is exciting, eighty explosions must be *eighty times as exciting*!

The narrative premise is that the aliens are here to steal our precious fluids – water, specifically – which they use directly to fuel their technology. 'Our planet is the only place in the known universe with liquid water' claims one stare-eyed TV scientist, which made me wonder from which institution of higher learning he had earned his degree. This 'water' notion is a puzzler, actually. At one point our guys come across a shot down alien flier, the wrecked innards of which display ruptured pipes from which water is dribbling. This suggests that the aliens simply fill their fuel tanks with untreated brine and are ready to go ('the ocean levels are already starting to drop!' claims the on-telly expert, in another belief-beggaring aside). As to how this technology works, or why, given that the aliens need water, they are moving *inland* from the California coastline towards the Mojave desert – why, indeed, they are invading LA at all rather than somewhere wetter like Hawaii, or Manchester…. well, the film doesn't give us enough information to answer these profound and challenging questions. 'Our planet is the only place in the known universe with liquid water' indeed – as if aliens with the technology for interstellar flight, and whose weapons discharge heat-ray like blasts, haven't figured out *how to melt ice*, a substance with which the universe is copiously supplied.

But, of course, it misses the point to read this plot element in terms of its semantic coherence. It works, rather, symbolically: 'we' invaded Iraq for the oil, which directly fuels our technology. We pitched up there, out of the sky, with terrifying technological superiority, blew a lot of stuff up and killed a lot of people. Now, after the mission accomplished banner has been unfurled, and indeed folded away again, it's possible that 'we' feel bad about that. *Battle: LA* employs the logic of inversion and condensation (as Freud might put it) to rework trauma as wish-fulfilment fantasy. 'We' are no longer colonial aggressors; now we are affronted and righteous representatives of civilization fighting – as the squad Lieutenant puts it, in his brief *Henry V* moment, 'for our lives, our families, our homes, for our *country* goddammit.' Accordingly, and however assiduously the film valorises the ethos and bravery of US Marines, it can't help putting its protagonists into Al-Qaeda situations: the brave officer who turns himself into a suicide bomber in order to take down a clutch of enemy aliens for instance.

During his tour of Iraq, Aaron Eckhart's Staff Sergeant lost men under his command. He carries the grief for this throughout the film, manfully repressed, except for one scene in which he gets to vent it. This he does in a properly manly way – by standing very close to one of his Marines, and yelling into the guy's face the names, ranks, *and serial numbers* of all those who died, which, handily, he has memorized for just such an occasion. Yelling, surely, *is* the best way to handle negative emotions. Yelling and shooting stuff. Anyway, this scene results in Eckhart's men becoming even more dedicated and loyal to their NCO, their Corps, and their *country* goddammit. The scene had a different effect on me, I must say. It made me think that for such a conventionally handsome man Eckhart has a really, *really* long face and proportionately very small eyes. There's something of the Simon MacCorkindale about him, facially. And also something of the aardvark.

So, yes, my preening, effete European liberal view is that this is not a good movie. Some of the design work is pretty cool – both the aliens themselves and their various craft – and very occasional moments of tension or excitement can be found within the relentless hammer drill monotony of the big explosions. I liked the noise the aliens made, too: a sinister stream of gurgles and snickers, halfway between a rattlesnake and a blocked drain. Or like a 33 rpm recording of Bill and Ben played at 45. But one explosion is very much like another, and ten thousand rifle rounds slamming into metal alien war machinery is nine thousand, nine hundred and twenty too many for dramatic effectiveness. Speaking roughly.

It put me in mind of *Stolz der Nation*, 'Nation's Pride,' the film-within-a-film in Tarantino's *Inglorious Basterds* about the heroic sniper who kills goodness knows how many enemies. Indeed, *Battle: Los Angeles* does feel like that, although without the saving grace of Mélanie Laurent's giant face appearing near the end to taunt the audience. Which was a pity.

Nation's Pride was never going to be this film's title, of course. Originally it was going to be called *Battle for Los Angeles*; and then it was *World Invasion: Battle Los Angeles*. *Battle: Los Angeles* is snappier, although I have also seen it advertised as *Battle LA*, which perhaps runs the risk of sounding a bit Welsh, or even of suggesting that the film will be all *Battle-la-di-dah*, which, really, it isn't. Actually when I saw the film, the poster had dispensed with the punctuating colon altogether and gone with the no-nonsense *Battle Los Angeles*, conceivably on the grounds that colons are for pussies.

I did think of making mock of the film's almost literally *blah* titular acronym, 'BLA'. But then I remembered that my last novel, *By Light Alone*, has exactly this acronym. Which made me realise what a dignified and effective acronym it is, actually.

David Lodge, *A Man of Parts* (2011)

Here's a younger David Lodge (quoted in Malcolm Bradbury's *The Modern British Novel 1878-2001*):

> This rising self-consciousness was one remarkable quality of mainstream British fiction over the Sixties; we can justly say a significant rediscovery of the novel and its possibilities was now occurring... But where was it leading? The novelist, David Lodge famously said in 1969, now stood at the crossroads: 'the pressure on the aesthetic and epistemological premises of literary realism is now so intense that many novelists, instead of marching confidently straight ahead, are at least considering two routes that branch off in opposite directions', one towards neo-documentary, fiction as history, history as fiction; the other towards fabulation. [p. 411]

There's never been any doubt in *my* heart that the latter is the right way to go; but Lodge, having made his name with a string of successful Campus novels (*Changing Places: A Tale of Two Campuses*, 1975; *Small World: An Academic Romance*, 1984; *Nice Work*, 1988 and the underrated *Thinks...*, 2001) appears to have decided on the former. *Author, Author*(2004) was a carefully researched facto-novel about Henry James; *Deaf Sentence* (2008) a fictional autobiography about Lodge's own experience losing his hearing, lightly dusted with a sort-of-thriller plot; and this year's *A Man of Parts*, though subtitled 'A Novel', is actually a scrupulously researched biography of H. G. Wells. The two main narrative strategies are, on the first hand, a process of docudramatisation of Wells's life as narrative, and on the other, a slightly stiff notional interview between Wells and an unnamed individual who poses questions **in bold type**. Conceivably this is Wells's **own conscience. I'm not entirely sure and can't remember if the novel makes it plain.** Anyway, much of the book concerns Wells's relentless pursuit of sex (hence the parts, private in nature, dangling about the book's title); although various other aspects of the public Wells gets handled (oo-er! 'handled'!) here – lots on his early life; a great chunk about his engagement with the Fabians – and some interesting material on his later life as a world-famous man.

I interviewed Lodge (and, as it happens, Stephen Baxter) at an event organised by the British Library in July 2011. Despite his deafness, and thanks in part to a very cool advanced-tech hearing aid, he was fluent, eloquent and on the ball. The novel itself is consummately crafted, and full of fascinating detail, without ever, quite, coming alive. I wonder if, in some sense, this has to do with the way this is a novel that goes down route A, in 1969-Lodge's fork in the road, even though it is *about* an individual whose most important contribution to world culture was the way he paved route B. I asked Lodge why he concentrated in this novelmentary on Wells's non-SF life – his politicking, Fabianising, New Women novels and other mainstream writing. SF gets mentioned (as how could it not?) but you get the impression that Lodge really does prefer *Ann Veronica* and *Boon* and *Mr Britling Sees It Through* – I was surprised to see this last title get such a resounding endorsement ('Whatever you say, *Mr Britling Sees It Through* was a good novel. Britling lives' [p. 478] ... really?). His answer, whilst conceding the influence the SF has had, was basically that it was the other kind of Wells novels that interested him. Wells's life is full of fascinating busy-ness, but despite its high fucking quotient, and its interpolated Wells/Conscience interviewing, the focus here remains public and exterior, as a neodocumentary surely must. It lacks the element of fabulation that might have enabled it to do what metaphor can do, and what factuality rarely can, howsoever scrupulously pursued – infused the Frankenstein spark into the monster and have it lurch to life.

Christopher Priest, *The Islanders* (2011)

It's an extraordinarily good piece of writing. Now, now, wait a minute. I hold Priest in high esteem as a writer. He's one of the authors the reading of whose novels (as a kid) inspired me to want to write myself. I've met him, too, on several publisher-party occasions, and he's always been very cordial and encouraging towards me personally (he doesn't much like what I write, and has reviewed my stuff accordingly, but that's fair enough). This is by way of a rather roundabout full-disclosure, since fans rarely provide the disinterested objectivity vital to sound reviewing, however much they may try. Nonetheless, *The Islanders* seems to me one of the later Priest's very best novels: beautifully put-together, absorbing and compelling as well as elegantly wrong-footing and sour-sweetly off kilter.

It is set in the 'Dream Archipelago', a planet-wide assortment of island communities, the scene of some of Priest's best early stories, as well as his 1981 novel *The Affirmation*. My memory of the early short stories – since my house move, I can't lay my hands on my old bashed-about paperbacks of *An Infinite Summer* and *The Dream Archipelago* to check, so my memory may be playing me wrong – is that the Archipelago used to have a more Aegean feel to it. In this latest novel, and although there are islands in every latitude, the broad flavour seems to me more Scandinavian, or Scots, especially in the book's latter stages. It's not just the names (the theatre where a crucial crime is committed is the *Teater Sjøkaptein*, for instance), or the comfortable, Nordic-middle-class quality of life many of the characters enjoy. It's also to do with the cool, even Bergmanesque tone of the writing itself. On the other hand Priest himself says on his own website:

> The Archipelago itself is not a transplant from a single place, but is an amalgam. You can find archipelagian images and recollections of Guernsey and Sark, the Greek islands, Harrow-on-the-Hill, the French Riviera, the Harz mountains in Germany, Hastings, the Pennines, even Dartmoor and the Isle of Wight.

So I may be barking up what the Swedes call the *wrong trä*. The novel takes the form of a gazetteer of islands in the Archipelago, fifty or so of them, from 'Aay, the 'Island of Winds" to 'Yannet' known as 'Dark Green' and 'Sir'. In listing the histories, flora, fauna, tourist spots and other interesting things about these various places, Priest starts to pick out a series of interlinked character narratives, mosaically assembling these from different contexts, and different perspectives, such that each new cell of the story changes our sense of the larger tale, its rights-and-wrongs, its meanings. The Priestalike ('sacredocish'?) writer Chaster Kammeston is one mysteriously opaque figure, and several other individuals are constellated around him. Many of the specifics are recognisable mundane and contemporary, although there are a few (immortality for some, 'temporal distortion zones' and the like) which are more fantastical. But the focus is less on these.

One of the things I loved about *The Islanders* is that pretty much all the Priestian fascinations and preoccupations are here: doubles; mirrors; dreams; stage magic; the unreliability and instability of narrative, and several intriguing and underplayed metafictional touches (a young [female] novelist writes fan letters to a tetchily unpredictable Kammeston; when her first novel is published she sends a copy to him. It is called *The Affirmation*). It coheres, or more precisely refuses quite to cohere, very stylishly indeed.

It's an archipelagic novel in more than one sense (always assuming that the word *has* more than one sense), formally embodying its scattered loosely connected strings of island subjects in loosely connected strings of narratives. There's a distant family relationship with Borges, perhaps; or Ballard's anthology of 'condensed novels', *The Atrocity Exhibition*. What else? Not so much Primo Levi's *Il Sistema Periodico* (1975), which, although it adheres to its 'Periodic Table' structuring conceit, is a collection of separate short stories, where *The Islanders* is fully a novel. One book that did keep popping up in my head as I read is Milorad Pavić's *Hazarski rečnik* (1984; published in English 1988 as *Dictionary of the Khazars: A Lexicon Novel*). That novel is more modishly postmodern, and has less by way of connecting story, or indeed story of any kind. (At least, that's my memory of it: I read it because it was a hip campus novel at the time when I was a university student myself, but 1988 is – now that I come to think of it – a frighteningly long time ago, and my memory may be wrong). I have heard of, but haven't yet read, Han Shaogong's widely-praised *A*

Dictionary of Maqiao, although from reviews it looks like Priest's novel has a little more in common with it. And Bolaño's *Nazi Literature in the Americas* is on my TBR pile. *The Islanders*, though, has a very different mouthfeel to all of these titles.

We're talking, really, about what the critics call Ergodic literature, a phrase coined by the Norwegian critic Espen J. Aarseth; or to be a little more precise, we're taking about novels that stir interesting patterns out of the mix of traditional narrative, and more freeform ergodic structures (many critics interested in ergodic narrative structures trace them through video games and hyperlink texts). The key thing, though, is books that 'produce a semiotic sequence which may differ from reading to reading'. 'Ergodic' not only from 'ergos', 'work', but also from 'hodos', 'path', you see. We often think of narrative as a kind of path. *The Islanders* presents itself to be read linearly, from start to end, and that's certainly how I read it. But the elements of the various narratives are not laid out in a linear sequence; they appear here and there, and I fitted them together into my larger sense of the story, having to revise my sense of what was going on and how people really were as I went (that creative tension between sjuzhet and fabula that's technically quite hard to do but which can be immensely satisfying to read) – a little like Ford's *The Good Soldier* in that way, although much more kaleidoscopically rendered. One of the things that grounds this is precisely Priests' cool command of traditional style, world and character, and there's a scrupulousness with which everything is set out – the doubleness and uncertainty of the book's treatment of *naming*, for example (most islands and many people have more than one name here) – that only enhances the artfully fractured misdirection. As if to say: you think of a story as being like a journey, and maybe it is. But perhaps it's less like a march along a road, putting one step in front of the other like Bunyan's pilgrim progressing. Perhaps it's like an odysseusing tour of a large group of islands, passing from one to another, losing track of time and orientation, visiting some several times, only glimpsing others, tantalisingly, in the distance. Stories are islands, and we, the readers, are the islanders; but the archipelago of story is far, far too large for us to explore in its entirety, and although we roam widely and try our best, the accretion of our fuller perspective is still partial and fog-bound. And that's enough metaphors in this review for now.

Lavie Tidhar, *Osama* (2011)

Since I'm going to praise this novel I'd better start off with a full disclosure: Tidhar is a friend of mine. So, I'm going to go ahead now and assume you've pinched your salt, and are keeping it handy as you read.

Osama is a bold, gripping, atmospheric and thoughtful novel; easily the best thing of Tidhar's I've yet read. The protagonist is a Chandleresque private eye, called (of course) Joe, living in a Greene-ily rendered Vientiane, in Laos. He is hired by the requisite bombshell mystery woman to locate a writer of pulp fiction, one 'Mike Longshott', author of a variety of low-rent adventure or porn-y novels, not least a series of novels about 'Osama Bin Laden: Vigilante'. So, yes, in this alt-Earth Bin Laden is a fictional character. Interspersed between the chapters of Joe's varied, kinetic adventures are excerpts from Longshott's novels detailing the terrorist attacks in 'our' world (Dar es Salaam, the shoe bomber, London's 7/7 and so on) with which we are familiar. In other words, Tidhar does that *The Grasshopper Lies Heavy* thing of giving us a perspective on our actual world from the point of view of an alt-historical location (that's not quite right, though, because, although the world of *The Grasshopper Lies Heavy* is closer to 'our' world than the world of *The Man in The High Castle* there are nonetheless key differences between reality and Dick's novel-within-the-novel. But the analogy is close enough for government work. And there is a Dick-ish flavour to Tidhar's work here, in a good way. OK; this parenthesis has gone on long enough now).

Tidhar's novel generates an impressive degree of emotional traction by setting his deftly replicated pulp noir 'tec idiom (the frame novel) against a carefully rendered neutral reportage rendering of terrorist atrocity in the interleaved sections. The violence of the main novel figures after the manner of pulp adventure violence – dramatic, but more-or-less consequence-free – but the violence described in the embedded section genuinely shocks. And although I'd have said I know Tidhar *pretty* well, I didn't know this about him (from *The Arty Semite* blog):

> Because I couldn't not write 'Osama.' As it happens, I have a very

158

personal history with that loose, and little understood, network of operatives that uses the collective name Al-Qaeda. I was in Dar es Salaam, in Tanzania, recovering from malaria in a small hotel room in 1998, when the American embassy was attacked. I was in Nairobi a week later, watching the remains of the embassy there, surrounded by soldiers after the fact. And my wife, who was with me there, was in the Sinai in 2004 when a set of bomb attacks rocked the tourist coast of the Red Sea. A car bomb exploded less than a kilometre away from where she was, and I remember that night vividly, trying to establish contact, find out that she was alive, with the phone lines jammed and people passing on messages to each other, reassurances that such-and-such is fine, that they're alive. Just as I remember being in London in 2005 when four suicide bombers blew themselves up, spreading out of King's Cross Station, where my wife travelled every day on her way to work (she was out of London that day, and had to travel back through the scene of chaos)... Most recently, a colleague of my wife's, an aid worker like herself, was kidnapped in Afghanistan and later killed by a US soldier's grenade in a failed rescue attempt.

So, Joe goes first to Paris, then via London and New York to Afghanistan tracking down the elusive Longshott, and has the sorts of adventures a private detective has in private detective novels – drinks with hookers in bars, meetings with sinister fat men, getting roughed up by mysterious thugs trying to warn him off. Along the way, as perhaps we might expect, the black-and-white distinction between the reality where Osama is only a character in a novel and the reality where he is (was) an actual agent in the world becomes blurred.

Tidhar's assured handling of this two-tone form enables him to do something conceptually clever, I think. Where Spinrad's *Iron Dream* (a novel I thought of several times, reading *Osama*) is only able, really, to elaborate one satiric point – the quasi-fascistic nature of a lot of SF, the uneasy proximity of the more grandiose SFnal dreaming and Hitlerian fantasy – *Osama* doubles up, with consequent increase in the richness of effect. In terms of its form, the novel prioritises a sort-of American world in which things like 9/11, though nightmarish, don't feel quite *real*, aren't really comprehensible, feel like intrusions into reality from a trashy, violent novel. But in terms of tone, and, of course, in the book's relation to real life, not to mention the nicely judged final sections, *Osama* is saying: something the reverse is true. The grievances and motivations of terrorists are the stuff of news reportage; the realm that denies them is a kind of exotic fantasy. And, more generally, this is a novel that interrogates the extent to which 'fantasy' governs our political as well as our personal lives. The members of Al Qaeda who thought that knocking down the Twin Towers would cause the US to pull out of the Middle East, or indeed do anything other than bring prolonged misery down on many, many Arab heads, were indulging a fantasy just as acutely, and direly, as those US policymakers who fondly pictured American troops entering Saddam's Baghdad and being acclaimed as liberators, like 1944 Paris.

There are other ways in which this book represents a step forward in Tidhar's career. He is, if I may, pot-like, address him as kettle for a moment, a very prolific writer, somebody who generates ideas in impressive profusion. With some of his earlier work, there has occasionally been a kind of impatience or even slapdashness in the execution of these many cool ideas. But *Osama* is a much more assured, carefully worked piece of writing; and some of the descriptions of place and mood are superbly rendered: atmospheric and vivid. Here's Joe in Paris:

> The sunlight hurt his eyes. In the square the pigeons seemed suspended in mid-flight. Above the fountain the saint was frozen in the act of slaying a dragon. The water seemed to hover like mist. [pp. 80-1]

Nice. The passage goes on:

> A girl was painting the Notre Dame cathedral in the distance

Wait: is the girl or the cathedral in the distance? (And that first 'the' is superfluous).

> The wind picked up out of nowhere, snatched a hat from a man passing by and threw it in the air. Joe followed the girl, who made for the narrow, twisting alleyways of the Quartier Latin. He lit a cigarette and blue smoke followed him as he passed, like the steam being snatched from a moving locomotive.

Good, although a more pernickety writer might have balked at the close proximity of two uses of 'snatched', and of 'followed', here. But Pulp Noir perhaps ought not be written like Nabokov, so I'll stop nitty-picking.

Despite the title, Osama Bin Laden is not actually a character in this novel. But that's as it should be; *Osama* the novel is in the largest sense about the way 'terrorism' is actually a mode of making war upon our imaginations, and not, however it might appear, upon our bodies and our infrastructure. Accordingly this is a novel about the power of fantasy, about the proximity of dreams and reality, about ghost people and ghost realities. Lavie Tidhar has written a fine, striking, memorable piece of fiction here; one that deserves to be widely read.

Connie Willis, *All Clear* (2011)

In 2011 Connie Willis shared SF's blue riband prize, the Hugo, with... well, herself. The joint winners were Connie Willis's *Blackout* and Connie Willis's *All Clear* – the two halves of a lengthy narrative about time travelling historians from 2060 in London during World War II. Some grumbled that giving the 'Best Novel' prize (singular case, after all) to two books wasn't fair. But we were told that *Blackout* and *All Clear* aren't two novels, but one novel chainsawed down the middle to accommodate the exigencies of commercial publishing. Living as we now do in the Age of Kindle makes this excuse, it seems to me, rather harder to justify than might otherwise be the case. But there you go.

Readers considering buying *All Clear* may wonder whether they can do so without first reading *Blackout*. I think they can. The back-story threads are very easily picked up: 21st-century historians Eileen Ward (real name Merope), Mike Davies and Polly Churchill, having been inserted into WWII Britain, are struggling to locate the 'drops' that will get them home, all the time worried that their actions might be altering the timelines and changing the course of the war. Since scores of historians have already gone back to such Big Tent events as the battle of Marathon and the French Revolution without causing any upset, the official belief is that nothing they might do *can* change anything. But nevertheless Eileen, Mike and Polly become increasingly anxious that the timelines are being perverted.

The result is an interesting 200-page novel about the ordinary heroism of British civilians during World War, bloated to 800 pages via an egregiously handled time-travel conceit, eked out with great jellied quantities of historical research, endless meandering conversations, long passages disposed into that tiresome typographical convention by which characters' inmost thoughts are spelled out *in italics*, and a string of inconsequential chapter-end cliff-hangers/immediate resolutions that got increasingly on my nerves as the book went on. There's little *overall* tension, and the time-travelling historians come over as both panicky and amateurish – a, one might think, undesirable combination where timelines are lying about ready to be mucked up.

The Hugos are voted for by fans, so Willis's win reflects her popularity in the genre. That said, *some* fans have shown themselves undelighted. UK commentators in particular have complained about faults in Willis's research: errors about the 1940s London Tube layout, and the like. These errors are certainly present, but I can't say they bothered me – for absolute accuracy is a chimera in fiction, and the presence of (to pick an example out of the air) chiming clocks in Shakespeare's *Julius Caesar* shows that even the most clanging anachronisms need not interfere with the suspension of disbelief on the part of the reader. And Willis's overall aim is a commendable one. Despite walk-on parts by General Patton, Agatha Christie and Alan Turing, the bulk of the characters in *All Clear* are ordinary people getting on with their ordinary lives. It's rare to chance upon a novel published in our restless, hectic days that is happy to pootle as gently along as Willis's does here. Since civilian life, even in wartime, is more gentle pootle than crash-bang, Willis's might be thought a commendable aesthetic strategy. But the problem is that *All Clear* lapses too often into actual dullness: hundreds of pages in which characters worry that so-and-so hasn't phoned, or that St Paul's Cathedral might have suffered slightly worse bomb-damage than was actually the case. The comedy is weak, and sometimes actively wincing; the tragedy oddly creaky and unconvincing. Nor are the 'ordinary' characters particularly well-drawn. In particular Wilis's cheeky cockney urchin 'Alf' is so dreadfully conceived and rendered that I grimaced with displeasure whenever he appeared.

So why did this slab of Blitz pudding and time-travel custard win the Hugo? It presumably has something to do with the fact that Willis herself, well-liked in SF fandom, has written many other good novels (including previous Hugo winners *Fire Watch* (1982) and *Domesday Book* (1993), both about the same time-travelling institute, the former also concerned with the fire-bombing of St Pauls). And it can't be denied that the subject here, the heroism of ordinary people in testing times, is worthy and honourable. Conceivably Hugo voters thought that giving this novel the prize (or half of it) was a way of registering their respect for the collective sacrifice of wartime Londoners. Which is fair enough; although perhaps a better way of honouring them might have been to write a tighter, less self-indulgent novel in the first place.

Part 2: Fantasy

'...f-ff-f-ff-ff-f...'

Hannibal Lecter, *Silence of the Lambs*
(dir. Jonathan Demme, 1991)

Two Hobbits

I first read *The Hobbit* in 1974. Actually, it would be more accurate to say I first *heard* the novel in 1974, my parents having given me as a birthday present a cassette-tape talking-book version, narrated by the never-knowingly-underacted Nicol Williamson, to which I listened obsessively over and over and adored as a child. I still adore it (the novel, I mean), and stand much too close to it for objectivity. What to say about a text where my critical faculties are so compromised?

Well, one thing I can note is that Tolkien wrote two versions of the story of *The Hobbit*. In the first, a troop of dwarves, to use what Tolkien insisted was the proper plural form of the word, are planning to trek to a distant mountain in order to steal a great pile of treasure guarded by a lethal fire-breathing dragon – or more properly, to steal it *back*, since they claim it belongs to them. They are looking for a professional thief to help them in this dangerous business. The wizard Gandalf, for reasons that appear largely capricious, tricks the dwarves into hiring Bilbo Baggins, an ordinary, sedentary, unadventurous hobbit, and likewise tricks Bilbo into going along. This situation is played broadly for laughs, because Bilbo is so patently unfitted to the business of adventuring. 'Unfitness' also seems to characterise the dwarves, mind you: the party stumbles from disaster to disaster as they journey, escaping death by hairs' breadths half a dozen times at the hands of trolls, goblins, wolves, spiders and hostile elves. They are saved from their early misadventures by Gandalf's interventions, for though eccentric he is considerably more competent than they. Later, though, Gandalf goes off on his own business, and the party has to rescue itself. As they continue to stumble into a series of potentially fatal pickles, they somehow manage, by a combination of luck and hobbit-judgment, always to get away. Indeed, following Bilbo's development from massively incompetent to marginally incompetent is one of the pleasures of the narrative. At one point in the story, as the group passes through subterranean tunnels and caves underneath a mountain range, Bilbo gets separated from the others, and meets a fellow called Gollum. The two play a gambling game, guessing one another's riddles, and when Bilbo wins Gollum hands over what he had wagered – a magic ring that makes the wearer invisible.

Ownership of this ring, and a very shallow learning curve, gradually make Bilbo better at thieving and sneaking about. When, against the odds, the party reaches the dragon's Mountain, the quest *is* achieved, much, *much* more by luck than judgement. Bilbo does use the magic ring to creep into the dragon's lair and to steal one cup from the great hillocks of piled pelf, but that's as much as he can do. Luckily for all of them, the loss of this single piece happens to enrage the dragon, causing him to leave the mountain with the furious intention of burning up the local town of men. One of the defenders there, warned by a talking bird, shoots a lucky arrow that kills him. After this there is a big battle: armies converging on the mountain and its now undragoned hoard. The leader of the dwarf-band is killed, but otherwise things work out well for everybody. Finally, having spent almost all the novel adumbrating the 'there' of the novel's subtitle, the story sprints through the 'and back again', hurrying the materially enriched Bilbo home in a few pages.

I stress the 'incompetence' angle in my retelling here because, really, that's what characterises the main players. It's an endearing incompetence, used partly for comedy; partly for dramatic purposes (by way of ratcheting up the narrative tension and keeping things interesting) and partly to facilitate the readers' – our – engagement. Because we can be honest; we'd be rubbish on a dangerous quest. We're hobbitish types ourselves, and *our* idea of fun is snuggling into the sofa with a cup of cocoa and a good book, not fighting gigantic spiders with a sword. Or more precisely, we enjoy fighting giant spiders with a sword *in our imaginations only*. The book has sold as many copies as it has in part because the Hobbits are able (textually-speaking) so brilliantly to mediate our modern, cosseted perspectives and the rather forbidding antique warrior code and the pitiless Northern-European Folk Tale world.

That there *is* something haphazard about the larger conception of this adventure is part of its point: obviously, it makes for a jollier tale if a clearly unsuitable comic-foil is sent on a dangerous quest than some super-competent swordsman alpha-male. The bumbling, homely qualities of Bilbo, and the pinball bouncing trajectory from frying pan to fire to bigger fire of the narrative, are loveable aspects of the whole. And that's right: the motor of the story is the idea that *adventure will come and find you*, and winkle you out of your comfortable hidey-hole. It's a beguiling idea, in part because it literalises the action of story itself. We settle ourselves to read, in physical comfort, but the story itself transports us imaginatively out of our hole and away, upon all manner of precarious, exciting, absorbing and diverting journeys.

This is *The Hobbit* that appeared in 1937, to both acclaim and commercial success. But there's another *The Hobbit*. I don't mean the upcoming film. I mean a second *The Hobbit* written by Tolkien, comprising revisions to this first edition, additional material written for the *Lord of the Rings* and the appendices of *The Lord of the Rings*, plus other material – most importantly two separate prose pieces, both called 'The Quest for Erebor' that were collected in the posthumously-published *Unfinished Tales* (1980). JRRT's first revisions were confined to the 'Riddles in the Dark' chapter: for after writing the first *Hobbit*, Tolkien came to the conclusion that 'the Ring' was more than just a magic ring, more even than a ring of Gyges: that it was indeed the most powerful artefact in the whole world, one with which people became so besotted they lost their souls. Gollum, he reasoned, would not freely give up such an item. So he rewrote the scene. But this is symptomatic of something larger – a reconceptualising (Tolkien purists might say: a distillation or focussing) of the now-celebrated JRRT-legendarium: no longer a folk-story, now a grand sacramental drama of incarnation, atonement and redemption. I can't say I'm particularly fond of Tolkien's coinage 'legendarium', by the way, which to me sounds like a Blue Water store selling lead Warhammer miniatures. Not, I might add, that there's anything wrong with Warhammer miniatures. My point is this: Tolkien's celebrated 1939 essay 'On Fairy Stories' actually celebrates *two* modes of Fantasy, homely and transcendental. Traditional fairy tales, which Tolkien sees as beautiful and profound narratives of escape and resacralisation; and the New Testament, which he thinks shares those qualities with fairy stories but which he also thinks exists on a higher, truer and more important plane. This is how he puts it: 'the Evangelium has not abrogated legends; it has hallowed them, especially the 'happy ending.' The Christian has still to work, with mind as well as body, to suffer, hope, and die; but he may now perceive that all his bents and faculties have a purpose, which can be redeemed. So great is the bounty with which he has been treated that he may now, perhaps, fairly dare to guess that in Fantasy he may actually assist in the effoliation and multiple enrichment of creation.'

My beef, if I may slip into a non-vegetarian idiom for a moment, is not with Tolkien's religious beliefs, which (although I do not share them) are clearly essential to the dynamic of his art. My beef is with the notion that *all our bents and faculties have a purpose*. In Tolkien's second version of *The Hobbit*, it is precisely the haphazardness, the intimations of glorious, human, comic incompetence that must be sanded, smoothed and filed away. It is no longer enough for Gandalf to turn up on the doorstop of the world's least likely adventurer merely because that is the sort of thing batty old wizards do. Now he must do so because he has a larger plan. In the first version of the story it doesn't really matter why Gandalf chooses a hobbit, of all people; or more precisely, his whylessness of choice is actually the point of the story. ('I am looking for someone to share in an adventure that I am arranging,' Gandalf says, with what sounds to me rather like desperation, 'and it's very difficult to find anyone.') This is because the novel is not about Gandalf's whys, it is about Bilbo's adventure: why he is chosen matters less than the way he acquits himself on his journey, and the extent to which he sheds his unheroism and becomes a better fellow. That's what matters because we are he. That's how the reading experience goes.

But in Tolkien's second version of *The Hobbit* everything has to happen for a reason. Gandalf was not idly arranging an adventure; he was setting in motion one crucial play in a larger strategy of a grand war against Evil:

> I knew that Sauron had arisen again and would soon declare himself, and I knew that he was preparing for a great war. [...] The state of things in the North was very bad. The Kingdom under the Mountain and the strong Men of Dale were no more. To resist any force Sauron might send to regain the northern passes in the mountain and the old lands of Angmar there were only the Dwarves of the Iron Hills, and behind them lay a desolation and a Dragon. The Dragon Sauron might use with terrible effect. Often I said to myself: 'I must find some means of dealing with Smaug.' [*Unfinished Tales*, p. 322]

Just to be clear; I have no problem with retconning; not in the least (for I take 'text' to be fundamentally fluid and adaptable). I can go further, and say that one of the things that gives Tolkien's art depth and resonance is precisely the way he layers medium and deep historical pasts into his present-set tale, and having this secondary perspective on the material of *The Hobbit* adds echoey, plangent splendour to the whole. But that's not to say that this piece of retconning makes sense. On the contrary: it compels us to believe that Gandalf, deciding that it was a strategic priority that Smaug be eliminated, thinks not of sending an army, and certainly not of going himself and tackling the dragon with his, you know, magic and that. Rather he thinks: 'I'll go to the *extreme other end of the continent*, recruit a number of dwarves, some of them manifestly not up to the task (Bombur?), plus a hobbit *without any experience or aptitude for a mission of this sort whatsoever*, and send them off travelling halfway across the world past unnumbered perils in the hope that somehow *they'll* do the old worm in.' Why the dwarves? Well, I suppose they can at least be persuaded to go, since they regard Erebor as rightfully theirs, although you have to wonder whether a military strategist who wasn't *actually* senile mightn't think first of approaching the men of Dale. But there is no reason in this scenario why Bilbo would be anyone's first, or thousand-and-first choice. In his second version of the story, Tolkien comes up with three reasons why it's a good idea to wager the entire success of the operation of Bilbo – a figure of whom Thorin rightly says 'he is soft, soft as the mud of the Shire, and silly', a judgement with which Gandalf concurs ("You are quite right' [*Unfinished Tales*, p. 325]). Those three reasons are:

1. That Hobbits don't wear shoes, where Dwarfs do ('suddenly in my mind [I pictured] the sturdy, heavy-booted Dwarves ... the quick, soft-footed hobbit'), a consideration, certainly, since Dragons have good hearing; although you might think that advising the Dwarves to *take off* their boots might be less precarious than hanging the success of the enterprise around the neck of a sort of Middle-Earth fur-footed Homer Simpson.
2. That Smaug would not know Bilbo's scent, where he would recognise the smell of Dwarves, although apparently Tolkien added this as an afterthought to his MS ('a scent that cannot be placed, at least not by Smaug, the enemy of Dwarves'). A scent that cannot be smelled at all by Smaug would make more sense, but OK. The fact that he smells a thief in his lair but can't immediately place the thief's provenance might confuse him for... six seconds or so. The third reason is the most arbitrary of all –
3. Gandalf just feels in his water that it would be a good idea:

'listen to me Thorin Oakenshield [...] if this hobbit goes with you, you will succeed. If not you will fail. A foresight is on me' [p. 325]. Hard not to see this as code for 'I've already written this story and know how it turns out', which comes dangerously close to a cheat.

The story of *The Lord of the Rings* is that even 'the little people' (that's us, of course) have their part to play in the great historical and martial dramas of the age – and it is a potent and truthful story, well told. But *The Hobbit* is that story only in its second iteration. In its first, the one we are chiefly considering here, *The Hobbit* is not about the great dramas of the age; it is about us-sized dramas of people being taken out of their comfort zone – whisked away by Story.

I'm happy that there are two versions of *The Hobbit*, and feel no desire to try and force them into some notional procrustean 'coherence'. Only narrative fundamentalists, the textual Taliban, believe that all stories must be brought into that sort of rigid alignment. But of the two stories, really I prefer the one (homely, funny, a little bit slapstick and a little bit wondrous) over the other (grand-verging-on-grandiose, theological, epic and strenuously, to coin a phrase, *eutragic*). Although I do love them both. And I love the Dwarves vastly more than any number of elves. I love precisely their lack of graceful elegance. Thorin Oakenshield has some noble speeches in *The Hobbit* it's true; but his Dwarves are better at stuffing themselves with food and drink, and getting (with endearing incompetence) into ridiculous scrapes. Consulting the Dwarf family tree, in the appendices to *Return of the King*, I discover that amongst Thorin's relatives are 'Borin' and 'Groin'. A little more groin would have done *The Lord of the Rings* no harm at all, I think. Not borin' in the least.

Maurice Sendak, *Where the Wild Things Are* (1963); David Eggers *Where the Wild Things Are* (2009)

Sendak's *Where the Wild Things Are* is one of my holy books. I'm not alone in that, of course: it's a widely adored picture book. But I can make a boast true of few Sendakophiles: I have rewritten *Where the Wild Things Are*, as a novel (called *New Model Army*): very far removed from the original in terms of its manifest content, very much closer, perhaps too obviously so, in terms of its latent symbols and mood.

I have yet to see Spike Jonze's movie version; but I have now read David Eggers's novelisation. It's not a bad novel, exactly (though neither is it a very good one), but it gets the original very wrong, I think, and more pressingly it gets the process of *adapting* the original wrong. What I mean by this latter observation is that it puts all its energy into the surface details of the picture book, and seems weirdly blind to the deeper currents of the text... it maintains and elaborates, sometimes at pitifully diluted length, the manifest content of Sendak's original, and misrepresents and distorts the latent elements. Since it's the latent elements that give the book its extraordinary potency, this is little short of disastrous.

Of course, maybe I am saying nothing here. It could be that I'm talking not about Maurice Sendak's original book, only the hybrid of it twined bindweedily around the stem of my imagination. Eggers is under no obligation to write a novel about my imagination, after all. And lots of the specifics of the novelisation are cannily worked out: Max is the son of a bitter single mother, and has an older sister who doesn't want to play with him anymore. The forest grows not in his room, but exists actually outside his house (he's warned against entering). He runs away, into this forest, takes the boat from there, and ends up where the wild things are. The book calls them 'infant-like, almost cute, and at the same time pathetic, tragic', which isn't how they strike me. But let a thousand flowers bloom, and all that. Anyway, the wild things themselves have a strange selection of names – strange, that is, for wild things (I suppose that's Eggers's point): Carol, a male, is the main figure, but there's also Douglas and Catherine. There's a lot of 'I'll eat you!' running about. Max burns their forest down. They build a fort. Towards the end, to escape the wrath of Carol, Katherine does eat Max, and the lad is later cut from her stomach. Then he goes home.

Where the Wild Things Are is a boy's book: it's a book about the joys of playing rough, of consciously misbehaving, and being a beast. But much more potently than that, it's a pure narrative distillation of Fort-Da. The boy's mother stops his fun, and he casts her, metaphorically, over the side of his cot, via the brilliant expedient of generating a whole new imaginative world that doesn't contain her. But of course the logic of Fort-Da is that he must, symbolically, spool the mother back in to him – or in this case draw in the real world of his room again.

Sendak's original has so many beautiful and eloquent moments, and is so potently economical I could spend many thousands of words talking about it. But I'll limit myself to noting only a couple of things, because they strike me as illustrative of the way in which Eggers's re-tread wholly misses the forcefulness of the source text. In Sendak, it's the case that the land of the wild things is more immediate and vivid than reality – look at the way he portrays Max's initial mischief in tiny boxes of illustration surrounded by several inches of white margin, and the way the size of the picture grows along with the forest in his bedroom, until it fills the entire page. (That the final image of Max in his room, with the meal waiting for him still hot, also fills the page suggests to me that he has been somehow enriched by his sojourn in the Wild Things' land). Watch what Sendak does with the moon in his illustrations. There's nothing so nuanced in the expository blubber of Eggers's prose.

But more fatally, Eggers wholly fluffs, or misses, the two crucial beats of the story. The first immediately follows the three-page Wild Rumpus (Eggers includes the Rumpus, although shifts its tenor from sheer jouissance to fright and chase). Then:

> 'Now stop!' Max said and sent the wild things off to bed without *their* supper. And Max the king of all the wild things was lonely and wanted to be where someone loved him best of all. Then all around from far away across the world he smelled good things to eat so he gave up being kind of where the wild things are.

I never cry at books (I almost never cry at anything at all: my upper lip being so stiff) but there's something in the piercing directness of that articulation, about Max wanting to be where someone loved him best of all, that makes my eyes hot with incipient tears. There's nothing equivalent in Eggers's novel, which is to say, the moment of loneliness is smeared and diluted and spread over the whole section.

Then there's my favourite moment of all from the original book. My 2 year-old's fond of this bit too: I think it speaks (to him) of the awesome power he has recently discovered, and which he utilizes a great deal. The power of saying 'no!'

> But the wild things cried, 'Oh please don't go –
> We'll eat you up – we love you so!'
> And Max said, 'No!'

So he gets back in the boat and sails home. Look at the picture: Max is smiling. He's happy. He understands that wildthingishness is not violence, or malevolence, or fear, or existential dread, or anything of the things Eggers talks about. It's a purer joy. 'We'll eat you up – we love you so!' is so perfect a line: it captures both the extraordinarily *edible* quality of little kids, the way our (parental) love for them almost spills over into wanting to devour them, they're so delicious. And it also captures the childish perspective too: where apprehending the world is most completely and immediately done orally, where eating is the most immediate sensual pleasure. Egger has nothing so brilliant in *his* account.

> When he awoke he saw all of the beasts, all but Carol, before him. They had untied his boat and had prepared it to sail. Max rose from Katherine's lap and stood, still feeling light-headed.
> 'So you're going,' Douglas said...
> Max nodded.
> Douglas extended his left hand. Max shook it.
> 'You were the best thinker we ever had,' Douglas said.
> Max tried to smile.
> 'I'm sorry for all this,' Ira said quietly. 'I blame myself.'
> Max hugged him. 'Don't.'
> Judith and Max exchanged glances. She made a face that said *Oops, sorry!* then emitted a high nervous laugh. 'I never know what to say in these situations,' she said. [p. 273]

To be clear: Eggers reads this superb, intense, poetic moment, almost the climax of Sendak's book, in terms of downbeat social awkwardness and embarrassment. Has he ever *met* a child? Has he ever *been* a child? And Max said: NO.

The Name of the Wind (2007) by Patrick Rothfuss and *The Children of Húrin* by J.R.R. Tolkien (2007)

Here are two titles for booksellers to shelve under Fantasy. Both follow the adventures of an essentially good though morally (slightly) complicated hero around a medievalised imaginary world. Both embody a sort of under-narrative about revenge, upon which are constructed varied and peripatetic adventures. There is, in both books, Evil to be combated, magic to be performed, and artefacts that have special powers. One (the Rothfuss) is an example of a genre pretty much wholly invented and defined by the other (Tolkien). Nevertheless they are absolutely as different from one another as could be imagined. One of these is, in its way, a great book. The other is a competently constructed time-whileawayer. See if you can guess which description fits which novel.

Rothfuss's tale, or yarn, or tome, or whichever term you prefer, concerns Kvothe – pronounced, we're told, 'nearly the same as 'Quothe' – who is the hero of all and the narrator of most of this sumo-sized volume. Living incognito as a humble tavern-owner in a quiet backwater, he's tracked down by a chap named Chronicler, who wants to write down Kvothe's heroic life story. Chronicler, actually, is attacked on the road by nasty evil-magic ceramic spider beasts (Kvothe rescues him) and whilst he is convalescing he transcribes our hero's story – which, with occasional interjections or requests for clarification from Chronicler, fills up almost all the rest of the book.

It's a varied and eventful tale. We get an account of our hero's childhood in a troupe of travelling players; his growing-up, his achievements and his reverses (he spends a time as a street-rat-kid in a crime-riddled city), and we get his ambition to enrol in a legendary university of magic and learn the true names of all things so that he can control them. His destiny is to become 'the greatest magician the world has ever known.' But it's not a straightforward path. It wouldn't be much of a story if it were.

Readers with even the most rudimentary experience of the genre will recognise all these elements from other books, and Rothfuss is clearly aware of the danger of *staleness*. Accordingly he tries to inoculate his book against accusations that it is merely derivative. From one of the sections where Kvothe reflects on his own story:

> 'I was wondering why you didn't go looking for Skarpi?' [...] Kvothe drew a deep breath and sighed. 'The simplest reason is the least satisfying one, I suppose. The truth is this: I wasn't living in a story.'
>
> 'I don't think I'm understanding you, Reshi,' said Bast.
>
> 'Think of all the stories you've heard, Bast. You have a young boy, the hero. His parents are killed. He sets out for vengeance. What happens next?'
>
> Bast hesitated, his expression puzzled. Chronicler answered the question instead. 'He finds help. A clever talking squirrel. An old drunken swordsman. A mad hermit in the woods. That sort of thing... he finds the villains and kills them.'
>
> Kvothe leaned forward. 'If this were some tavern tale, all half-truth and senseless adventure [...] but whilst that might make for an entertaining story, it would not be the truth. The truth is this [...]' [pp. 304-5]

This is the author patting the reader on her shoulder, saying, 'fools may be content with the old storytelling clichés, but *you* and *I* have more sophisticated tastes...' Except that it's a lie: not only is Kvothe's tale thoroughly storybook in every particular, even the opposition invoked here between real and 'literary' is precisely a *device*, a storytelling trick used by innumerable writers, not least Tolkien himself in *The Lord of the Rings* (Sam and Frodo, you'll remember, discuss how the heroic tale of their quest would differ from the actual hardships they are experiencing).

Rothfuss is a skilled writer with good storytelling instincts and the ability to drop just enough specific detail into his worldbuilding to make his Central Casting characters come alive (or at least half-alive, like Pinnochio dolls), but not so much that it bogs down the narrative or bores the reader. There's nothing wearisome here, except possibly the sheer weight of the book itself in one's hands; overall it's a smooth-rolling reading experience that passes the time, is fairly entertaining, and has a few moments of excitement. But here's the thing: it's a fundamentally cosy book. It flatters the reader. It winks at her, promising her the real thing rather than some sanitised storybook version, at the same time sanitising anything that might genuinely unsettle, or unnerve, or wrong-foot her readerly expectations. It, like many works of contemporary fantasy, panders to a sort of imaginative tourism, a safe entry into an escapist imaginative space defined by its reassuring familiarity. Cosiness is a good quality in sweaters. It is not a merit in books.

I read *The Name of the Wind* as a bound proof. The cover of this pre-edition is as black as Spinal Tap cover art, save only for a white-printed letter from Elizabeth R. Wollheim, DAW's President and Publisher. Now, the purpose of this letter is to let booksellers know what a great book *The Name of the Wind* is:

> *Dear Bookseller,*
> *You hold in your hands an Advance Reading Copy of the most brilliant first fantasy novel I have ever read in over thirty years as an editor. After reading the first hundred pages of Patrick Rothfuss' THE NAME OF THE WIND, I knew I had to publish this book... A tale told in classic high fantasy style, THE NAME OF THE WIND is a masterpiece that carries a fresh and earthy originality all its own. It transports the reader to the interior of a wizard's soul and to the world that helped create him. It is the story of a legendary hero and the truth that lies behind his legend. Kvothe is a genuine hero created to walk alongside the greatest heroes of our imagination... Join me in welcoming a writer who ranks with Tad Williams, George R R Martin, Terry Goodkind, Robert Jordan and Terry Brooks as a great writer of high fantasy. Exciting and rousing, intimate and personal, THE NAME OF THE WIND doesn't just describe what it is to be heroic, it is heroic.*
> *Enjoy!*
> *Elizabeth Wollheim*

There's a slight awkwardness in praising the book for its 'fresh and earthy originality all its own' and then listing the authors (Williams, Martin, Goodkind, Jordan, Brooks) of whom it is – as she rightly says – very, very reminiscent. But we understand that this is a kind of code, and we take it as such. It says, 'You like Robert Jordan? You'll like this!' – information presumably useful for people who still enjoy Robert Jordan despite having wheeled themselves all the way to the end of his enormous, time-sucking series. I suppose there are such people in the world. That's not the problem I have with this letter. The problem I have with this letter is this part: *A tale told in classic high fantasy style [...]*

But no. *The Name of the Wind* is a tale told in the bourgeois discursive style familiar from the modern realist novel. A passage picked at random:

> I settled onto the stone bench under the pennant pole next to my two friends.
>
> 'So where were you last night?' Simmon asked too casually.
>
> It was only then that I remembered that the three of us had planned to meet up with Fenton and play corners last night. Seeing Denna had completely driven the plan from my mind. 'Oh God, I'm sorry Sim. How long did you wait for me?'
>
> He gave me a look.
>
> 'I'm sorry,' I repeated, hoping I looked as guilty as I felt. 'I forgot.'
>
> Sim grinned, shrugging it off. 'It's not a big deal.' [p. 427]

This could be three pals from any novel set in the 20th or 21st century, and hundreds and hundreds of similar passages serve only to show the author has not entered into the pre-industrial medieval mind-set that his medieval pre-industrial world requires – to, for example, understand the crucial point that not guilt ('I looked as guilty as I felt') but *shame* was the key moral dynamic for the period. But to understand that would involve shifting about the psychological portraiture of the entire project; it would have meant writing characters less like, and therefore less appealing to, a 21st-century readership disinclined to make the effort to encounter the properly strange or unusual.

This speaks to a broader state of affairs in which style – the language and form of the novel – is seen as an unimportant adjunct to the 'story.' It is not. A bourgeois discursive style constructs a bourgeois world. If it is used to describe a medieval world it necessarily mismatches what it describes, creating a milieu that is only an anachronism, a theme park, or a World-of-Warcraft gaming environment rather than an actual place. This degrades the ability of the book properly to evoke its fictional setting, and therefore denies the book the higher heroic possibilities of its imaginative premise.

The Children of Húrin, on the other hand, *does* feel real. It's a book by a man who knew intimately not only the facts and paraphernalia but the mind-set, values, and inner life of his relevant historical period – more Dark Age than medieval, this time, but assuredly not modern. The most obvious, although certainly not the only, level on which this registers is that of the style, which actually does approach the classic elevation that Wollheim wrongly identifies in Rothfuss. *The Children of Húrin*'s syntax is compact, declarative and unafraid of inversion ('Great was the triumph of Morgoth'). Its vocabulary is almost entirely purged of words not derived from Old English sources: so much so that the occasional Anglo-French term – for instance, the phrase 'Petty-dwarf' with its *petit-*derived qualifier – jars a little. More, it is a prose written with a careful ear for the rhythms of English; a prose with a very satisfying balance of iambic and trochaic pulses, sparingly leavened with unstressed polysyllables (it reads well *aloud*). It also distils frequently into compact phrases of surprising resonance and power. Here is the seven-year-old Túrin in conversation with the family servant Sador and trying to come to terms with the death (from sickness) of his beloved little sister Lalaith:

> 'Then Lalaith will not come back?' said Túrin. 'Where has she gone?'
>
> 'She will not come back,' said Sador. 'But where she has gone no man knows; or I do not.'
>
> 'Has it always been so? Or do we suffer some curse of the wicked King, perhaps, like the Evil Breath?'
>
> 'I do not know. A darkness lies behind us and out of it few tales have come [...] it may be that we fled from the fear of the Dark, only to find it here before us, and nowhere else to fly to but the Sea.'
>
> 'We are not afraid any longer,' said Túrin, 'not all of us. My father is not afraid, and I will not be; or at least, as my mother, I will be afraid and not show it.'
>
> It seemed then to Sador that Túrin's eyes were not the eyes of a child, and he thought: 'Grief is a hone to a hard mind.' [p.43]

That last eight-word phrase has a poetic feel in part because the unfamiliar formality and alliteration of Tolkien's style provides us with some of the estrangement that poetry does, and partly because its rhythm (two dactyls and a spondee) make it sound like the second half of a Homeric hexameter. It's appropriate, too, encapsulating in little the theme of the novel as a whole; the way a heroic temper such as Túrin's responds to continual hardship and grief by becoming harder and more edged. Which is a roundabout way of saying that Tolkien was a very skilled writer of this sort of prose.

The Children of Húrin is set in Tolkien's First Age, thousands of years before the events of the Third-Age *Lord of the Rings*. There are no hobbits, wizards, ents, or Tom Bombadils. There are, however, elves, men, and orcs – lots of the latter. Sauron is mentioned in passing, because at this point in Tolkien's imaginary history Sauron is only the lieutenant of a far greater evil: Morgoth, or Melkor, a character who is, essentially, Satan himself. Húrin, a man from Mithrim, takes part in the battle of Nirnaeth Arnoediad, in which elves and men confront Morgoth's hordes. The bad guys win. Captured by Morgoth, Húrin's family is cursed, and then he is tormented by being placed in a magic chair that preserves him from death and compels him to watch as this curse works its malign influence upon his wife, son, and daughter. This takes us up to chapter 3 (of 18). Most of the rest of this book is given over to Húrin's son Túrin, and a little bit to his daughter Niënor.

In the two paragraphs that follow this one I outline the story, with many spoilers; but I have fewer qualms about this than I otherwise might because the story will already be familiar to many people. For one thing, it has appeared in print before, several times, in *The Silmarillion* (1977) as 'Of Túrin Turambar' (prose); in Unfinished Tales (1980) as 'Narn i Hîn Húrin' (prose) and in *The Book of Lost Tales, Part II* (1984) as 'Turambar and the Foalókë' and 'The Nauglafring' (both prose); in *The Lays of Beleriand* (1985) as 'The Lay of the Children of Húrin' (verse in alliterative long lines) and then yet again in *The War of the Jewels* (1994) as 'The Wanderings of Húrin' (prose). Clearly this was a story that wouldn't leave Tolkien alone. There's another sense in which the story may ring bells with readers, for it is an amalgamation of a number of celebrated mythic precedents: one is the story of Kullervo from the Finnish epic *Kalevala*; the other is Siegfried from the Nibelungen epic. But where the familiarity of Rothfuss's story registers as belatedness and tiredness, the familiarity of Tolkien's gives it the resonance and inevitability of myth.

The book traces the increasingly terrible lives of Húrin's children under the withering curse of Morgoth. Son Túrin is high-minded, noble, taciturn, and darkly charismatic. Daughter Niënor is a much less successful piece of characterisation, little more than a passive beauty (it's almost as if Tolkien *can't do* women...). Túrin flees his northern home and takes refuge for a time with the elves, who love him, but his haughty manner and his disinclination to speak up for himself leads to him being – unjustly – banished. Armed with a terrible and magical black sword, he takes up with some outlaws, leads men, becomes a prince of the hidden city of Nargothrond, and finally –in some very powerful chapters given added heft by the sheer density and momentum Tolkien's focussed prose accumulates as it goes along – fights and kills the terrible dragon Glaurung.

But Túrin's destiny is consistently infelicitous. His pride contributes to the fall of the city he is sworn to defend; he accidentally kills his best friend, and later he inadvertently marries and impregnates his sister who, when she learns what has happened, drowns herself in a river. At various moments in the narrative Túrin comprehends what he has done, and is driven from his wits, but he recovers them, propelled as he is by the ferocity of his will to revenge. But after this last incestuous transgression has been revealed to him by the dying Glaurung, he finally gives up.

> Then he drew forth his sword, and said: 'Hail, Gurthang, iron of death, you alone now remain! But what lord or loyalty do you know, save the hand that wields you? From no blood will you shrink. Will you take Túrin Turambar? Will you slay me swiftly?'
>
> And from the blade rang a cold voice in answer: 'Yes, I will drink your blood, that I may forget the blood of Beleg my master, and the blood of Brandir [Túrin's best friend] slain unjustly. I will slay you swiftly.'
>
> Then Túrin set the hilts upon the ground, and cast himself upon the point of Gurthang, and the black blade took his life. [p. 256]

This is based on Kullervo's suicide, also preceded by a conversation with his magical sword. Moorcock's Elric is only one of many contemporary fantasy variants of this venerable notion.

The Children of Húrin is relatively short; novella length, although published here in a thoroughly gorgeous volume (lovely paper, beautiful typeface generously spaced, a fold-out two-tone map, and eight handsome full-colour illustrations from Alan Lee) that has been plumped-up with a preface, introduction, note on pronunciation, family trees, and a couple of appendices. I knew the story before I picked it up, but I read it nevertheless with enormous and unexpected pleasure. It commanded my full attention and it generated the emotional charge of a much longer novel. It is a tragedy, not in the Aristotelian sense (for there is precious little catharsis here) but in the northern-European sense of humans encountering an overwhelming fate with defiance. And that is at the heart of Tolkien's conception of heroism: precisely *not* achievement, but a particular and noble-hearted encounter with failure; not how you triumph, but the spirit with which you resist the fate you know to be unavoidable.

The question is whether Tolkien's style here is accessible enough to attract the sort of readership likely to enjoy Rothfuss's more calculated blandness of tone. Or to put it another way: what must a writer of Fantasy do to reach the many Fantasy fans whose potential enjoyment of (say) *Njal's Saga* or Chrétien de Troyes is blocked by the works' archaic style? How to make a bridge between our modern sensibilities and the medieval matter? Rothfuss's solution, for good and ill, and mostly for ill, is simply to write the pre-modern as if it is modern. In *The Silmarillion* Tolkien was widely criticised for writing his antique matter in an unadorned antique style ('like the Old Testament,' reviewers complained; although actually it is rather unlike the Bible in tone and much more like the northern Sagas). Plenty of ordinary readers couldn't stomach it, although Old English specialists and medievalists, who are used to reading this kind of thing, usually speak of the book in much warmer terms.

The Lord of the Rings was amongst other things one attempt at a solution to this problem, constructed by braiding together modern perspectives (the cosy bourgeois hobbits) and pre-modern (the medieval Gondor, the Old English Rohan), not only in terms of story but style – the hobbit chapters are of course written with a kind of early 20th-century contemporaneity of narrative voice, where the later sequences inhabit a more antiquated and high-flown idiom, full of inversions, dated vocabulary, invocative and rhetorical stiffness, although at the same time rather splendid and suitably heroic.

But it's surprising how few writers have attempted to imitate Tolkien's stylistic strategy in this, although of course they have stolen plenty of other things from his writing. There are other ways of tackling this problem: for instance, rather than sacrifice a modern style many

Fantasy writers have given up the medieval setting: there's clearly no problem with using a 19th-century novelistic voice to describe a basically 19th-century world, as in the work of Ian MacLeod and China Miéville. But though vibrant this remains, I suppose, it is a minor part of the market for Fantasy; Wollheim pitches her 'Dear Bookseller' letter at a climate she knows is still hungry for Heroic Fantasy.

Heroic Fantasy, we know, takes as its setting a pre-industrial world, in which some of the conveniences accorded to modern humanity by machines fall within the purview of magic, whilst others are dispensed with altogether. The former strategy enables escapist fantasy about the empowerment of magical skill; but the latter strategy also enables escapism, by giving the readers access to an earthier, more authentic, more empowered, more physical existence than they have as pale wage-slaves snagged in the webs of Civilisation and Its Discontents.

Now, the standard defence of escapism goes something like this: 'what's wrong with escapism? Who is it that opposes escape? Jailers!' It's an incomplete logic, although there is a grit of truth in it. If you are a parent, and your teenage child spends eight hours a day upon their bed in heroin-induced lassitude as a strategy for escaping the anomie of modern teenagerdom, you don't need the soul of a jailer to want him, her, to stop. Art is about modes of engagement with the world, not modes of avoiding it. The key thing is that some forms of engagement are liberating, and others enslaving, and simple 'distraction' falls under the logic of the latter.

Escapism isn't a very good word, actually, for the positive psychological qualities its defenders want to defend; it's less a question of breaking one's bars and running away (running *whither*, we might ask?); it's more about keeping alive the facility for imaginative *play*, that faculty that only a fool would deny is core to any healthy psychological makeup. Kids are good at play, and have an unexamined wisdom about it; adults, sometimes, forget how vital it is. What's wrong with Art that insists too severely on pressing people's faces against the miseries of actual existence is not that we shouldn't have to confront Darfur or Iraq, poverty or oppression; it's that such art rarely gives us the imaginative wiggle room to think of how things might be improved, or challenged, or even accepted. Imaginative wiggle room, on the other hand, is something SF/Fantasy is very good at.

An art that simply depresses is liable to be an ineffective art because it will tend, by putting people off, to disable rather than enable imaginative engagement. But even more depressing than reading Celan on the Holocaust is reading the blithe, upbeat, *escapist* holocaust-fiction of (say) the *Left Behind* series. I am not, in this review, saying that Tolkien is simply a better writer than Rothfuss; although, as it happens, I think he is. But Rothfuss is certainly an accomplished storyteller; it's just that he has not thought-through the implications of writing Heroic Fantasy in the way Tolkien did.

The irony is that the readers who read Fantasy because they want the uplift of a heroism with which they can identify – and who believe that heroism has no place in the modern world – are actually reading about precisely *modern* heroes. Kvothe, an individual who overcomes various life obstacles to triumph has plenty in common with Lance Armstrong or that guy in *The Pursuit of Happyness*. His is a didactic and a feel-good heroism. Túrin, on the other hand, is an individual who fights against a doom greater than he, despite knowing that he cannot win, simply because defiance in the teeth of an inevitable doom is the strength given to humans. His world –where triumph and glory are localised and temporary, and always give way to subsequent defeat – is in the deepest sense our world. That is what it means to be mortal. We are all going to die; it's demeaning to waste our energy in schemes or fantasies that tell us otherwise. What matters, as with Túrin, is the character with which we face that annihilation. Of the two heroisms presented by these books, his is the greater, and the most relevant.

J R R Tolkien, *The Legend of Sigurd and Gudrún* (2009)

Sigurd and Gudrún is the latest title from the seemingly bottomless supply of posthumous Tolkieniana to be edited for publication by his son, Christopher. (The last being the aforereviewed *Children of Húrin*). *Sigurd and Gudrún* is a rather different sort of beast: 170 pages of heroic poetry, written in a scrupulously imitated pastiche of Anglo Saxon alliterative verse, attended by 200 pages of detailed editorial commentary, retelling the tragic story of the Volsungs (Tolkien calls them 'Völsungs' following his OE sources, but since that rather gives them the look of a heavy metal band, I'm going to stick with *Volsungs*).

The story, in other words, is an actual Norse or Germanic legend, rather than the mythopoeic Tolkienian imaginings of Middle Earth. Fans of the latter might be disappointed by this fact, and might, moreover, find the dense, allusive verse in which Tolkien has rendered his tale pretty indigestible compared to the expansive flowing prose of *The Lord of the Rings*. But that's not to say they shouldn't give it a go.

Now I have no doubt you, reading this, are a highly cultured individual. You will, therefore, of course be familiar with the story of the Volsungs and the Niblungs; perhaps from the original Sagas, or Snorri Sturlson's medieval *Prose Edda* – or perhaps in one or other modern retelling. The most celebrated of these are both later 19th-century: Englishman William Morris's *The Story of Sigurd the Volsung* (1876) – once a fairly famous poem, and one Tolkien certainly knew; and, most famously of all, Wagner's operatic recasting of the legends, *Der Ring des Nibelungen* (1869-74). But it's a complicated legend that involves a whole chunk of story, and before I discuss the merits of Tolkien's version I'm going to summarize it here. Those familiar with its ins-and-outs can skip ahead to section 2 of this review. But since it isn't really possible to talk about the poem without reference to the legend Tolkien is retelling, and since these legends perhaps aren't as well-known as they might be, I hope you'll bear with me.

The story starts, as the best ones do, with an enormous pile of treasure. The Norse god Odin has been imprisoned by a chap called Hreidmar – no ordinary fellow, this: he and his sons can take the form of animals, if they choose – because Odin killed Hreidmar's son Otr (in the form of an otter). To get free again, Odin ransoms himself with a hoard of treasure that he, in turn, takes from the dwarf Andvari. Now the dwarf is unhappy about having to relinquish his gold, and begs Odin's middleman (Loki) to be allowed to keep one ring. Denied this, he curses the whole hoard, and the ring especially ('My ring I will curse/with ruth and woe!'). Hreidmar gets his gold, though, and Odin goes free.

That, in effect, is the backstory. Tolkien's focus is not so much on these supernatural beings as the mortal dynasty of the Volsungs, but it's worth touching on what happens to this gold in the meantime. Hreidmar's remaining sons, Regin and Fafnir, desire it, and kill their father to get it. Regin demands his share, but Fafnir wants to keep it all to himself, so he pops on a 'Helm of Terror' to scare his brother away. Fafnir then takes the form of a terrible dragon, and curls up on his pile of gold in a lair, which is, as we all know, how dragons like to enjoy their wealth. We'll come back to the treasure in a bit.

Enter Odin's grandson, Volsung, and his eleven children; most especially his son and daughter, Sigmund and Signy. Signy marries a neighbouring king, Siggeir of the Gauts. But Siggeir is a bad sort: he betrays the alliance and chains up all ten sons of Volsung in the forest to be eaten by wolves. Only Sigmund survives, and he takes his vengeance on nasty Siggeir with the help of a son conceived upon his sister Signy, wife of his enemy and Queen of the Gauts. The Gauts are slaughtered, but Signy chooses to die with her husband, which, since she hates him, is a rather puzzling decision.

Sigmund returns to his land and rules as king, and here (a) his incestuously conceived son is killed, and (b) he marries again and fathers Sigurd. Since Sigmund dies in battle before his son is born, and since his mother also dies, Sigurd is raised in the forest by Regin (from the backstory). Now we get onto more familiar, Wagnerian ground. Sigurd grows up to be the greatest warrior in the world. Regin decides to use him to get his hands on the treasure hoarded by his dragon-brother, sending him to do what Regin is too weak or cowardly to do himself: to kill Fafnir. Regin plans, after the deed, to eat the dragon's heart – thus gaining supernatural wisdom – and afterwards dispose of Sigurd. And indeed Sigurd kills the dragon, and on Regin's instruction cuts out and cooks the heart for him. But the fat spits and burns Sigurd's hand. When he instinctively puts this wound to his mouth

Sigurd tastes the dragon and acquires the ability to understand the birds. They tell him of Regin's evil plan and Sigurd doesn't muck about. To quote Tolkien's version:

> *Round turned Sigurd*
> *and Regin saw he*
> *in the heath crawling*
> *with hate gleaming.*
> *Black spilled the blood*
> *as blade clove him*
> *the head hewing*
> *of Hreidmar's son.* [p. 114]

The treasure is now Sigurd's. What next? Well, some birds tell Sigurd that the most beautiful woman in the world, the celebrated Brynhild, is lying on a mountaintop, surrounded by a wall of fire, waiting for the mightiest warrior in the world to brave the flames and claim her. So off Sigurd goes, leaps the fire and wakes Brynhild with a kiss. The two fall in love, and swear oaths of fidelity to one another. This takes us up to the end of Wagner's opera *Siegfried* (Siegfried being the German form of Sigurd's name).

Now Gudrún enters the tale. She is the daughter of king Gjúki and his sorceress-queen Grímhild. When Sigurd comes to stay (now we're into the story of Wagner's *Götterdämmerung*) Grímhild decides he'd make a good husband for her daughter. That he is in love with, and sworn to, Brynhild is clearly an obstacle, but Grímhild gets around this by giving him a memory-erasing magic potion. I say memory-erasing, although presumably the only portion of Sigurd's memory that gets erased is the bit about having met and fallen in love with Brynhild. Anyway, under the influence of this potion Sigurd agrees to marry Gudrún. Since this makes Brynhild once again marriageable material, Grímhild decides that her son, Gudrún's brother Gunnar, can marry her. The problem here is that Gunnar isn't the mightiest warrior in the world (that's Sigurd) and so can't broach the wall of fire to get to her. But by means of another handy magic potion, Grímhild gives Sigurd the outward appearance of Gunnar. He then – obligingly – rides off and claims Brynhild on Gunnar's behalf. Brynhild is, as you might expect, a bit confused by this, but goes along with it; and Sigurd-in-the-likeness-of-Gunnar seals the deal by giving Brynhild the cursed ring from Andvari's hoard.

Brynhild, coming to the court of Gjúki as Gunnar's betrothed, is understandably narked to find Sigurd already there, pledged to Gudrún. Things get, narratively, a little confused at this point. You might think Gunnar would be grateful to Sigurd for taking on his form and braving the wall of fire to win him the world's most beautiful woman. But instead he decides he's going to kill him, and although he's too squeamish, or scared, to do so directly, he persuades his half-brother Gotthorn to stab Sigurd in his sleep. (According to the legend, the dying Sigurd chucks his sword at Gotthorn and cuts him in half.) When grief-stricken Brynhild goes off to throw herself onto Sigurd's funeral pyre, everyone seems happy to see her go, which again seems odd given the trouble they all went to get her in the first place: 'Crooked came she forth/from cursed womb/to man's evil/and our mighty woe' [pp. 176-7] – surely a little harsh in the circumstances.

That's the end of Sigurd and Brynhild. The remainder is Gudrún's story. Grief-struck at this turn of events, she is nevertheless married off to 'Atli' (Attila the Hun, no less) in a dynastic treaty-style wedding. But Atli has heard of the huge hoard of gold. He wants it; and when he invites Gudrún's brothers Gunnar and Högni – the two men in the world who know where the treasure is – to a mighty feast, he is actually planning to torture them into revealing its location. Gunnar and Högni come with their war band, and there's a major rumble at Atli's court, with a good deal of hewing, smiting and slaying. Eventually the Huns capture both brothers. Gunnar promises to tell Atli where the treasure is, provided he brings him his brother Högni's heart, cut out of his breast. Atli cuts out a slave's heart and tries to pass it off as Högni's (although why he should wish to spare Högni is far from clear), but the heart trembles with fear when its presented to Gunnar, so he knows it can't be Högni's. So finally Atli chops out Högni's actual heart. It doesn't tremble, so Gunnar knows his brother really is dead. Then he refuses to tell Atli what he wants to know (even though he promised to), and, wrathful, Atli throws him in a pit of snakes.

Naturally upset by the deaths of her brothers, Gudrún decides on revenge. She and Atli are parents to two children, the rather sweetly-named Erp and Eitill. (Don't you think that 'Erp and Eitill' sound like two glove puppets hosting a CBeebies show?) Sweetness isn't their fate though: Gudrún kills them, makes their skulls into cups, makes smoothies out of their flesh and feeds them to her husband. After Atli has supped she tells him what she has just done; the horrified man takes to his bed (not even pausing to punish Gudrún for her crime) and Gudrún creeps in later that night and knifes him to death. Then she burns the palace down, wanders in the woods for a while forlorn, and finally drowns herself in the ocean. That's the end.

2.

This is the story Tolkien decided, probably in the early 1930s, to retell in verse. He did so, in Christopher Tolkien's opinion, in part to come up with solutions to the various problems, narrative chicanes and oddities of motivation the original presents the reader, amongst which are: why does Sigurd bugger off after winning Brynhild the first time? Why not marry her straight away? Why, since she is already betrothed to Sigurd, does Brynhild agree to marry Gunnar? Sure, he breaches the wall of fire (it was actually Sigurd in his likeness, though Brynhild doesn't know that), but not only does she not want to marry him, she's already sworn herself to somebody else. After he wins Brynhild why does Gunnar decide to kill Sigurd? And having done so, why does he let Brynhild immolate herself? And finally, after traveling together to Atli's court, and fighting side by side against Hunnish treachery, why does Gunnar demand the heart of his beloved brother Högni?

The Legend of Sigurd and Gudrún offers answers to most of these questions, although sometimes a little obscurely. And although Tolkien's meditations on Eddaic and heroic poetry are interesting, and although reading this book will certainly bring you closer to a number of interesting topics (the Volsung saga and the transmission of Old English and Old Norse poetry in particular), it isn't in its own right a very effective piece of writing.

In part this is a function of the poem's extreme terseness. Events are compressed, elided or even omitted altogether, such that going through *Sigurd and Gudrún* feels like reading the epitome of a longer poem. The result is overly sketchy, clotted with unfamiliar names and wrong-footing zeugma:

> *Son Sinfjötli,*
> *Sigmund father!*
> *Signý comes not,*
> *Siggeir calls her.*
> *Where I lay unwilling*
> *I now lay me glad;*

I lived in loathing,
Now lief I die. [p. 86]

There's too much of this *who-did-the-what-now?* and *hang-on, which one was* he *again?* stuff in the poem to make it a smooth read. It's a challenge to get your Högnis straight from your Hjallis, sorting the Gautars from the Gunnars, Grams, Gjukis and Grimhilds, and distinguishing between all the many *Sigs* (Sigmund, Signy, Siggeir, Sigurd and Sigrdrif, to name only five of them). I knew the story already – knew, that is, Morris's and Wagner's versions, though not the original sagas – but nevertheless I could only pick my way through by leaning heavily on Christopher Tolkien's commentary. I suppose the poem is in this respect like the original sagas *to a modern audience* (although presumably not like the originals to their *original* audience). Which is to say, it reads as a series of condensed textual and interpretive puzzles to be solved. And though the commentary enables the attentive reader to do precisely this, the process entirely congeals the necessary motion and fluidity required by the heroic narrative. This in turn robs the poem of tragic momentum. Never mind that the characters are ciphers, and their motivations often cloudy; everything happens in an airless, rather claustrophobic narrative space.

I don't want to be too negative: there are various moments of genuine poetic impact in *Sigurd and Gudrún*. The thing is that these tend to be touches of epiphanic intensity that remove themselves from the sweep of the whole, rather than focusing the integrity of the Eddaic narrative. For example, I liked this Ted Hughes *avant-la-lettre* moment right at the beginning:

> *The falls of Andvari*
> *frothed and murmured*
> *with fish teeming*
> *in foaming pools.*
> *As pike there plunged*
> *his prey hunting*
> *Dwarf Andvari*
> *From his dark cavern.*
>
> *There hunted hungry*
> *Hreidmar's offspring:*
> *the silver salmon*

sweet he thought them.
Otr in otter's form
there ate blinking
on the bank brooding
of black waters. [p. 67]

That's vivid and suggestive verse, right there. But turn to the commentary to discover the identity of Andvari, Hreidmar and Otr – to pin down their place in the tale, how the Sagas treat them, what Tolkien takes and what changes from his sources – and much of the magic evaporates. Then again, at the other end of the poem some of the battle scenes escape this problem, and retain a vehement vividness:

'Wake now, wake now!
War is kindled.
Now helm to head,
to hand the sword.
Wake now, warriors,
wielding glory!
To wide Valhöll [Valhalla]
ways lie open.'

At the dark doorways
they dinned and hammered;
there was clang of swords
and crash of axes.
The smiths of battle
smote the anvils;
sparked and splintered
spears and helmets.

In they hacked them,
out they hurled them
bears assailing,
boars defending.
Stones and stairways
streamed and darkened;
day came dimly –
the doors were held. [p. 286]

One reason this works, I think, is that the troping of the fighting men as 'smiths of battle' connects with the smith-like *bang!-bang!* double pulse of each line of verse. Tolkien's contemporary Robert Graves talked about two European poetic traditions: the epic metres of Homer and Virgil which, he thought, rhythmically embody 'the slow pull and push of the oar', and Celtic traditions that 'match the rhythms of the smiths' hammer.' There's certainly a distinct feel of the hammer and anvil in this poem.

The whole thing, 'The New Lay of the Völsungs' together with 'The New Lay of Gudrún,' adds up to 4030 lines of verse. That isn't a very long poem, as long poems go (Morris's version runs to 13,000 lines). And actually it's *not* 4030 lines. Christopher Tolkien has decided to print the poetry in a stanzas of short two-stress lines, rather than (as is more conventional when printing Anglo Saxon alliterative verse) in longer lines with a caesura in the middle. There may be some scholarly justification for printing each half-line separately and in effect of doubling the length of the poem, but there are certainly practical ones. On p. 42 the editor notes that Tolkien's manuscript is written mostly in long-line form, although he also scribbled a marginal note to the effect that the 'short line [...] looks better.' This is how the first stanza of part 1 is laid out:

> *Of old was an age*
> *when Ódin walked*
> *by wide waters*
> *in the world's beginning;*
> *lightfooted Loki*
> *at his left was running,*
> *at his right Hœnir*
> *roamed beside him.* [p. 66]

As to whether this really looks better than–

> *Of old was an age when Ódin walked*
> *by wide waters in the world's beginning;*
> *lightfooted Loki at his left was running,*
> *at his right Hœnir roamed beside him.*

– I suppose is merely a matter of personal taste. I prefer the latter, particularly for reading at length, although that's partly because I'm more familiar with it. If that format *had* been adopted, of course, it would have meant Harper Collins publishing a 2000-line poem. A comparison: the first 2000 lines of Tolkien's verse version of *The Children of Húrin* – only one of the several long poems in 1985's *The History of Middle Earth III: The Lays of Beleriand* – takes up 70 pages, commentary included. Printed as compactly, *Sigurd and Gudrún* would have been a pamphlet. Not so viable, commercially speaking, clearly.

The more important point is that 2000 lines are, frankly, too few to cover the whole long, involved multi-generational saga I summarised above, and getting through everything forces on Tolkien a too-packed and oblique style. Reading the result is a laborious process, and though it *is* rewarding, it's made harder than it need be by Tolkien's unabashed antiquity of idiom, for instance with respect to subject and object. In an inflected language it's possible to identify subject and object by word endings, but modern English is not such a language, and in our tongue – the one Tolkien is using, after all – 'a wall saw Sigurd' [p. 119] does not mean the same thing as 'Sigurd saw a wall.' 'Gand rode Regin/and Grani Sigurd' [p. 108] is liable to confuse, and even when you've worked out which names refer to horses and which (the second and fourth) to men, the image is still liable to ludicrous haunting by the thought of a saddled Sigurd bearing a stallion on his back. The poem is oblique enough as it is without giving the reader knots of signification to untie of this 'Grim was Gunnar/on Goti riding/under haughty Högni/Hölkvir strode' (p. 134) sort.

3.

There are few Professors of Anglo-Saxon who could expect to see their dabblings in poetic pastiche published at all, let alone handsomely produced by a major publishing house and intruding into bestseller lists. That *Sigurd and Gudrún* has been thus presented for our reading pleasure, in 2009, has everything to do with Middle Earth and nothing with Snorri Sturlson. But although there will be interest (naturally enough) in the elements Tolkien 'adapted' from the Volsung saga for *The Lord of the Rings*, these two poems actually have very little bearing on the more famous book. Tolkien himself repudiated suggestions that Sauron's ring was a version of the Nibelung ring ('both rings were round and there the resemblance cease,' he snapped in a letter to Allen & Unwin in 1961: 'the 'Nibelung' [...] has nothing whatsoever to do with *The Lord of the Rings*'. [*Letters*, pp. 306-7]

In one sense it is, I admit, impertinent of me to criticize this poem for its pastiche archaisms. Such archaism is deliberate, not inadvertent, because Tolkien wrote the poem to test out interpretive solutions for an ancient mythic narrative, not to create something new. But, even bearing that in mind – and indeed specifically with regard to those Tolkienian solutions – I'd say this is a text that falls down in crucial ways. I'm going to conclude this review by looking at a couple of Tolkien's solutions to the narrative 'problems' of the Volsung saga, and by saying why I think these are less than satisfactory. I should warn you now that this involves bringing Shakespeare into the mix.

The main lacuna in the Volsung story is accidental. The earliest version of the tale is today preserved in a document called the *Codex Regius*, now kept in Copenhagen. It's in two parts, because 'after leaf 32 a gathering, probably of eight pages, has been lost.' [p. 28] Tolkien thought these eight pages, containing a significant chunk of 'the Long Lay of Sigurd' had been deliberately stolen. Without it we have two separate stories. Story A takes the conventional, satisfying form of the hero overcoming the monster and getting the girl: Sigurd slays Fafnir, and wins the beautiful Brynhild. That looks like a very serviceable Happily Ever After, don't you think? But wait, here's Story B: Brynhild will only marry the bravest warrior in the world. She loves Sigurd, who fits that bill. But Sigurd is betrothed to Gudrún; and Brynhild is won instead by Gunnar. The braided wires of these four lovers' destinies go into the black box of the story and come out the other side with Sigurd murdered in his sleep, a grieving Brynhild throwing herself on his funeral pyre, and Gudrún heartbroken.

Now, the big question (the missing chunk of *Codex Regius*) is how we get from Story A to Story B. But the black box portion of Story B is a problem too. As far as that goes, Tolkien jotted down 'notes [...] on his interpretation of the tangled and contradictory narratives that constitute the tragedy of Sigurd and Brynhild, Gunnar and Gudrún,' reproduced here by his son (written, apparently, 'very rapidly in soft pencil, and difficult to read'). Tolkien's sequence of events, rather clearer in his notes than in his actual poem, is: Brynhild finds out about the deception (that it wasn't Gunnar, but Sigmund-in-the-likeness-of-Gunnar, who won her) and is 'mortally wounded' in her pride; so wounded, indeed, that she decides not only to kill Sigurd, but to 'avenge herself upon Gunnar' for his part in the deception. Accordingly she 'lies terribly against Sigurd and herself', and tells Gunnar that when

Sigurd – in Gunnar's form – rode through the flames, he had sex with her. This, not being part of the deal, outrages Gunnar, who has Sigurd killed, but once this is accomplished Brynhild comes out with the truth, so revealing that Gunnar has unjustly slain his sword-brother and widowed his sister.

It all makes sense, although according to a rather stiffly limitedly consecutive logic of human motivation. But it doesn't address the bigger problem of how Brynhild is still behind the wall of flame waiting to be claimed *after* Sigurd has already ridden the wall of flame and claimed her *in his own name*. How, in other words, do we get from Story A to Story B?

How can Sigurd, having once sworn himself to Brynhild, then go on to swear himself to Gudrún? There are two possible answers to this question. One of them is simple and psychologically interesting. The other is implausible, awkward and much less interesting, psychologically speaking, but because it preserves a sense of Sigurd's 'noble heroism' it is the one Morris, Wagner and Tolkien follow. This second explanation has already been mentioned: Sigurd unwittingly drinks a magic potion that makes him forget his first love – a device as cheesy as the use of temporary amnesia to paper over plot-cracks in the first season of 24. But it doesn't have to be that way. There's a much simpler and more satisfying explanation available to us. Why does Sigurd act this way? Because *especially where matters of love and sexual desire are concerned, men's oaths are not necessarily to be trusted.* This has the advantage not only of being, you know, true; it also turns Sigurd from a type into a character. It stops him being an improbable epitome of manly virtue, and presents him instead as genuine, resonant and three-dimensional; shifts him from being a static icon from myth. Turns him, in other words, from an antique statue into a modern individual.

Actually, I know of no version of the story that spins things this way. Our investment in Sigurd's dull Heroic Nobleness and absolutely unimpeachable honour is, perhaps, too profound. And something of the same marionette-like logic rusts Tolkien's Brynhild too: her only motivation her own wounded pride, her method dependent upon an assumption of absolute truthfulness.

It puts me in mind of *Hamlet*. Bear with me a moment.

The story that Shakespeare worked into his celebrated play is an ancient one, and found in many cultures. In the sources that

Shakespeare used it is fairly straightforward: Hamlet is the king's son; his father is killed by his uncle in a palace *putsch*. There's nothing secret about this – it's an open coup d'état – and to consolidate his power the usurper executes key figures of the old guard. Hamlet, as the old king's son and heir, is evidently at danger of death, and to avoid this he lights on a clever plan. He pretends to be mad, in effect saying to his uncle 'you don't need to bother yourself executing me, your highness – I'm mad, me. Harmless!' The ruse works, and Hamlet is able, under the disguise of madness, to kill his father's murderer.

Now what's crucial here is the way Shakespeare adapts this story. In his version Hamlet is still the son of a royal father killed by his uncle in a palace *putsch*. But the coup d'état is secret; Claudius murders Old Hamlet in his garden and everyone thinks the old king died in his sleep. One of the first things Claudius does in Shakespeare's play is announce to the whole court that young Hamlet is next in line to the throne, effectively adopting him as his son. So rather than facing his imminent death, Hamlet finds himself royal heir and a prince of the realm. He has no need to protect his life by pretending to be mad.

But he pretends to be mad anyway. Why? In Shakespeare's play it's hard to be certain (though you may have your theories); more to the point it's hard to be certain in the terms of the play's *sources*, because those sources treat characters as logical and rational agents. If characters in those sorts of stories do something, there must be a straightforward reason why. Shakespeare's Hamlet is a much more profound piece of characterisation. The play precisely requires us to try and puzzle out *why* Hamlet acts the way he does. To what extent is his madness play-acting, and to what extent has grief forced an actual irrationality to the surface in his behaviour? Shakespeare understood what Freud, centuries later, was to build a career elaborating: that often our motives are hidden even from ourselves; that our subjectivity is made up as much of the irrational as the rational (of the unconscious as the conscious). That, moreover, this is particularly true with respect to traumatic events like bereavement, or to repressed and taboo desires. Even Hamlet doesn't really understand why he gets so very, very furious with his mother in her bedroom. He rationalizes his rage as a commitment to public chastity, especially for the over-forties; but that's not the *real* reason he gets so murderously het-up. Where sex is concerned it can be hard for us to untangle our motives.

Shakespeare turns Hamlet from a canny 2D character into an immensely complex, nuanced 3D individual. He is one of the first properly modern figures in world literature. This, indeed, is a large part of the titanic reputation of this text. Medieval literature has its fair share of colourful and engaging characters (and much more than a fair share of blank ciphers and cardboard heroes), but there's no one in it like Hamlet; and we are much more like Hamlet than we are like Chaucer's knight.

And how *does* this relate to Tolkien? Well, *Sigurd and Gudrún* is an exercise in conscious archaism not just in subject matter, and not just in poetic form and idiom. It treats its characters in flat, archaic ways. It didn't have to do so. What makes *The Lord of the Rings* much more than an exercise in reheating old mythology under an invented nomenclature and geography is the way its main conceit parses a much more interesting and much more contemporary dilemma. Of course some of Tolkien's players are as brightly-coloured and as stiffly static as any from the *Edda* – Aragorn, say, or Elrond. But at the heart of the narrative are three figures which are as modern, in their way, as Hamlet: Frodo, Sam, and above all, Gollum. In other words, what makes *The Lord of the Rings* particularly valuable as Fantasy is the way it bridges old Anglo-Saxon fascinations with heroism, doom and catastrophe with modern fascinations with guilt, desire, power, compromise, and the hidden springs of psychological life. There's nothing so nuanced or complex in *Sigurd and Gudrún*. No bridge, but an embalmed limb of the dead past.

M D Lachlan, *Wolfsangel* (2010)

Hwæt! Ic novela cyst secgan wylle,
hwæt mē árǽdatte tō midre nihte,
syðþan cildren reste wunedon.
Þūhte mē þæt ic gesāwe syllicre wulf
on bóc áwritan, lēohte langtwidig,
bóc-fantasia beorhtost. Eall þæt átellanung wæs
begoten blódgéotende; wulfas stōdon
fægere æt foldan scēatum, swylce þær þríe wæron:
Vali and Felig, lífgetwinnan, Adisla gefǽmne
Behēoldon þær þríe wulfsengel dryhtnes ealle:
werwulfen ofer moldan, ond eall þēos mære gesceaft.

M D Lachlan, *Fenrir* (2011)

Þys boke ys issue and generacioun of þe moost-praysed saga of
wulfmen & Norsmen ycleppit *Wulfesangelus*, verilye þe howlinge soule of
Fantasia binden bitween two boords. Ne better boke ypublisht was, nor
ys, þeis yere or þe last of þe fascion or matter of Fantasy; and newist þe
facte of fulle disenclosure (for þe auctor ys freend to mee and myne)
shd gif ye stynt nor pause but to buyen þes boke wiþ al haste.

Þe scene yt is: Anno Domini 886, at Paris, sich citie be onder seggen
of þe Norsmen, þem by King Sigfred wealden; and þat mightig citie
forestonds þe asaut. Yet þe Norsmen nicht for grenehede, nor spoyle,
but misse lefer an wyf of high estat, ycleped þe Ladie Aelis. An heileg
Prest, yclept Jehan, ablenden ond crippled, most her avise to tradice
herseln and pass to þe Norsmen entir. Yete he wol nat, for dreden the
paynim will her sacrifise & lot, liken Isak by Abram; and she is loth.
Prest mid mayden, hem tua voyden þe citie. For þe troth of þe matiere
is stranger, far, and ferlie. For þe fals goddes Odin and Loki and the
wulf yclept Fenrir foughten the nones, a greet battel of wyttes and will,
gildir and ytrapping arond the lifes of þreo mortall men. Þiy died, Odin
þwerted was, and Loki did wynn; bot þe whele tornes anew, and peples

souls reborne sich þat þe game beginneþ againe.

Grete ys þe Wold, grete þe firm *auctoritas et potentia* of Lachlanes Lettrure; selden is boke as doughtie and mightie. Brod in reach and scop; bricht in *imaginatio*; yea þe dramatis personae, sich Aelis, Jehan, Leshii and Ofaeti, all be an weolthe of qhat þe rhetoritians do calle *characterisatio*. Pythagoaras þe Grece spake of Re-incarnatio, and Lachlanes boke also. þis is þe world in dare, and þe darken of Lachlanes soule is stark and stronge. As þe poete sayde, and richtig: Þe more strenghþe of ioye myn herte strayneȝ. An grete boke: ye most beye yt.

Ben Aaronovitch, *Rivers of London* (2011)

It's easy to see why this has become a bestseller; it's very good indeed, a sort of modern-day *Jonathan Strange and Police Procedural*. The narrator, Peter Grant, is an ordinary copper in contemporary London who becomes involved in the investigation of a murder outside St Paul's: some poor geezer having had his head knocked clean from his shoulders. This in turn brings him into contact with a hidden world of magic, supernatural beings, vampires, revenants and other such in-the-night bump-goers. He is transferred to a semi-official and rather endearingly amateur 'magic' branch of the Met, and becomes the apprentice of a wizard-policeman called Nightingale. The story is well-told but the real triumph here is one of *tone*. Aaronovitch creates a genuinely likeable voice for Grant, and the whole book is carried off with tremendous charm. I mean that word in a more than flippant sense; charm is more than niceness (charms are the currency of magic, after all). It cannot be faked, and it cannot be taught at creative writing school. But it makes a story glide very agreeably along.

The book also works as an entertaining gazetteer of London, a city Aaronovitch groks, in a way that – to pick a name at random from my London hat – Peter Ackroyd, doesn't quite. Aaronovitch knows the topography and lore, gets the multicultural vibe and glamour and friction right, and captures the scuzzy along with the magical very neatly. In particular, the *rivers* are important: not just the Thames but the various tributaries, now mostly bricked over. I liked the fact that, at one point, Grant drives his cribbed-from-Morse jag over Staines Bridge. I wrote a novel a couple years ago in which Staines Bridge gets blown up. And, actually, if you've got a moment, I'd like to take this opportunity to agitate for a new literary movement in Fantastic Literature, after the manner of the New Weird or the Mundane, to be called 'Staines Bridgers'. The manifesto would require novels to make some mention of Staines. And / or to have a title that can be sung to an XTC track – I found myself humming *Rivers of London* to the tune of 'Towers of London', and it works quite well. Beyond that, the details of the Manifesto have yet to be, er, worked out.

Not to get distracted.

Anyway, my purpose here is not to review *Rivers of London* (beyond saying: really very good, read it), so much as to shoot off at an angle and think about Fantasy more generally. Charlene Harris is quoted on the back of the dust jacket praising Aaronovitch's book as 'fresh and original', which it isn't, really (isn't *trying* to be, really – it's an expert midrash upon a venerable body of magic-intersects-reality fictions that re-imagine London: Dickens, Carter, Gaiman, Miéville, *Harry Potter*, Susan Clarke et al. This is a feature rather than a bug, and Aaronovitch handles his intertexts cannily, often wittily and adds depth and texture to his writing through them). In particular, and despite wearing the coat of a police-procedural/crimey/murder-investigation plot, *Rivers of London* shares one quality with fantasy that we do not find in noir. I'm going to call this quality *amplitude*. Here's how Aaronovitch opens his novel:

> It started at one thirty on a cold Tuesday morning in January when Martin Turner, street performer and, in his own words, apprentice gigolo, tripped over a body in front of the West Portico of St Paul's at Covent Garden. Martin, who was none too sober himself, at first thought the body was that of one of the many celebrants who had chosen the Piazza as a convenient outdoor toilet and dormitory. Being a seasoned Londoner, Martin gave the body the 'London once-over'– a quick glance to determine whether this was a drunk, a crazy or a human being in distress. The fact that it was entirely possible for someone to be all three simultaneously is why good-Samaritanism in London is considered an extreme sport – like base-jumping or crocodile-wrestling. Martin, noting the good-quality coat and shoes, had just pegged the body as a drunk when he noticed that it was in fact missing its head.

This is how Chandler or Hammet would have written this opening:

> Martin Turner, noting the good-quality coat and shoes, clocked that the body was that of a drunk. Only then did he notice it was missing its head.

This isn't a *better* way of starting a novel, naturally, except in the general horses-for-courses sense that applies to all writing everywhere. But it would be a mistake to think that Aaronovitch writes 150 words instead of 25 because he has more specific detail to communicate to the reader. The point is not in the content; it is in the tone – the voice of the novel. It is a voice that sets its face against terseness and reticence in favour of a generous discursive expansiveness.

This isn't to say that I'd describe Aaronovitch's treatment of his murder mystery as 'leisurely': there's plenty going on, and the novel rarely feels flaggy or slack (I might have done with a little less of the sub-Harry-Potter 'learning magical spells' stuff, but I'm a grump). *Rivers of London* isn't trying to do the hard-boiled thing. On the contrary, it is trying, and succeeding, to flesh-out a world in which mundanity is underlaid by magic, with plenty of detail and atmosphere and tone and not a little humour too. Indeed, we lose sight of the initial murder for quite long stretches. In fact – I wonder if this is linked to the thought that there are a great many brilliant SF short stories and hardly any Fantasy short stories worth mentioning – this amplitude is precisely what many readers of Fantasy go to their chosen genre *for* in the first place.

It goes without saying that this amplitude can easily become bloat. But my point is that we may go astray if we single out (for example) the latest Robin Hobb or Branden Sandandersenbrand novel and say 'there's a fit, lean 250-page novel hidden somewhere inside this flabby 1000-page monster'. Critics certainly do this; on occasion I've even done it myself. But perhaps it is missing the point. Not everybody considers 'size zero' to be an aesthetic ideal, after all.

I really am moving away from Aaronovitch when I say this: his novel is a trim 400 pages and there's a lot going on between its covers. Rather, I'm trying to put my finger on something critics of the novel, content-obsessed as they often are, sometimes miss – and arguably critics of SFF titles are *more* likely than not to fixate on the manifest content of a title and to ignore the form, style, voice and the like. So, to step away from genre for a moment. You see, I was chatting with a writer friend of mine recently about the case of Sir Walter Scott.

Here's the thing with Scott: he was, in the 19th century, bigger than you can imagine. Everybody read him. Many people read his (very ample) complete works right through, from start to finish, *every year* (Henry Crabb Robinson talks about the pleasure of maintaining a sort of on-rolling Scott read, of closing the last page of his last published novel knowing that he could now open the first page of *Waverley* yet again). Scott was the first international mega-celebrity of letters, rivalled only by Byron (whom he outsold, and outlasted). Aha, but nowadays who reads him? It's hard enough getting English literature students, people who have specifically chosen to read books, to trudge through *Waverley*, never mind the rest of the Scotty oeuvre. The problem is that he is *prolix*. Things do happen in Scott's fiction, and some very interesting questions of history and politics, of identity and modernity and fantasy, are worked through in complex ways. But the ratio of 'things happening' to 'great wodges of prosy prose' is weighted, for modern tastes, disadvantageously on the latter side of the scale. As a result, Scott has gone from being the most famous novelist in the world to (outside academia) almost total desuetude.

The trick to understanding the prodigious success of Scott in the 19th century is the realisation that he was popular not *despite* being so prosy, *but because of it*. You don't read Scott's prose for its sharpness, for its quotable zingers or apothegmic wisdom. Opening the covers of a *Waverley* novel and starting to read is, or ought to be, like sinking into a warm bath. It is the very amplitude of Scott's art that explains its success. One of the striking things about Scott's career is that he had a significant stroke in later life, yet continued writing – great screedy novels like *Castle Dangerous* (1831) and *Count Robert of Paris* (1832) which read like regular Scott novels with all the *actual stuff-happening* taken out. Nobody seemed to mind. As if Scott didn't really need a fully functioning brain to produce the sort of verbal art that made his name.

My point, I suppose, is that although Scott himself has fallen from favour, the taste for amplitude in our verbal art hasn't. Many readers don't want their fiction to work as a brisk, cold shower. Many really want to sink into that warm bath.

There are times when it's hard for me to quite get my head around just how ubiquitous Walter Scott was for Victorian readers (everybody loved him; everybody not only read him but re-read and re-re-read him); hard because, although I've read a great deal of Scott, and enjoyed much of it, I can't really see how it is that people fell so completely for him. He's so often prolix, and dilute, and underpowered. He's not, surely, worthy to touch the hem of Dickens's garment.

Now and again, though, I get flashes, like distant lightning, that illuminate for me at least the possibility of falling more deeply under Scott's enchantment. One of the incidental joys of Chesterton's superb little monograph on *Dickens* (1906) is the comparison between Scott and Dickens in his tenth chapter; a reading that quotes a line of Scott's from *The Antiquary* that seems to me one of the most profound things the 19th century produced. Here, at length:

> At the very beginning of this review I remarked that the reader must be in a mood, at least, of democracy. To some it may have sounded irrelevant; but the Revolution was as much behind all the books of the nineteenth century as the Catholic religion (let us say) was behind all the colours and carving of the Middle Ages. Another great name of the nineteenth century will afford an evidence of this; and will also bring us most sharply to the problem of the literary quality of Dickens.
>
> Of all these nineteenth-century writers there is none, in the noblest sense, more democratic than Walter Scott. As this may be disputed, and as it is relevant, I will expand the remark. There are two rooted spiritual realities out of which grow all kinds of democratic conception or sentiment of human equality. There are two things in which all men are manifestly and unmistakably equal. They are not equally clever or equally muscular or equally fat, as the sages of the modern reaction (with piercing insight) perceive. But this is a spiritual certainty, that all men are tragic. And this, again, is an equally sublime spiritual certainty, that all men are comic. No special and private sorrow can be so dreadful as the fact of having to die. And no freak or deformity can be so funny as the mere fact of having two legs. Every man is important if he loses his life; and every man is funny if he loses his hat, and has to run after it. And the universal test everywhere of whether a thing is popular, of the people, is whether it employs vigorously these extremes of the tragic and the comic. Shelley, for instance, was an aristocrat, if ever there was one in this world. He was a Republican, but he was not a democrat: in his poetry there is every perfect quality except this pungent and popular stab. For the tragic and the comic you must go, say, to Burns, a poor man. And all over the world, the folk literature, the popular literature, is the same. It consists of very dignified sorrow and very undignified fun. Its sad tales are of broken hearts; its happy tales are of broken heads.
>
> These, I say, are two roots of democratic reality. But they have in more civilised literature, a more civilised embodiment of form. In literature such as that of the nineteenth century the two elements appear somewhat thus. Tragedy becomes a profound sense of human dignity. The other and jollier element becomes a delighted sense of human variety. The first supports equality by saying that all men are equally sublime. The second supports equality by observing that all men are equally interesting.

In this democratic aspect of the interest and variety of all men, there is, of course, no democrat so great as Dickens. But in the other matter, in the idea of the dignity of all men, I repeat that there is no democrat so great as Scott. This fact, which is the moral and enduring magnificence of Scott, has been astonishingly overlooked. His rich and dramatic effects are gained in almost every case by some grotesque or beggarly figure rising into a human pride and rhetoric. The common man, in the sense of the paltry man, becomes the common man in the sense of the universal man. He declares his humanity. For the meanest of all the modernities has been the notion that the heroic is an oddity or variation, and that the things that unite us are merely flat or foul. The common things are terrible and startling, death, for instance, and first love: the things that are common are the things that are not commonplace. Into such high and central passions the comic Scott character will suddenly rise. Remember the firm and almost stately answer of the preposterous Nicol Jarvie when Helen Macgregor seeks to browbeat him into condoning lawlessness and breaking his bourgeois decency. That speech is a great monument of the middle class. Molière made M. Jourdain talk prose; but Scott made him talk poetry. Think of the rising and rousing voice of the dull and gluttonous *Athelstane* when he answers and overwhelms De Bracy. Think of the proud appeal of the old beggar in the *Antiquary* when he rebukes the duellists. Scott was fond of describing kings in disguise. But all his characters are kings in disguise. He was, with all his errors, profoundly possessed with the old religious conception, the only possible democratic basis, the idea that man himself is a king in disguise.

In all this Scott, though a Royalist and a Tory, had in the strangest way, the heart of the Revolution. For instance, he regarded rhetoric, the art of the orator, as the immediate weapon of the oppressed. All his poor men make grand speeches, as they did in the Jacobin Club, which Scott would have so much detested. And it is odd to reflect that he was, as an author, giving free speech to fictitious rebels while he was, as a stupid politician, denying it to real ones. But the point for us here is this that all this popular sympathy of his rests on the graver basis, on the dark dignity of man. 'Can you find no way?' asks Sir Arthur Wardour of the beggar when they are cut off by the tide. 'I'll give you a farm... I'll make you rich.' ...'Our riches will soon be equal,' says the beggar, and looks out across the advancing sea.

Chesterton goes on to suggest that whilst he is manifestly Dickens's inferior in so many ways, in *this* regard (in the sense of the beggar's haunting, chilling observation) Scott was the greater author. Indeed, that moment in *The Antiquary* is one of my favourite moments from the whole of the 19th century.

Ursula K. Le Guin, *Lavinia* (2009)

Ursula K. Le Guin's beautiful, haunting new novel, published in the UK in May 2009, had been published in America the previous year. Accordingly, the bound proof I read (to review) came pre-endorsed for the Britreader: 'a winning combination of history and mythology featuring an unlikely heroine imaginatively plucked from literary obscurity'[*Booklist*]. That rather undersells it, actually. 'Deserves to be ranked with Robert Graves's *I Claudius*'[*Publishers Weekly*]. That's more like it. Although Le Guin's pre-Roman first-person narrative has a very different flavour to Graves's Imperial Roman first-person narrative, they are of a similar stature: classics in essence as well as theme. 'Arguably her best novel'[*Kirkus*]. Arguably so. Certainly I enjoyed this novel more than any Le Guin since the 1970s, and that (it's almost tautological to add this) means that I enjoyed it more than pretty much any novel since the 1970s. It possesses a depth, clarity and wonder greater than most of the fiction being published nowadays.

Lavinia is a Latin princess, living in pre-Roman Italy. She was the woman who married Aeneas, the Trojan prince who fled his burning, defeated city to settle his people and his household gods in a new land. Virgil's Aeneas. To be precise, Virgil's *Aeneid* ends (with Aeneas's killing the local warrior Turnus in a sudden and deplorable loss of self-control) *before* his marriage to Lavinia, but since his and her descendants are destined not only to found Rome but to rule it and the world as Caesars, we know the marriage is coming.

The *Aeneid* (a genuinely core text, I need hardly remind you, of western culture) divides broadly into two. Books 1 to 6 are sometimes called 'Virgil's *Odyssey*,' since in imitation of Homer's journey-epic they detail Aeneas's escape from Troy and his voyages around the Mediterranean in search of another homeland. Fate has decreed he will settle in Latium, in central Italy, and at the beginning of Book 7 he and his people finally pitch up there. Books 7-12, the second half of the epic ('Virgil's *Iliad*'), reconfigure Homer's famous epic of war: instead of Trojan Hector fighting Greek Achilles, it is Trojan Aeneas fighting Latin Turnus, and instead of Achilles winning, Aeneas triumphs. Le Guin's Turnus dies by p. 160 of her 250-page account, which is to say, her treatment overlaps. She gives us 'Le Guin's Virgil's *Iliad*' in the first half of her novel, followed by 'Le Guin's Livy's *Ab Urbe Condita*' in the second. I concede that Lavinia is a better title than *Le Guin's Virgil's Iliad Followed by Le Guin's Livy's Ab Urbe Condita*. Her voice, very different to but just as strong as Virgil's (and capable of much more variety), inflects her source in fascinating ways.

Indeed her reworking of Virgil involves more than just the *Aeneid*: the poet is a spectral character in, as well as the textual frame for, her narrative. It's all exquisitely done, as another pre-endorsement put it:

> Everywhere Le Guin catches the rhythms of the great epic, echoes them, riffs. In a way, this is a jazzy book, playing in odd syncopation with a massive canonical work [...] I found myself delighted, even stunned, by the freshness of Le Guin's prose. [*Los Angeles Times*]

Enough quoting other reviews, even to endorse their judgments. Because actually, although her prose *is* extraordinarily fresh and effective, 'jazz' isn't the right comparison to make here, I think. There is a stately sureness of step to Le Guin's writing, beautiful, mournful, and plain, more like a late Beethoven string quartet than Keith Jarrett.

Le Guin clearly knows the *Aeneid* backwards (knows, we could say, the *Dienea*), so clearly she's obviously aware how slight a figure this heroine makes in Virgil's account. When 'Lavinia virgo'– the maiden Lavinia – crops up in the original poem, her eyes are demurely downcast ('oculos deiecta decoros' 11:480). The most Virgil does by way of description is to say how very prettily she blushes ('Lavinia heard her mother's words, her burning cheeks steeped in tears, while a deep blush kindled its fire and mantled o'er her glowing face. As when one stains Indian ivory with crimson dye, or as when white lilies blush with many a blended rose – such hues her maiden features showed.' 12.64 ff.: I'm quoting the Loeb translation here). That's just about it for Virgil's interest in Lavinia, except that in book 7 her hair catches alight in a miraculous portent of her future greatness, and the oracle says that she must not marry a local, but must wait for a foreigner ('Strangers shall come to be thy sons, whose blood shall exalt our name to the stars and the children of whose race shall behold where the circling sun looks on either ocean, the whole world rolls obedient beneath their feet' *Aeneid*, 7.96 ff.). Indeed, despite being the ostensible cause of conflict between Aeneas and Turnus, she's so minor a player in Virgil's poem that K.W. Gransden's critical study of books 7-12 of the

Aeneid doesn't even mention her once.[3]

Out of this unpromising raw material Le Guin has done something very clever. She has taken a marginal figure as a means of reflecting upon a great work of literature without thereby writing a novel about the marginal – as, for example, Marion Zimmer Bradley did in her Morganacentric Arthurian novel *The Mists of Avalon* (1979). Bradley's enormous novel is at heart a polemic about the marginalisation of women, and, in its way, a powerful one. But Le Guin, though of course aware of the limitations of female existence and the arbitrariness of male power, has a broader aim in this novel. What she has done is to evoke the actual quality of lived experience: the qualia of people and their being-in-the-world. It is *life*, in the sense of that thing that goes on from day to day, with all its variety, its joys and anxieties, that is at the heart of this novel. Lavinia is the best person to focus this perspective because she is not, as many of the male characters are, distracted by grandiose stories of Fate or Destiny, Pride or Honour; she has the clearest perspective on life as a whole. That's what comes across in the fiction. She lives, sees war come to her country. She sees Turnus killed, and then marries Aeneas and has a happy marriage – that rare quantity in contemporary fiction, beautifully and convincingly rendered here. Then she sees her husband killed, and goes on with her life, coming under the authority of his heir, her stepson Ascanius. She negotiates the awkwardness and danger of that relationship. She raises her own son Silvius. She grows old.

In addition, Lavinia's world is interpenetrated with the supernatural – with omens and prophecy, with the ghost of a poet not to be born for centuries, and with an ending in which (spoiler redacted). But what I would say about this is that, unlike most Fantasy, where the magic exists discretely as a glamour or addition to an otherwise mundane mise-en-scène, Le Guin's pre-Roman Italy is rendered as a place where the distinction between the mundane and the magical doesn't really obtain. The magic feels completely natural, which has the consequence the natural world becomes magical. This is a much more remarkable achievement than I am perhaps suggesting, because Le Guin achieves it despite wholly jettisoning Virgil's gods and goddesses, so important (and so liable to intervene in the doings of humans) in every single book of the *Aeneid*. Le Guin's author's note puts it plainly: 'the

---

[3] *Virgil's Iliad: an Essay on Epic Narrative* (Cambridge University Press: 1984)

Homeric use of quarrelsome deities to motivate, illuminate, and interfere with human choices and emotions doesn't work well in a novel, so the Greco-Roman gods, an intrinsic element of the poem, are no part of my story' [p. 253]. This is a very good call. It means, amongst other things, that the magic in Le Guin's novel is not anthropomorphized, and therefore not particularized, except in the localized sense that it clings particularly about certain landscapes, about certain families and communities. Instead there is a *pervasively* numinous quality to Le Guin's imagined world; finely rendered and completely believable, it makes for a brilliantly compelling textual universe.

Putting Virgil himself into the narrative as a character is a bold move. It works, not despite but because it turns the novel into a self-reflexive meditation upon poetry, or writing more generally. Aeneid 6 ends with Virgil's famous, but nevertheless rather baffling, distinction between true dreams and false dreams, the one set emerging from the underworld via a gate of horn, the other via a gate of ivory. Le Guin's Virgil frets over his own veracity, or validity, when he appears before Lavinia. 'I am a wraith... my body is lying on the deck of a ship sailing from Greece to Italy, but I don't think I'll get to Brundisium even if the ship does. I am sick, I'm dying [...] or else I am a false dream. But they come from down under there, don't they, the false dreams? They nest like bats in the great tree at the gates of the kingdom of the Shadows, so maybe I am a bat that has flown here from Hades. A dream, that has flown into a dream' [p. 39]. Bats fly, but they don't fly straight.

Against the hesitant figure of Virgil, and the intricate, backward-spiralling verse-narrative of the *Aeneid*, Le Guin draws Lavinia as a narrator whose tale moves swiftly straight. No bat, but an owl: 'I fly among the trees on soft wings that make no sound. Sometimes I call out, but not in a human voice. My cry is soft and quavering: *i, i*, I cry: go on, go' [p. 250]. I love that shift from the Latin '*i, i*' to the English 'I': it embodies in little the most profound of shifts from being-in-time to egotistical subjectivity. Lavinia is surrounded by people, from Virgil, to her father, to her suitor Turnus and her stepson Ascanius, who trace out their lives in spiral tangles of ego. Lavinia herself sails through, always conscious of the fact that the key salient for life is not that it coalesces around particular moments, or particular subjectivities, but that *it goes on*. It is this that makes narrative the key mode of art for apprehending life. That's why Le Guin's story rolls smoothly not only past the death of Turnus (where the *Aeneid* stops), but also the death of Lavinia's loved husband Aeneas – very touchingly understated, here – and onward. That's why it ends so beautifully, inverting the solidly masculine I of *I, Claudius* and ending instead with the Molly-Bloomish *i, i*, of the hooting owl. Virgil has a story to tell, but he is a poet first, and his poem continually risks distilling into gem-like stuck moments. Le Guin is capable of very affecting poetry, but she is a storyteller first. Her novel is a narrative, and is about narrative: about the fact that life goes on after setback, disaster, and death.

It is harder to praise books than knock them. To criticize in a negative sense necessitates the self-generating structure of being specific: in what ways does the book fall short, where is it wrong? That doesn't transfer to the wholly positive review. We might ask, in what ways is this book so very good? But the temptation would be to reply: *in all the ways*. There's a quality to this fiction that I cannot capture in a review. You'll have to read it for yourself to find out what I mean.

Margo Lanagan, *Tender Morsels* (2009)

And here we go again. For the second piece in a row, I butt my bear-ish snout up against the problem of writing a praising review. This novel is very good indeed. What else is there to say except, buy a copy, read it? You *won't* regret it; you *will* find yourself wholly immersed in Lanagan's miraculously well-realised double-world (a medievally 'real' world and a medievally 'fairy tale' world, linked by a weird portal). The matter of the traditional fairy tale, in this case Snow White and Rose Red, is treated with all the sophistication and thickness of an unillusioned modern novel, but it is wholly to Lanagan's credit that this rather enhances than undermines the magic. 'This is a very good novel' hardly cuts it. It might, perhaps, make sense to establish a grading scale of veries out of ten; such that I could say 'this is a very, very, very, very, very, very, very, very good novel'. That could certainly simplify the business of reviewing.

Why is it so very good? Partly because it's just extremely well written: very vividly realised and cleverly made; and partly because the characterisation, though simple (as befits fairy tale provenance; I don't mean 'simplistic', by the way) is genuine and authentic and engaging such that you really care what happens to the agents. Although it does not spare its players (or us) any of the horriblenesses to which mortal life, especially female mortal life, is sometimes prone, it is nevertheless a warm book: I was reminded less of Angela Carter's rather brittle, chilly modern-recastings-of-fairy-tale, and more of Sheri Tepper's wise, lovely *Beauty* (1991), one of my favourite books. There is wisdom here, too: not only about the way people cope with trauma by relocating themselves, to one extent or other, in an imaginative realm, but also about precisely the *limitations* of that sort of idealised living, about the way it starts to chafe after a while. I was particularly impressed by the way Lanagan handled her weight of textual precedence. There have been lots of fairy-tale-based modern novels, after all, and lots and lots of portal fantasies where one world leaks into another. But, as far as both antecedents are concerned, the novel deftly and cleverly parleys its influences into something far beyond mere belatedness.

So why only eight veries, and not ten? And why, perhaps more importantly, do I carry on pretending the plural of 'very' is 'veries', when we all know it to be 'verii'? I can't answer the second question, but can have a go at the first. In part the novel is a victim of its own extraordinary success: specifically, its opening stretch – in which poor put-upon Ligia is raped first (repeatedly) by her father and then by a lairy crowd of village boys – is *so* extraordinary and powerful, the reader feels a slackening when the book moves past it into its middle section. It sounds like a grim way to start a novel, no pun intended, and it *is* grim, but it manages to be both properly horrifying and non-exploitative without ever being off-putting. Indeed, the thing that impressed me the most was the way Lanagan renders Ligia's point of view in terms of bewilderment, nausea and a low-level, oppressive sense of being trapped and having no way out. At the moment she is driven to suicide, Ligia translates (perhaps) into fairyland, and is gifted a threat-free, flawless version of her previous life in which she can raise her two daughters, the Snow White Urdda and the Rose Red Branza. The end of the novel is very well judged too: genuinely moving. It generates its charge in part by virtue of a kind of accumulating sense of horrible inevitability about the way real life, with its danger and glamour, increasingly bleeds into the fantasy realm, and about the way Branza is herself drawn to it. But also the novel toys precisely with our expectations: will things end happily, fairy-tale fashion, or unhappily, according to the logic of the modern novel, a form over which Lanagan demonstrates such impressive command?

But, yes, there's a slight sense of sag about the central sections, well-written and absorbing though they are. I also wondered if Lanagan's versions of maleness, personified here via a fairly venal man of restricted height and two (male) bears, is a touch limited. She apprehends bearish masculinity as a cuddlesome, clumsy, inarticulate thing in one of the bears, and it is well done; she apprehends it as something more threatening, potentially violent and sensual in the other bear, and it is even better done. But that's as far as the men go, really; the whole gender otherwise becomes a background collection of rapists and users. Although, that said, the focus of the novel isn't on the men; it is, rather, on the women; and in a sophisticated, accomplished way, I think.

One final thing: I read the novel in a 2010 Vintage paperback edition. I bought it because it piqued my interest in the bookshop, not for any other reason. Nevertheless, it surprises me that it is nowhere mentioned, anywhere upon the cover of this edition, that *Tender Morsels* won the 2009 World Fantasy Award. I wonder why not?

One final, final thing: I propose to you that you fire up Google and track down an interview in the online journal *Clarkesworld*, between Lanagan and Jaff Vandermeercat, about this novel and other things. It is well worth your time, and is especially markworthy on account of Lanagan's use of the excellent word 'boofhead'. I intend to start using that one in my day-to-day. It's a fine word.

There is no final, final, final thing.

Pierre Pevel, *The Cardinal's Blades* (2009)

Well, this is a jolly novel: essentially the *Trois Mousquetaires* plus dragons. So, to be clear, that's Alexandre Dumas, *père*:

– not a slim man, as you can see – and dragons. We're in a fantasied-up 17th-century France. Pevel's Cardinal Richelieu plots and schemes; gentlemen fight duels, quaff in taverns, roister and doister, and the Parisian streets are coated in *merde*. In this world there are dragons – not only actual dragons ('the ancestral breed') but tame dragons, used as a sort of flying horse, and lots of cat-sized dragons who roam the streets of Paris like, well, cats. There are also half-dragon/half-human types, who look human except for something lizard-like about the eyes, and who reminded me rather of the aliens-in-disguise in the original version of TV's *V*. Now, these dragons, together with a sinister, shadowy human conspiracy called 'the Black Claw', are threatening France; so Richelieu reassembles the disbanded 'The Cardinals' Blades' in the national interest. This is a group of brilliant swordspeople, including the heroic Antoine Leprat ('Tony the Twit' in English); the half-dragon Saint-Lucq (confusingly, not actually a saint in this tale), Ballardieu (whose name is presumably a SF in-joke by Pevel, modelled on the 'Clapton is God' graffiti) amongst others, under the leadership of grizzled old Capitaine La Fargue ('Captain Fog' in English). And off they go, on various adventures.

The result is an enormously thigh-slapping, cheering, toasting, roaring, puking, bawling, galloping, adventuring *hearty* piece of fiction. If it were any heartier, it would actually suffer from inflammatory cardiomegaly. Perhaps I might have liked a little more about the dragons themselves, if only to justify the decision to write the book as Fantasy rather than straight historical melodrama, but the novel instead chooses to focus mostly on Captain Fog's varied crew, and the scrapes they get into. And into scrapes they do get indeed. Scrapes they do get in – they do get themselves scraped-up in… um.

They get into scrapes.

There's lots and lots of swordfighting, but it's rather more *cliché* than *touché* (aha! you see what I did there? Ha-ha! Ha. Ah). The whole book, in fact, is prodigiously, momentously clichéd, but so energetically, so forcefully does Pevel inhabit these clichés, and with such aplomb, that you don't mind. It's all melodrama, all the time; everything is turned up to *onze*. Moments that would, in another novel, break the tension through sheer ludicrousness ("Dead?' Belle-Trogne asked, to put his mind at rest. 'Yes. Strangled while he shat.", p. 221) here only endear the reader to the novel. Except for a few bit-parts, the men are all dashing, and except for a few matronly types the women all gorgeous. This latter fact is not unproblematic, incidentally – by including badass female characters such as the Baroness Agnès de Vaudreuil, Pevel seems to think he is entitled to unload the sort of sexist claptrap that used to be, and I suppose still largely is, a feature of the sub-genre's representation of its female characters. Take for instance this hideous celebration of the male gaze, which reads like a set-up paragraph in a porn tale:

> Marciac immediately attracted the notice of four pretty young ladies who were sitting about in casual dress. The first was an ample blonde; the second a slim brunette; the third was a mischievous redhead; and the last was a Jewish beauty with green eyes and dusky skin. The blonde read from a book, while the brunette embroidered and chattered with the other two […] he was welcomed with fervent cries of joy.[p. 73]

There's not *too* much of that sort of thing, though.

Now, the novel originally appeared in France as *Les Lamas du Cardinal* (2007) – *The Cardinal's Llamas*, a title the otherwise competent English translator Tom Clegg has incomprehensibly rendered as *The*

Cardinal's Blades. Clegg has also excised all actual llamas from the storyline; although look carefully and you can see one in the background of the original Bragelonne cover-art. Also, characters are constantly getting out their swords and saying '*en garde!*' – an obscure French idiom that Clegg, astonishingly, omits to translate. These small blots aside, I enjoyed *100% Blades* a great deal. Good vulgar fun.

Gosh, wasn't Papa Dumas fat, though?

Kit Whitfield, *In Great Waters* (2009)

1

I came to this highly praised novel with great expectations. And, having read it, I can see why it's been so highly praised; it's very good. It didn't *quite* take the top of my cranium off, though.

It's an alt-historical fantasy set somewhere around the 1500s in a world where mermaids and mermen actually exist (Tudorpunk; Splashpunk; Walk-the-plankpunk; not sure what the best neologism would be). The premise is actually something along the lines of: in a world in which traffic by water was vital, the 'deepsmen', as Whitfield calls her wet ones, would surely be in a position to grab themselves serious political power. And so they have, in *In Great Waters*: deepsmen and landsmen having interbred to produce hybrid humans who dominate the royal houses of Europe. The novel then tells the stories of two such hybrids – deepsborn Henry cast out by his pod, and the aristocratic Anne, raised in an English court – illuminating as it does so the world of high-born politics and scheming, flashes of beauty, blots of cruelty and hideousness. All very evocatively done.

Now, the danger with a project like this – which is to say, *The Mermaid Tudors* – is that it could so very easily become cheesy, or twee, or worst of all *both* ('cheestwee'). And the first thing to note about *In Great Waters* is that it assuredly, even triumphantly, avoids those dangers. It is, if I'm pressed for one word to describe it, a very *classy* piece of work. Whitfield's deepsmen bear the same relation to conventional 'mermaids' that *Blade Runner*'s replicants do to creaky actors-in-tinfoil androids of earlier cinema, or that the Batman of *Begins* does to the Batman of *& Robin*. The writing is fluent, and spotless, and if it's a little diffuse (and occasionally a tad too discursive) for my taste it is also capable of exquisite moments of really beautiful expression; sentences or passages of distilled stylistic excellence that are very striking.

But there's a problem, and it has to do with the worldbuilding. This alt-Renaissance world is one in which deepsmen have forced themselves into the ruling dynasties all over Europe. Early in the novel, we're given some backstory: how deepsmen and Venetians clashed centuries earlier, how the deepsmen got the better of the landsmen, forcing them to accept a mermaid Queen, and after subsequent generations of inter-breeding, deepsman/landsman hybrids ruling every country. But I didn't believe it, and since the whole novel is premised on this situation that's awkward. Specifically I didn't believe the deepsmen would be so indefatigable, militarily speaking; something that struck me as both inconsistent with the way they're portrayed elsewhere in the novel (for otherwise they're enormously dim, easily tricked, unambitious and lacking in initiative) – as well as inconsistent with what we know of human military persistence and ingenuity. The Venetians, I think, would not have given up so easily.

Now as I read the first quarter of so of the novel, this kept getting in the way of my ability to suspend my disbelief. Then I thought: but what if I'm taking this the wrong way? Maybe the point here is not so much the worldbuilding as the metaphorical potential? We get only Venice and the English channel, rather than the rest of the world, not because Whitfield is incapable of showing us other seas and coasts, but because Venice (where, as Browning famously noted, St Mark's is, where the Doges used to wed the sea with rings) and England were both such important *maritime* powers. The point of a human/fishman-linked dynasty is in the ways it dramatizes the importance of the sea to this world. In other words, I wondered if the novel is about how important the sea is to the land of England. Conrad has written about that, and done so by representing the world of maritime England. Whitfield does it, perhaps, by metaphorizing it.

And the literalising of metaphor is of course the core SFF textual strategy. So, I told myself: take the book this way. See if the eloquence of her central metaphor, as a way of talking about human connections between sea and land, supersedes creakiness in the nuts-and-bolts representation. And up to a point it's good to read the novel that way, something helped by Whitfield deliberate rooting her similes and metaphors oceanically (There are lots and lots of examples of this, but I liked: 'on the day of the wedding, Anne was packed into the heaviest dress she had ever owned, caked with sharp jewels like a barnacled hull', p. 80). Nevertheless by the end of the novel I found myself unsatisfied, and I think the reason for this was that the novel isn't *quite* true enough to its metaphoric, poetic vision. It keeps getting itself bogged down with the merely metonymically representative: all the twisty ins-and-outs of personal and political interaction, all the nooks and crannies of the worldbuilding. I should add that these are the precisely the satisfactions most readers of Fantasy look for, so it's hardly a mistake of Whitfield to provide them. And I could add further that, actually, it's a close run thing: there's a great deal in this novel that is precisely poetic, hauntingly and transportingly to the process of metaphorization. Just not, for me, in the end, quite enough. Very good, though, and very much worth reading. You should buy a copy. You could, if you liked, buy two. One will probably be enough for you, though.

2

One thing the novel is very good on, though (especially in its storming first section) is using the positions of ocean-dweller and land-dweller each to illuminate the other in estranged, powerful and beautiful ways. In this, I'm guessing Whitfield took some impetus from Leigh Hunt's splendid linked trio of poems 'The Fish, the Man and the Spirit', which really ought to be better known. She quotes a few lines from it as epigraph to her tale, but it's short enough to quote in full.

I especially like the second one:

A MAN ADDRESSES A FISH
You strange, astonished-looking, angle-faced,
Dreary-mouthed, gaping wretches of the sea,
Gulping salt-water everlastingly,
Cold-blooded, though with red your blood be graced,
And mute, though dwellers, in the roaring waste;
And you, all shapes beside, that fishy be –
Some round, some flat, some long, all devilry,
Legless, unloving, infamously chaste:–
O scaly, slippery, wet, swift, staring wights,
What is't ye do? What life lead? eh, dull goggles?
How do ye vary your vile days and nights?
How pass your Sundays? Are ye still but joggles
In ceaseless wash? Still nought but gapes, and bites,
And drinks, and stares, diversified with boggles?

A FISH ANSWERS
Amazing monster! that, for aught I know,
With the first sight of thee didst make our race

For ever stare! O flat and shocking face,
Grimly divided from the breast below!
Thou that on dry land horribly dost goWith a split body and most
ridiculous pace,
Prong after prong, disgracer of all grace,
Long-useless-finned, haired, upright, unwet, slow!
O breather of unbreathable, sword-sharp air,
How canst exist? How bear thyself, thou dry
And dreary sloth? What particle canst share
Of the only blessed life, the watery?
I sometimes see of ye an actual pair
Go by! linked fin by fin! most odiously.

THE FISH TURNS INTO A MAN, AND THEN INTO A SPIRIT,
AND AGAIN SPEAKS
Indulge thy smiling scorn, if smiling still,
O man! and loathe, but with a sort of love;
For difference must its use by difference prove,
And, in sweet clang, the spheres with music fill.
One of the spirits am I, that at his will
Live in whate'er has life – fish, eagle, dove–
No hate, no pride, beneath nought, nor above,
A visitor of the rounds of God's sweet skill.
Man's life is warm, glad, sad, 'twixt loves and graves,
Boundless in hope, honoured with pangs austere,
Heaven-gazing; and his angel-wings he craves:–
The fish is swift, small-needing, vague yet clear,
A cold, sweet, silver life, wrapped in round waves,
Quickened with touches of transporting fear.

Kevin J Anderson, *The Edge of the World: Terra Incognita Book One* (2009)

Well, *[sigh]*, this isn't very good. The even-*I*-think-he's-too-prolific-(and-I-know-prolific) Anderson slides a nautical-Fantasy saga down the slipway with this enormous volume, and there it sits, low in the waterline. It's set in a schematic Fantasy world divided between two tribes – Aiden in the northern hemisphere, Urec in the south, their landmasses linked by an isthmus on which is located a holy city called Ishalem. When this sneezily-named place gets burnt down, it's War! *War!*, and off we go.

As is usual for this manner of slop-chest-novel, there's pretty much everything and anything that the conventions of Fantasy require. There are some swords, and a quantity of sorcery; a dozen or so characters; lots of filler about windlasses and gunwales and lubbers; sea-serpents; beautiful ladies captured by slave-traders; sexy witches; heroic princes; voyages to the edge of the world; a magical compass; a quest for the Golden Fern; episodes of yaddita; incidents of yaddita; and big battles that are all yaddita-yaddita. Everything in this book is taken from somewhere else, *Pirates of the Caribbean / Sinbad the Sailor* meets George R R Martin or David Eddings. But the real provocation for the sigh with which this review starts is the poor, poor, *poor* quality of the writing. This, from early on:

> On the Aidest side of the city, the architecture showed familiar Tierran influence, similar to what one might find in any coastal village, while in the Urban District, on the opposite side of the isthmus, the buildings looked alien, with unusual curves and angles, stuccoed rather than timbered, the roofs tiled rather than thatched. [pp. 13-14]

That's a terrible sentence. I challenge you to read 'similar to what one might find' without thinking 'the play what I wrote'. But worse, this undisciplined, additive, clause-piled-on-clause comma-orrhea is entirely characteristic of Anderson's approach to the larger business of putting the novel together. He piles stuff upon stuff, and at the end we're presented a hardback-bound big pile of stuff. And all of it rendered in dead, humourless, grey prose: describing characters, describing character's thoughts and motivations, describing actions, everything on the kindergarten level excepting only the violence. Sometimes the prose is baffling ('the cook's hemorrhaged eyes were blank', p. 175), and sometimes more straightforwardly inept, as in this impossible metaphor: 'tides pushed and pulled the currents like watery pendulums' [p. 428]. Or else in this passage, in which the attempt to ratchet-up the tension is undermined by the momentary transformation of the character into Dr Zoidberg with his claws up, scurrying sideways:

> [He] counted to a hundred. He still couldn't be sure he was safe, but he knew he had to go. At last he moved with all the stealth he could manage. Covered with dirt he crab-walked out of the hollow. [p. 396]

All of it, all, terribly written. *[sigh]*.

Greer Gilman, *Cloud and Ashes: Three Winter's Tales*
(Small Beer Press, 2009)

It cries to be read slow and savoured, so I read it fast and hard. And its wordage came a spate that smithed sparkles and round diamonds from the rocks in falling, but ever, as moon chased sun and sun chased moon over the dark ploughed field of the sky, I thought to myself: 'now-now, see, *is* that titular apostrophe in the right place, though? But – *is* it, though? Shouldn't it rather–?' But the spate hushed and rushed me away. Ah! Like fire, quoth the wisewife, like fire, alliteration is a savvy servant but a mouldy master. And, oh! How lovely the binding! *The weight of the paper touched by fine type*, says the red-man, the rib-man. *How lovely the making of books when a fashioner of books has wrought, as this Small Beer has wrought.* It was a chase, following the chaste prey on the hareroad. I followed that hare and by moonlight, when my eyes shivered with tiredness, by the starfire of electricity penned in its glass shell, the sickle coil of spright's gleam. I followed that hare, when the warren's round mouth turned gold and shining in the daysky, and I read upon trains, and in my chair, and at odd moments. I read it fast, and hard.

A Riddle.
What's Lear without the King? *O write me a book*, my Ma might chant, *O write me a book and bind it in art, that readers might look and break-up their heart.* Lear without the king is an O – an O such as a writer might deploy who doesn't know the difference between the vocative O and the exclamatory Oh – might repeatedly deploy, perhaps, to bait the pedant, O pedant, O red-man. Lear without the king: an egg, a world, a noon. A quasi-Jacobean fantasy of pagan nearly-England, of earth and blood, starlight and goddesses, death having no dominion but rebirth being bloody and hard and cold as frost. One winter's tale; three winters' – and the first tale calling, and called:

One: Jack Daw's Pack
A daw that steals Tom Bombadil's gold ('He holds her ring up, glancing

through it with his quick blue eye; and laughs' p. 11)[4] and speaks Hughes' Tedtongue like a blooded puppetmaster ('the crows make carrion of halfborn lambs, their stripped skulls staring from their mothers' forks' p. 6). And the descriptive prose sounds like this:

> *Between the scythe and the frost he's earthfast, and his visions light as leaves. He keeps the hallows of the earth. And winterlong he hangs in heaven, naked, in a chain of stars. He rises to her rimes. When Ashes hangs the blackthorn with her hail of flowers, white as sleet, as white as souls, then in that moon the barley's seeded and the new green pricks the earth. He's scattered and reborn.* [p. 11]

And for a moment – a moment, mind – the charm wakes to its work, and the spirit of Dylan Thomas rises. But then the charm crumbles, for the dialogue sounds like this:

> *'Called thee.'*
> *'Canst play us a dance on thy crowdy catgut? Light our heels then.'*
> *'What, is thy candle out?'* [p. 4]

And magic flees harefast from prithees and nonny-nons, deep into the thickets of thous and thees. But it matters nought; for as soon as begun it is ended, as a child's life snuffed, and:

Two: A Crowd of Bone.
'Margaret do you see the leaves? They flutter, falling'. [p. 23] And at this goldengrove's unleaving the salady words pile, they pile. The thread is woven longer, and we come to the world of Cloud, where mortals live, though your Mag's grandnan was a goddess. There is more of story here, and the characters glimpsed as scatterlings in part 1 return, or their children return, and they tell one another tales, and meet and part. What else does the story say but that pretty girls make Robert-graves, and the maiden, mother and crone dance upon the tight roadline of Law? The fox darts quick in the chalk-white winter garden, like a flame. The play falls within the play. It speaks, with Thea, of a 'world warped with water' [p. 41]. It is magic, O magic! – but tangled and witchily so. The shearer shaves wool from sheep as the carpenter planes curls and

---

[4] 'Frodo, to his own astonishment, drew out the chain from his pocket, and unfastening the Ring handed it at once to Tom. [...] Suddenly he put it to his eye and laughed. For a second the hobbits had a vision, both comical and alarming, of his bright blue eye gleaming through a circle of gold.' [*Lord of the Rings*, bk 1, ch. 7]

tangles from the wood; and the prose is still:

> *He saw a scutter and lop of coneys, and at his feet the fumblings of a dawstruck mole. A-sway on the nodding corn, the gressops leapt and chirred. He saw the plash of poppies falling, and the blue-eyed blink of corn-flowers, clean petticoats of bindweed. He saw the scurry of the denizens laid bare to light: whitespinners, jinny-long-legs, harvestman.* [p. 85]

– to make the heart leap up (that bindweed!) But the alacking dialogue is still: "twill do that errant part wherein thy mother did betray me' [p. 100] – and is still: 'no art i' that, thy fortune's i' thy fork': wha tellt thee it were thine? Caggy awd thing wha'd want it? [p. 88]. We run and stumble and we're into:

Three: Unleaving
The longest of the longing threads,
That runs through good and ill
Is magic made of Margaret's words:
For th'scriptive prose is still:

> *Margaret bent her neck to the crow-clawed waiting women, Grieve and Rue. They tugged her laces, twisted up her hair from off her shivering nape and shoulders, pinched her slight pale buds in mockery of ripeness. The gown they'd put her in was rich and strange, of cloud-changing shifting silk: steelblue, stormblue, dizzying with musk and wormwood, old and yet unworn. Her jacket and her petticoat, her stout nailed shoes, were locked away. They turned her round in this garb, as they would buy her on a stall.* [p. 216]

And the red-reader thinks: but this dress is Gilman's prose! Old and yet unworn, silk smooth, cloud cold! Such finery! But there's woefilling and infalling, for the dialogue is still:

> *'Lasses gang. I's not got a tallywag atween my legs.'*
> *'Thou's not yet wanted one.'*
> *'Thou's not yet bled.'*
> *'Thou'd nobbut ask for a babbyhouse.*
> *'I'd want nowt. Just to be lating i't the dark, and see t'stones walking, and t'stars awhirl'* [p. 256]

Though mayhap it fashes us not, even unto the thous of it. The book, entire, shines its newness in its studied antiquity; for there is nothing like it, quite, on bookstalls: and that is a very good thing. It is a fatasy finnegans wake, and *there*, quoth the crow, now *there* was a book and a writer-of-books who knew what to do with a titular apostrophe. A woman's book, a goddess' tale, a molly book that pours forth a studied, creaturely écriture féminine, and its half-glimpsed (though you're looking at them the whole time) characters and world are striking: its lovelinesses womanifold and womenny.

Yet; yet. It is menny too, in length and crush, that the woe fall. For as the back cover and the last page embrace, and the reviewer thinks, as the sisters mingle close as moon and dark of moon, and the garland becomes a hey of light [p. 439], that the lyric mode is a powerful and beautiful thing when shaped by a gifted writer, as Gilman assuredly is, but that the lyric mode cannot be sustained at such density over such length without compacting into something overdense, overdone, something choking and stifling, something thrown around the windpipe to block the tune anon and ever, and the red-reviewer dangling from the suffocating cord.

— *But why did you read the pages so hard and fast, red-man, rib-man?*
— *It was done because they are too menny.*

229

Robert Jordan, *The Wheel of Time* (1990-2005)

I know the gags, of course ('help, I'm trapped like a hamster in the *Wheel of Time!*') but I've decided to give it a go anyway – reading it, I mean. It may or may not be significant Fantasy in an aesthetic sense, that remains to be seen. But there's no questioning its commercial success. *The Eye of the World* is sitting in front of me on my desk right now. This is what the copyright page tells me: first published in the United States by Tom Doherty Associates Inc, 1990; first published in Great Britain in 1990 by Macdonald & Co; this Orbit edition published 1991. Reprinted 1991, 1992 (twice), 1993 (twice), 1994 (twice), 1995, 1996 (twice), 1997, 1998, 1999, 2000, 2001, 2002 (twice), 2003, 2004 (twice), 2005, 2006 (twice), 2007. People keep buying it, evidently. I bought it myself – in a charity shop, for £1:49

So on one side of the scales is my curiosity. On the other side, obviously, is the enormousness of the task. Fourteen volumes, most of them more than 800 pages long. Think of it as one 11,000-page novel. Phew. I daresay there's a lot of *stuff* in that sedimentary cliff-face of text: many characters, a peck of business, a Cook's-tour (or perhaps several) of Jordan's imaginary world. Should I anticipate Tolstoyan depth and richness; or Nabokovian prose; or even Dostoevskian intensity? Wouldn't that be to perpetrate a *category error*? But it's clearly *long*, at any rate. We can probably go further and say that some of the appeal of this series is precisely *its length*. The back of my second hand Orbit paperback carries this endorsement, from the (UK) *Sunday Times*: 'Epic in every sense.' The truth is probably that it's epic in no classical sense at all, but 'epic' now is taken as a synonym for 'very long', and *The Wheel of Time* is clearly, undeniably, indisputably – very long.

1. The Eye of the World (1990)

So, I read the first volume and was heartened. It turns out that *The Wheel of Time* is not long at all. It may *look* long to the inexperienced eye, but it's actually fairly short. The whole series (I thought to myself) will be a doddle.

Here's what I mean. *The Eye of the World* is 53 chapters, each chapter being 15-20 pages long. But the plot traced out by those 53 chapters is unthreateningly simple, and even the narrative, though clearly puffed and tumoured a little in terms of length, is not much longer. Jordan's 800 page novel is actually a 300 page novel. For example: Jordan's protagonist is making his way through the forest with his dad when he sees a mysterious dark horseman. Here's how Jordan writes the sentence 'Rand stumbled and nearly fell':

> Abruptly a stone caught his heel and he stumbled, breaking his eyes away from the dark horseman. His bow dropped to the road, and only an outthrust hand grabbing Bela's harness saved him from falling flat on his back. With a startled snort the mare stopped, twisting her head to see what had caught her. [p. 4]

And here's how he writes 'when he looked up again, the dark horseman had vanished.'

> Tam frowned over Bela's back at him. 'Are you alright son?'
> 'A rider,' Rand said breathlessly, pulling himself upright. 'A stranger, following us.'
> 'Where?' The older man lifted his broad-bladed speak and peered back warily.
> 'There, down the…' Rand's voice trailed off as he turned to point. The road behind was empty.
> Disbelieving, he stared into the forest on both sides of the road. Bare-branched trees offered no hiding place, but there was no glimmer of horse or horseman. He met his father's questioning gaze. 'He was there. A man in a black cloak, on a black horse.'

The writerly-technical term for this is 'padding'; but the prolixity is such a fundamental part of what Jordan is doing that I suspect it misses the point to object. Lots of writers do it, after all. Now, this has specific textual effects; and the one that struck me, on reading through it, is of upholstery. It's a comfortable sort of style, like settling into a bath; a mix of stiff little archaic touches and chattily modern waffle.

The other thing that leaps out, having read it, is the wholly saturated *derivativeness* of it all. According to *The New York Times* (quoted on the front cover of my copy), 'with the Wheel of Time Jordan has come to dominate the world Tolkien began to reveal.' That 'reveal' is rather annoyingly precious, but we can take this as code for '*The Wheel of Time* is massively derivative of Tolkien.' And indeed it is. Great Odin it is. The only substantive thing it adds to *Lord of the Rings* is increased length, and since each of Tolkien's 1100 pages is ten times as dense as Jordan's 11,000, that resolves into no additional substance at all. Otherwise there's a cosmic battle between good and evil; little people caught in the middle of incipient cosmic war, bestial orcs ('Trollocs'), istarian wielders of the true source. Does Jordan, in one jarringly un-American moment, have one character say 'I can feel it... I can bloody feel it!' [p. 684] because he thinks *that's how JRRT's compatriots swear?* The Professor would not have been pleased.

Still, best to take this novel as a self-conscious exercise in remix. Our hero is an ordinary chap, in a rural community ('Two Rivers', which is also, distractingly for me, the name of the main shopping mall in Staines, Middlesex, England) whose life is upended by the eruption of mysterious dark riders and orcs (Trollocs, sorry) into his sequestered backwater. Fleeing from them takes him, and his various companions, first of all, to a Bree-like town (Baerlon), then via a Mines-of-Moria-like dead metropolis (Shadar Logoth) to a brief kinda-Elvish-y sanctuary (Caemlyn). All through these journeys the forces of evil, servants of the disembodied Shaitan, harry Rand. They do this because they know him to be a reincarnation of their ancient enemy, and they try in various ways to bump him off: Trollocs and airborne Nazgul (I can't, off the top of my head, remember what Jordan calls his Nazgul, but big lizard-like flying evil creatures are certainly there) from without, treachery from within, not least the egregiously Gollum-like ('Gollumoid'? 'Gollumnar'?) pedlar Padan Fain. More than that, the evil one himself keeps appearing in Rand's dreams, wearing Über-melodramatic impossible-to-actually-visualise facial expressions, and calling him 'youngling'.

> Ba'alzamon's clothes were the color of dried blood, and rage and hate and triumph battled on his face. 'You see, youngling, you cannot hide from me forever!' [p. 493]

A couple of non-Tolkien elements are also thrown into the mix: one being the pseudo-militia 'Children of the Light' who, like New England Puritans, have taken opposition of 'the evil one' to self-defeatingly destructive and fundamentalist lengths. Prophesy tells of the rebirth of 'the Dragon', who will battle the evil one, but whose coming will wreck the world, and so is looked on with as much dread as anything.

Now, reading this was actually *not wholly a chore*. The whole galleon moves at a stately but not particularly boring pace through 40-odd chapters. Then Jordan seems to decide he needs to speed things up a bit; so he introduces some interdimensional portals called 'the Ways' to shift his characters out of besieged Camlaen and zoom them the great distance to his Mordor/Mount Doom-ish denouement without further faffing, which reads like a bit of a cheat, actually. And then it's into the wasted lands behind the mountains, pursued by myriad manifestations of evil, to get to the titular Eye of the World. This turns out to be a magical reservoir of the Magic Magical Energy, 'Saidan', that underpins Jordan's cosmos, magically. For a man to utilise this stuff is inevitable madness and death (women do rather better with it). But Rand has his stand-off with evil, wields the magic Saidan to destroy the armies of wickedness. The book closes with a quick flourish of duh-duh-DURR! – viz. Moraine, a sort-of female Gandalf, after consoling Rand that things will be OK, waits till she is alone and whispers, 'the Dragon is Reborn!'

Reading is a different pleasure to re-reading: the one exploratory, an encounter with newness; the other reassuring, an encounter with familiarity. But what Jordan has done here is produce a book such that the reader feels as if she is *re*reading it even when she is actually reading it for the first time. That doesn't especially suit me, I must say, since I prize the estrangement of literature over the comfy warm-milk-and-cookies pleasures of curling up with a novel that will give you precisely all the things you expect of a novel. But I daresay that's just me.

There were some things I enjoyed about it, mind. I quite liked the way we intuit, from early on, that the whole cycle is actually a far-future history. Buried behind the horizon of Jordan's world's history are the events of 20th- and I suppose 21st-century history remembered only as mythic fragments: the 1969 Lunar Exploration Module becoming 'Lenn [...] how he flew to the moon in the belly of an eagle made of fire', and a Russian-US nuclear war (Jordan shows his age and generation in this) reduced to 'tales of Mosk the Giant with his Lance of Fire that could reach around the world, and his wars with Elsbet, the Queen of All.' [p. 51] It's neither original nor particularly cleverly done, this, but it works quite nicely nevertheless.

Less clever is the way Jordan continually interrupts his narratives to have characters recite gnarly chunks of history, like this:

> Before Mordeth had been long in the city he had Balwen's ear, and soon he was second only to the King. Mordeth whispered poison in Balwen's ear, and Aridhol began to change. Aridhol drew in on itself, hardened. It was said that some would rather see Trollocs come than the men of Aridhol [...] The story is too long to tell in full, and too grim, and only fragments are known, even in Tar Valon. How Thorin's son, Caar, came to win Aridhol back to the Second Covenant, and [...] [p. 289]

Wait, didn't you *just* say it was too long and grim to tell? Why do that and then *go on and on for pages*? Or, this:

> 'I remember the making of it [the Eye]. Some of the making. Some.' His hazelnut eyes stared, lost in memory. 'It was the first days of the Breaking of the World, when the joy of victory over the Dark One turned bitter with the knowledge that all might yet be shattered by the weight of the Shadow. A hundred of them made it, men and women together. The greatest Aes Sedai works were always done so, joining saidin and saidar, as the True Source is joined...' [p. 744]

And so on.

Jordan's gender politics are marginally more progressive than Tolkien's, although the margin involved is slender, for his whole world is built around a small-c conservative and essentialist notion of the appropriate powers and responsibilities of male and female. There are no gay characters, and indeed I was struck, reading the whole, by how painfully *chaste* it all is. Pitched perfectly for religious-prudish Middle America.

One last thing. The book reads like the first instalment in a trilogy (as, Wikipedia tells me, it was originally planned). I don't see how Jordan and his heirs can spin this story out through *fourteen* fat volumes. But we'll see.

2. The Great Hunt (1990)
On I go; volume two slips under the belt. Like the first, this is actually a 250-page novel pretending to be a 700-page one, and also like the first book after a sticky start it settles into an unoriginal but I suppose

unobjectionable groove. Nevertheless I'll confess I found the business of reading this much less enjoyable than the first. It felt – not all the time, but for fairly long stretches – like a chore.

It doesn't help that the book starts so weakly, for prologue and opening chapters have a distressingly high 'reader-struggling-to-give-a-fuck' quotient: inconsequential and unengaging. And this is more deep-seated a problem, I think, than just readability. The book's prologue betrays the debilitating *thinness* of Jordan's ability to conceptualise what evil is. Here it's a kind of masked ball of medievalised Bond villains, through which the lord of wickedness floats like a hydrogen-inflated Mardi Gras person-shaped balloon. Later in the novel it's Horrid Violence Against Civilians, but even there J. can't quite keep his account free of bathetic lurches. Here's a description of Trollocs getting nasty in a village: 'Pleas for mercy and children's screams were cut off by solid thuds and unpleasant squishing sounds' [p. 197]. That's *squishing*, yes. That ineluctably evil word, yes.

Anyway, the opening seven-or-so chapters drag, as our three heroes dawdle about in foppishly-named Fal Dara fortress. The Aes Sedai, a sort of Bene Gesserit sisterhood, meet in infodumpy convocation. At one point two of them, Anaiya and Moiraine, chat about *something they both already know very well*. Notice the first four words of this speech:

> 'You must know that the Great Hunt of the Horn has been called in Illian, the first time in four hundred years. The Illianers say the last battle is coming' – Anaiya gave a little shiver, as well she might, but went on without a pause–'and the Horn of Valere must be found before the final battle against the Shadow.' [p. 52]

There are dozens of more pages like this, detailing various prophesies and plot-coupons, until discussion is cut off by the unpleasant squishing sounds of frustrated readers.

At any rate, this 'great hunt' is the titular premise of vol. 2. As one Aes Sedai helpfully explains to another who already knows it, 'the Horn of Valere was made to call dead heroes back from the grave. And prophecy said it would only be found just in time for the Last Battle' [p. 65]. Where *Eye of the World* was saturated in its Tolkien original, this novel is more parsimonious with its source-material: it lifts only Aragorn's ability to command the dead of Dunharrow, saving other things, I suppose, for future volumes.

The Aes Sedai have this horn but they carelessly lose it to the Evil at the start of this book, and many hundreds of pages of text must be given over to its recovery. To raise the stakes a magic dagger has also been half-inched, upon the recovery of which, for obscure magical Magic reasons, the life of Rand's pal Mat depends. So off they go, in search of these plot-coupon artefacts. Rand and his pals take an interdimensional short cut through a sort-of waking dream alternate reality called 'Tel'aran'rhiod' and get both horn and dagger back, lose it again (because there are still several hundred pages to fill) and finally retrieve it once more. Another friend of Rand's, called 'Reginald Perrin', although, tragically, not the Reginald part, is now a sort of werewolf and has golden eyes.

What else? Well, whenever the narrative sags, J. throws some battling orcs, sorry, trollorcs, sorry, Trollocs at our heroes, to leaven the questing/infodumping tedium with some fighting. But even though we're only at vol. 2 Jordan already feels the need to garnish his accounts of these repetitive fighty-fights so as to ameliorate their monotonous over-familiarity. So, for example, one hero-v.-Trolloc fight takes place in a firework shop, to the accompaniment of lots of fireworks going off. Bang! Crash! I felt this, however, completely failed to ameliorate the monotonous over-familiarity of these repetitive fighty-fights.

Then at the three-quarters point, a little jarringly, a whole new evil empire, from a place not even on the map on the book's flyleaf, invades, and everything kicks off. These 'Seanchan' have a big army augmented by various horrid monsters, and as the book ends our pals find themselves squeezed between these invaders on the one hand and the cruel Children of Light on the other. Handily, though, our guys have the horn. If you see what I mean. One toot on the magical horn from ailing Mat and the dead arrive (King Arthur, no less, himself amongst them). Then Rand has a further round of fighty-fight with Ba'alzamon. The writing, in this latter, is not what you would call restrained:

> 'I will destroy you to your very soul, destroy you utterly and forever... why are you grinning like an idiot, fool? Do you not know I can destroy you utterly?'
> 'I will never serve you, Father of Lies!' [...]
> 'Then die, worm!'
> Ba'alzamon struck with the staff, as with a spear. Rand screamed.

As he felt it pierce his side, burning like a white-hot poker. The void trembled, but he held on with the last of his strength, and drove the heron-mark blade into Ba'alzamon's heart. Ba'alzamon screamed, and the dark behind him screamed. The world exploded in fire. [p. 666]

Implicit in the aesthetic guideline 'less is more' is the injunction 'more is *not* more'.

In sum, such shine as the opening book managed to kindle in my imagination dulled for me in the second. The longer one reads this yarn the more unignorable it becomes that there's nothing really at stake in Jordan's battle of good and evil. The Evil are Evil because he says so, because they cackle and threaten like villains out of a theatrical melodrama, occasionally because they kill people, but most of all *because they wear black clothes*. Indeed, *black* hardly does the clothes justice. The black clothes of the Evil are none-more-black black ('those black clothes, blacker than black [...]' p. 186). On the other side of the divide, the good are characterised mostly by an Epic Blandness, an almost transcendental Blandness that goes beyond Bland into ÜberBland. Bland, sorry, *Rand*, the main protagonist, is the worst offender of all in this regard. There's some notional fretting on his part about 'not wanting to be used', and a little friction with his girlfriend; but no development, or conflict, or interest in the character in any meaningful sense. And the 'Horn of Valere' plot coupon feels *massively* arbitrary. I can't remember if it was mentioned in *The Eye of the World*. Conceivably it was, but it still feels plucked from the ether here: introduced, chased after, lost again, chased after, and then used; a sterile imitation of dramatic tension.

If I had a completely free hand in this I might easily find reasons never to pick up another *Wheel of Time* instalment again. But I've committed to reading the whole thing, and don't choose to be forsworn. Onward. Time to drown out any inward pleas for mercy with solid thuds and unpleasant squishing sounds.

3. *The Dragon Reborn* (1991)

For some reason, and I'm not *entirely* sure why, this wasn't such a chore to read as vol. 2. I say so despite the fact that nothing very much happens in the story: Rand, our hero, is the Dragon Reborn, but he's gone missing. His mates, especially his two best mates 'Reggie' Perrin and Mat Cauthon, go questing after him. Perrin is still only called 'Reggie' in my mind, but I keep hoping that J. will catch up with me and slap down the nickname for real. He is already calling his Evil Characters things like Neil and Julian (well: Niall and Juilin), so it's not as if naff names carry any stigma as far as he's concerned.

Anyway, eventually Rand comes back, has another show-down with the evil one, Ba'alzamon, and is *publicly* declared the Dragon Reborn, to much falfalla and parading. Along the way there's a good deal of stuff about the various sects of Aes Sedai magicianesses, some more stuff on the corrupt puritans, The Children of Light, and quite a lot of narrative dilly-dallying. Mat was under the evil influence of a wicked dagger, but he gets cured of that by the end. Otherwise it's pretty much all just padding out the circular plot. Maybe I'm now reconciled to the Jordanian shtick; maybe it's that where most volumes in this enormous series are 300-pages-pretending-to-be-800-pages long, this one is *200*-pages-pretending-to-be-*650*-pages. At any rate, it slipped down easily enough.

That's not to say it's any good, mind. This book has all the limitations of a YA novel and none of the focus or penetration. So, for instance, *The Dragon Reborn* remains coy on the subject of sex. In one chapter Mat is visited in his bedroom by the evil Selene ('so beautiful he almost forgot to breathe') which causes the young lad 'tingle and pain' [p. 227] as well it might, but nothing more explicit is stated. (Then again, chapter 42 is called 'Easing the Badger', which may well become my new favourite onanistic euphemism). There's spits and spots of violence, but this all feels been-there-done-that *tired* – already! and we're only in vol. 3!

> Perrin shouted wordlessly as he struck out with an axe; [...] the Trolloc fell, roaring and kicking. [p. 75]

Good YA books are generally less padded and meandering than 'adult' books; not, as here, more so.

An issue I had with the second vol. was intensified for me by this, third one: namely that Jordan has a problem representing, because conceptualising, evil. It's all second-hand and none of it alarming in any genuine sense: medieval Bond villains, beast-men, creaky but (see above) euphemistic old decadence. In the prologue an evil 'Fade' shows how e-e-evil he is by *gouging a table with his bare hands.*

The Myrddraal was drawing a hand across the tabletop, and thin tendrils of wood curled away from its fingernails. [p. 29]

Then there's a sort-of Dreamtime dimension in which the e-e-evil Ba'alzamon, gathering a conclave of his underling-baddies, gets to be both Freddy Krueger ("You all dream,' Ba'alzamon said, 'But what happens in this dream is real!'") *and* a Bond villain, both at the same time:

> 'You have been given tasks. Some of these tasks you have carried out. At others, you have failed. [...] You!'
> [...] The man screamed and began to quiver like a file struck against an anvil. [p. 411]

To be clear, that's *'like a file struck against an anvil'*. Boingg!

Otherwise a few more gobbets from general myth/culture are added to the stew: some more Arthuriana, in the shape of an Excaliburish magic sword that only the Dragon can wield, called (the 'Ex-' prefix having been filed away) 'Callandor'. There are also bits of Wagner ('the Maidens of the Spear') and some wolves. But most of it remains the same-old same-old. Characters still explain things to other characters who presumably already know those things:

> 'The soulless?' Egwen said, a tremor in her voice. [...] 'A Gray Man?'
> Sheriain [...] gestured to the corpse. 'The Soulless, the Gray Men, give up their souls to serve the Dark Lord as assassins. They are not really alive after that. Not quite dead, but not truly alive.' [188]

A bit like this novel, then. Or later in the narrative:

> 'Let us saddle the horses,' said Mat. 'Horses are gramnivorous quadrupeds with forty teeth, namely twenty–four grinders, four eye–teeth, and twelve incisive. They shed their coats in the spring; in marshy countries, shed their hoofs, too. Hoofs are hard, but requiring to be shod with iron. Their age can be known by marks in mouth.'
> 'Excellent,' cried Reggie. 'To horse we go!'

Well, I made that last one up. But you take my file-struck-against-an-anvil point. *Boingg!*

4. *The Shadow Rising* (1992)

Volume 4 is considerably fatter than the previous three: more than a thousand pages long. It's also less focused; a sprawl of different storylines going in different (physical) directions, great splodgy-wodges of second-hand worldbling, and, er, that's it. I enjoyed reading vol. 1; didn't enjoy 2 at all; quite (despite myself) enjoyed 3. 4 was pure slog.

The structural glitch of the previous novels – a too-slow start followed by a deal of too-detailed wandering about – is magnified here: the start is fantastically boring and taxing, and the subsequent wanderings hard to keep a mental handle on. In this volume our pals split up: 'Romaine' Rand going, via magical short-cut, to visit the Aeil; 'Reggie' Perrin back to his provincial home, the Two Rivers. Meanwhile, representatives of the various coloured Aes Sedai (blue, red, etc.) go hunting the evil branch of their movement. I'll leave you to guess what colour the evil branch is. Mat goes into dreamtime for a bit and comes back with some more magical artefacts (a magical spear and a protective medallion). If the novels continue accumulating magical artefacts at this rate, the three pals will be able to open an extensive antique shop at the end of it all. Rand meanwhile, is stretching his metaphorical magical muscles, making axes fly, ships crash and the like.

Did you guess 'black'? Clever you.

I read the book fairly rapidly, but I look back on it now trying to remember *what* all this diverse running-around, collecting, fighting and so on *amounted to*. To be precise: I look back trying *and failing* to remember. A fair bit has to do with the 'Aiel', a sort of Native-American/ Samurai/Fremen warrior race of people who live in the 'Aiel Wastes' and have some special spoken-by-prophesy relationship to the Dragon Reborn. But aside from taking us around their world and culture, and establishing to their satisfaction that Rand is indeed the Muad-Dib, sorry, the Dragon, I'm not sure what the force of this lengthy narrative detour was. There's also the Gipsy-like Tuatha'an, and a character called Slayer. A nasty character, naturally. Though not nasty enough to possess an electric guitar and amplifier.

Mat is menaced by the e-e-evil: 'Time to die, Hornsounder!' [p. 225]. I believe I once went to a tiny basement club in the Borough, or possibly Kennington, where the DJ was called 'Hornsounder.' I may be misremembering that. Anyway, as before Jordan intersperses his yawnly tale with lots of Trolloc combat to try and maintain flagging excitement levels. This fighting is ramped up ('fiery explosions tore at the trollocs', p. 729) from the previous books, in a diminishing-returns sort of way. Now, I like humans. And I like Trollocs. But which is better? There's only one way to find out…

A good chunk of the novel is given over to the notional 'development' of the main characters, but this is all teen-soap-opera nonsense, and rubbish to boot. There are *intimations* of sex in the book, but instead of actual sex we get a load of schoolyard crushes, mooning about, kissing, jealousies and the occasional bottom-pinch. Egwyne – Rand's girlfriend – announces that she doesn't love him any more ('People change, Rand. Feelings change […] I love you as I would a brother', p.147) which frees him up to snog other girls. There are also occasional instances of topless serving wenches, attractive women discussing things whilst naked in saunas and beautiful women chained naked in dungeons, which would be less creepy if it were more honestly handled (handled, that is to say, with less mendacious cod-propriety).

But my main grouse here is the *way it is all written*. Vol. 1 was written in a garrulous, occasionally creakily cod-archaic style, but was at least quite solidly written, according to the rather limited aesthetic criteria of that kind of writing. But Vol. 4 is really not very well written at all, even by those standards.

> Perrin and Faile had made no effort to be quiet in climbing the stairs, but the three men were so intent in their watching that none of them noticed the new arrivals at first. Then one of the blue-coated bodyguards twisted his head as if working a cramp in his neck; his mouth dropped open when he saw them. Biting off an oath, the fellow whirled to face Perrin, baring a good hand of his swordblade. The other was only a heartbeat slower. Both stood tensed, ready, but their eyes shifted uneasily, sliding off Perrin's. They gave off a sour smell of fear. So did the High Lord, though he had his fear tightly reined. [p. 79]

This isn't hopeless writing (aside from the eyeballs-in-the-sky-y 'their eyes slid off Perrin's' bit, which is indeed hopeless writing), but it reads like a first-draft that Jordan couldn't be bothered to revise. The smell-in-harness at the end; the cliché; the fumbling-bumbling piling up of clauses. That all needs polishing. The paragraph that follows it, on the other hand, is pretty much beyond revision. You need to bin this and

Adam Roberts

start again:

> The High Lord Torean, white streaking his dark, pointed beard,
> moved languidly, as if at a ball. Pulling a too sweetly scented
> handkerchief from his sleeve, he dabbed at a knobby nose that
> appeared not at all large when compared with his ears.

Now *that's* bad writing: clumsily wrong-footing and unevocative. From
whence did that knobby nose appear? Did the white streak his
beard *as* he moved languidly? Which is to say, did his languid
movement *shake free* some white from the upper reaches of the beard?
The writing is all like this, either undercooked or actively bad: 'a myriad
of scents danced in his nose' [p. 718]. 'Without touching her head she
knew she had on some sort of helmet' [p. 867]. 'Ogier's ears went stiff
with shock' [p. 257]. 'The woman frowned and lowered her chins' [p.
784]. You know the way that, when somebody throws a pencil at your
nose, it squeezes perspiration from the whole spread of your skin?

> Damp heat hit her like a stick between the eyes. Sweat popped out of
> every pore. [p. 584]

Now some of this, I'll confess, had to do with the rapidity of my
reading of the book. Encountering the phrase 'the fork bearded fellow
with a ruby the size of a pigeon's egg in his ear' [p. 227] I clocked the
fork, egg and ear-insertion and thought 'say what?' But in such cases I
can always re-read to get a clearer sense of what the writer is on
about. *Clumsily* on about in this case.

Another feature of the style is the way Jordan scatters the text with
cod-proverbial wisdom. He gets this from Tolkien too, I think; except
that where Tolkien's invented proverbs generally feel right ('grief is a
hone to a hard mind'), Jordan's feel either flabby or else goatblinkingly-
incomprehensible. Some examples.

> *'There's no time for winking at the men when you're busy bailing the boat.'* [p.
> 29] OK. I get this.

> *'On the heights, the paths are paved with daggers.'* [p. 43] Laid flat, this
> would surely result in a perfectly serviceable, if expensive, road. Laid
> edge-upwards, you'd probably want to walk alongside it rather than
> on it. Either way it seems self-defeating.

'As well you try to understand the sun, Perrin. It simply is, and it is not to be understood. You cannot live without it, but it exc.:ts a price. So with women.' [p. 417] I don't understand this one at all. What price? Is the meaning here: 'if you're staked out underneath a woman with your eyelids cut off you'll go blind?' Does that count as 'proverbial'?

The sling has been used. The shepherd holds the sword. [p. 775] Um. OK. This is one of those 'the wild geese fly south at noon' style statements.

A weeping woman is a bucket with no bottom' [p. 117] But this can't be right. 'When a woman weeps it's like all the water gushes out in one go and then she's dry'? Presumably not. 'Don't try gathering water in a weeping woman.' What?

'I could have shaved myself with one sneeze.' [p. 55] What?

Otherwise, despite the addition of a metric tonne of detail, Jordan's imaginary world feels more-and-more ersatz/theme-park and less-and-less authentically rendered.

[It was] a large room with a high ceiling. A rope strung along waist-high posts would keep anyone from going too close to the things displayed on stands and in open-fronted cabinets. [p. 199]

Can you imagine a room like that in Middle Earth? As the Old English proverb has it: better a dinner of herbs where authenticity is, than a stalled ox and a National Trust Property thereby.

5. *The Fires of Heaven* (1993)

None of the previous volumes in this series are what you would call fast-paced (although I concede the first one had a reasonable, if stately, momentum to it), but this book is slower than a slug on mogadon. By this stage in his series Jordan had evidently, and I think unwisely, decided to jettison 'stuff happening' as the organising principle of his fiction in favour of 'characters talking, backstorying, bickering, flirting, fretting over their motivations and wearing *painstakingly described clothing'*. Of course, Jordan's previous model of 'stuff happening' was 'meandering characters getting intermittently attacked by Trollocs.' But it was better than what we get here. The thing is, it so happens I have a very high tolerance for, and in some cases, deep love for novels in

243

which nothing happens. A novel in which nothing happens can be a wonderful read. But not this one. Nothing happens here in a maddeningly faffy, self-regarding, high-school-soap-opera sort of a way. Then at the very end there's a big set-piece Fighty-fight, although the notional drama of it bounced off my soggily worn-down imagination.

Tedium, oh tedium. Or, indeed, something stronger than tedium: coffeedium. Tripleexpressodium. Rand leads an enormous army of his super-warrior 'Aiel', and there's some dull, laboriously described but hard-to-visualise military stuff, all lead-up and no pay-off. More, Jordan assumes we will be fascinated by which adolescent crush is uppermost in his hero's life. Sex, which in the previous instalments had been non-existent or else Carry-On euphemistic, here comes out of the wardrobe, and it's a ghastly sight. Pantechniconloads of beautiful girls fling themselves at the main guy, Rand, and he worrits and ponders which of them, or which several of them, he fancies the most. Rand by name, Randy by nature.

But, oh, and woe, and oh *dear* the novel's sexual politics is offensively narrow and essentialist, to the point often of being actively gynaphobic: women in fancy dress granted notional 'powers' by authorial fiat, set up as 'strong women' in order to be humbled, magically enslaved, spanked or forced to perform humiliatingly menial tasks. J.'s male characters complain endlessly that they 'don't understand women', but I don't know why. The key Jordanverse women are either transparently vain, or man-hating, or both. And, gosh, but there are a lot of *boobies* in this novel. Really, lots and lots. Low-cut dresses, boobies, silk clinging to breasts, cleavage, lady lumps, bosoms. Jordan can't stop going on about them. It's embarrassing.

Otherwise, the Bene Gesserit characters go after their 'black' chapter, and Mat uses his nifty ability to channel all the Great Military leaders there have ever been in all time ever. Perrin doesn't appear to be in the novel at all. Or else Perrin is in the novel but my imagination and memory were so stupefied by the reading process that I don't remember him. But, then again, what *do* I remember about this novel? Its interminability, mostly. Its details hardly at all.

Now, see, I'll give you an example: two of Jordan's most powerful, if nascent, female magicians, Nynaeve and Elayne, *join a travelling circus* in this instalment. That either happened, or else my heat-oppressed brain has somehow muddled childhood memories of watching *Dumbo* in with memories of reading this book (Elayne *learns to walk on a tightrope!* Nynaeve has to *fend off the circus-owner who has a crush on her!*) Elayne and Nynaeve spend a lot of the novel bickering, whingeing and complaining. Characters wander about. The evil characters compound their banality and thinness with stupidity and incompetence. Nothing is resolved. This does not make for interesting reading.

Also, I have no idea why the novel is called 'Fires of Heaven', unless it is to mock me by reminding me of Mary Renault's similarly-titled but vastly superior novel. I don't recall there being any heavenly fires in Jordan's book. But it is conceivable that they're there, I read them, and all thought of them has fallen out of the gash in the back of my imagination caused by being rear-ended by this clanking juggernaut of a book.

6. *Lord of Chaos* (1994)

I originally posted these *Lonesome Dove*-style 'trekking through the wilderness dragging behind me the corpse of my interest' pieces on Jordan's *Wheel* on my blog weekly, every Friday. But that didn't mean I read them as regularly as this regimen perhaps suggests. I can be more specific: I read the first three *Wheel*-vols. pretty much one after the other; and then it was only a short interlude before I tackled four and five. But after that I didn't read another Jordan novel for quite a long time. Somehow I couldn't quite summon the energy to pick up the effectively cuboid, thousand-page ('megapage'?) *Lord of Chaos*. At the back of my mind was the thought: but even when I finish this one *I won't yet have reached the halfway point!* And at the front of my mind was 'No! No! No!'

That *Lonesome Dove* reference, there, dates me rather, doesn't it though?

Still, eventually I screwed my courage to the sticking point, or to be precise, stuck my courage to the screwing point, or screwpoint-and-sticked, and I read the thing. And the result was: dear merciful God. That pretty much sums it up. 'Oh God!' is an interesting utterance, isn't it? It can be spoken by someone at the very point of orgasm, as a signifier of extreme pleasure; or it can be groaned out by someone facing horrors, terrors, pains and an eternity of dullness. I leave it as an exercise for the reader to determine which usage applies in this case.

To be a little more specific: this seems to me a novel written by a man who has only too effectively painted himself into a corner. The overarching narrative is the battle of Good versus Evil. Evil has a seemingly never-ending supply of bestial Trollocs, various high-placed traitors and wizards, and all the cool black clothing. But by volume six Good has acquired not only the draconic magical leader destined by prophesy to overthrow evil, *but also* an enormous army of impossibly gifted warriors of a naturally martial race; a general who can channel all previous genius-generals; an invincible magical sword that can destroy whole cities; and a horn that can summon the greatest dead warriors of all time to help you out. The implication, it seems to me, is that 'Ayn' Rand, Jordan's hero, could wipe the floor with Evil's Minions *any time he liked*. But Jordan has many more fat volumes to fill. I suppose he could balance each of these laboriously acquired magical positives with magical kryptonite-equivalents to cancel them out, until the final showdown. But he chooses a different textual strategy: he dillies, and dallies. He dallies and dillies, misses the cart and, furthermore, he cannot find his way home.

Volume six is a lengthy exercise in treading water. Nothing at all happens for hundreds and hundreds of pages. And when the reader has got on top of that, nothing at all happens for hundreds of pages more. Finally there's a big battle, but by this point the reader's brainwaves will long since have assumed a perfectly sine regularity. For almost the whole of its length this is a novel that absolutely point-blank *refuses* to get off its arse and do something. Anything. Anything at all. Reading it is the equivalent of spending ten hours staring at a portly man slouched in a bean-bag.

What happens? Some more magical artefacts are discovered to add to the characters' lumber room: here a crystal bowl that affects the weather. Egwene, Rand's former girlfriend, hooks up with a fellow called Gawain. The Aes Sedai split into two factions, and Egwene is elected Grand Panjandrum, or Grande Panjandra, of one of these. There are various assassination attempts upon Rand's life (think how much more interesting the sequence could have been had one of these succeeded!) Then Rand is kidnapped, put in a small box, no, really, and carried away; and Perrin leads an enormous army on a rescue mission. There's another big dust-up, during which Rand gets free on his own without anybody's help, and then, after E-e-evil has been knocked on the head, that's your lot.

And finally Esther (and finally Cyril), this section's instalment of Robert Jordan's Proverbial Wisdom:

'*Never prod at a woman unless you must.*' Good advice.

'*Cheer the bull, or cheer the bear; cheer both, and you will be trampled and eaten.*' Since bulls eat grass rather than people, I would say that implicit in this proverb is 'eaten *by the bear.*' Or to paraphrase: the bear doesn't mind if you cheer him, or if you cheer the bull; but for some reason he gets *very* cross if you cheer them both. I daresay the bear has his reasons.

'*If the world is ending, a woman will want time to fix her hair.*' There's a word for proverbs like this. The word is 'sexist'.

'*Caution once forgotten could be forgotten once too often.*' Um... what?

'*If wishes were wings, pigs would fly.*' Because what pigs truly wish for is wings. Little curly wings.

'*The best way to apologize to a man is to trip him in a secluded part of the garden.*' The second best way is to say 'sorry'. But, really, you should go with Plan A in the first instance.

'*You put your cat in your hat and stuff it down your breeches.*' This one is attributed to that ill-starred Dr Seuss porno project you've probably read about.

7. *A Crown of Swords* (1994)

A heat wave has devastated the WoTland, and the parching climate is described at length, but I can't say I cared. Rand al'Thor, who has wangled himself three attractive girlfriends, spends quality time with one of them: Min of the Goon-Show Name. He plans an attack upon the blond-haired, scarred Evil-fellow, Sammael, and I can't say I cared. Then he gets stabbed with a magic dagger by evil former-pedlar Padain Fain, although not stabbed fatally, and I can't say I cared. I thought Padain died in a previous instalment, but I must have got that wrong. Must keep up. What else? Mat, Nynaeve, and Elayne look for a magic bowl with the power to end the heat wave, but I can't say I cared. Perrin does a lot of sniffing around; literal sniffing, since he's a half-

247

man-half-wolf, but I can't say I cared. The Evil characters plot and counterplot and plot some more, but I can't say I cared. There's some more awkward titillating nudity, and a lot of waffling about. I just can't say I cared.

Did I care about anything in this novel? Well, I cared about the quality of the writing, which seemed to me markedly worse than even previous instalments. In the prologue, e-e-evil Elaida talks with a subordinate called Alviarin, a lady described as being 'slim and cool-faced' [p. 5], though I'm not sure what that means.

> The Ajas sent to the Keeper whatever dribbles from their own eyes-and-ears they were willing to share.

Eeew! As for Alviarin, 'the slim woman merely smiled her cool smile' [p. 6]. Cool, you see. 'Her voice became cold [she] stood there, calm as a frozen pond [...] the woman's reply was cool and smooth as her face [...] if anything it should have coated the walls with frost.' You get the idea. Ah but it's ironic, see, because the world is suffering an unnaturally prolonged heat wave! D'you see the irony?

You do?

I started keeping note of some of the more out-leap-y examples of WoT-style:

> That old woman reminded Sevenna of a landslide plunging down a mountain. [p. 22]

> The threat hung in the air like a gleaming dagger. [p. 30]

> The birdlike fellow made Valda itch [p. 37]

> Suddenly he pressed the looking glass to his eye as a woman galloped a tall black horse. [p. 39]

> This had been his first real lesson as a soldier. You always had to pay the butcher. [p. 42]

> Shoulders wide enough to make him seem shorter than he was slumped under the weight of responsibility. [p. 45]

> Worry [...] ate inside him like a ferret trying to burrow out of his middle. [p. 45]

He sounded like a bumblebee the size of a cat instead of a mastiff. [p. 63]

A rabbit watching for a hawk might have been as intent, but never with that air of menace. [p. 77]

Min held herself stiffly and took ginger steps. [p. 102]

His nose strained for a scent of her, but the perfume was too strong, and the fear. She had a reason for being there on the dais, a good reason. She did. [p. 104]

Gently he took her by the shoulders and lifted her until those big tilted eyes were level with his [...] Berating himself for being an oaf he let her go, arms springing apart, but before he could apologize her fingers clutched his beard. [p. 119]

But after 120-pages of this I exhausted the patience necessary to interrupt my reading with jotting examples down in my notebook. I wanted to get through the damn thing as soon as possible. That's not to say that the writing get any better, for it does not ('cold eyes followed her in a bubble of silence', p. 493).

One thing that sticks most in my mind is the book's very un-Tolkienian, un-Herbetian obsession with *interior design and soft furnishings*:

The case clock balanced the door to her sitting room [...] the carpet covering most of the tiles came from Tarabon, patterned in red and green and gold; silk carpets were the most precious. In each corner of the room a marble plinth carved in unpretentious verticals held a white vase [...] [p. 3]

The furnishings were Domani, striped wood inlaid with pearlshell and amber, bright carpets in patterns of flowers and scrolls [...] [p. 27]

Tall gilded stand-lamps with mirrors on every branch ... scattered niches held bowls and vases and now and then a small statue, in gold and silver or alabaster [...] [p. 102]

Carved chairs heavy with gilt stood in paired lines to either side of a golden Rising Sun, two paces wide, set into a polished stone floor [...] a carpet spread for the occasion was green and gold and blue in a

> Tairen maze. [p. 305]

> Min watched him, rooting through the coats in the huge ivory-inlaid wardrobe. How could he sleep in this room, with all its black, heavy furniture? [p. 520]

Hideous bourgeois *Homes-and-Gardens* decor-porn, the lot. 'Egwene returned to her unsteady chair and pushed her breakfast tray aside [...] filled her teacup, setting it and the blue-glazed honeypot on the corner of the table.' [p. 197] Can you imagine Arwen eating off *a breakfast tray?* Aragorn?

8. *The Path of Daggers* (1998)

I was rather dreading this, actually ([voices off]: 'Then why are you reading it *at all*, fool?'), but once I got going it wasn't nearly as bad as I'd anticipated. I suppose these things rarely are. After about p. 250 it turned into quite a rapid, bump-less slide down a gentle slope to the conclusion. Not that it's page turning. It is a treading-water sort of book. It is treading out the vintage where the grapes of stultified stupefaction are stored.

So, Book 7 ended with Rand killing the 'forsaken' Sammael in characteristically understated fashion ('Screaming, Rand swept the balefire down toward the square, the rubble collapsing on itself, swept down death out of time – and let *saidin* go before the bar of white touched the lake of Mashadar that now rolled across the square, billowing past the Waygate toward rivers of glowing fray that flowed out from another palace on the other side bang crash wow! kaboom crsssh-crassh haha!'). Book 8 takes up the story, but does so in a one-step-forward-one-step-back sort of way. Or to be more precise, in a no-steps-forward-no-steps-back manner. An army of Seanchan rampages through the world. Some of Rand's own followers are plotting against him. Nynaeve and Elayne finally get hold of the bowl of the winds that they've spent, I suppose, two books looking for, and use it to heal the weather. Then there's a lengthy, minutely shuffling build-up to another big climactic battle. At the end of Wotviii we don't seem to be any further forward than we were at the end of Wotvii. Rand is still going bonkers, but very slowly. His mates are still noodling around, except for Mat, who wasn't in this one at all. Unless he was, and I missed him.

Is the novel too padded? Well, there's a great many characters' points-of-view that need to be orchestrated, and a lot of … Oh! Time for a tea-break!

> Careful of the silver pitcher's heat, Cadsuane poured a cup of tea, testing the thin green porcelain cup for warmth. As might have been expected in silver, the tea had cooled quickly. Channeling briefly, she heated it again. The dark tea tasted too much of mint; Cairhienin used mint entirely too freely in her opinion. She did not offer a cup to […] [p. 292]

Right. Always refreshing, a nice cup of tea. On we go. So, there's evil plotting, and several battles, and an explosion in the – ah! Stop! Time for another tea-break!

> Egwene went in to find everything in readiness. Selame was just setting a tea tray on the writing table […] The tea tasted of mint. In this weather! Selame was a trial […] [p. 353]

The question is not 'is it padded?' The question is: 'could it *be* more padded? When Jordan calls one chapter 'The Extra Bit' is he *kidding*? I thought I understood, broadly, the appeal of Epic Fantasy. *Surely* readers don't go to Epic Fantasy for endless descriptions of clothing, furniture, fabrics, and characters *constantly drinking cups of mint tea?* Does Jordan think his readership are all senior citizens?

No, but, wait: I spoke too soon! Here's some excitement! Adelas and Isman, two important Aes Sedai, have been assassinated! Stumbling across the dead bodies – Birgitte draws her belt knife – Nynaeve surveys the scene, and:

> Dipping her finger into the teapot, she touched it to the tip of her tongue, then spat vigorously and emptied the whole teapot into the table in a wash of tea and tea leaves. [p. 594]

Assassinated *by tea*! Fitting, fitting. Not so much *Epic Pooh* as *Epic Miss Marple.*

Why am I persevering with this series? Shouldn't I stop reading, since I'm not enjoying it. By insulting the *Wheel of Time* I insult those fans who love the *Wheel of Time.* At the very least, it would be worthwhile considering whether, since so many love it so, whether I am missing something important.

To be precise: I get that for many people the deal is escape. Leave your worries behind; you enter this better world. It's a world in which you don't work in the accounts department of a mid-size educational supplies firm; where, instead, you live in a palace and command servants and have magic powers and enjoy exciting sex with beautiful people and are able to vent your repressed aggression in fighty-fight. Jordan's twist on this venerable textual strategy is, partly, giving his readers much more detail than his market rivals, and partly, more cannily, creating the illusion of psychological depth. Simple wish-fulfilment gets old too soon, so Jordan's Alexander-the-Great-alike is troubled by the fear he's going mad. It's not much, but it's enough to separate him from the bulk of competitors. And otherwise, the wotworld is coloured and detailed like a Pre-Raphaelite painting, and to similar aesthetic effect – *viz.* the embourgeoisification and prettifying of a notional past:

> Across the harbour the wind roared, tossing small ships and large, across the city itself, gleaming white beneath the unfettered sun, spires and walls and color-ringed domes, streets and canals bustling with storied southern industry. Around the shining domes and slender towers of the Tarasin Palace the wind swirled, carrying the tang of salt, lifting the flag of Altara, two golden leopards on a field of red and blue. [p. 36]

But – I keep coming back to this. But – really, it screams from the books – but it *is all terribly written*. I don't just mean the style, although the style *is* awful. I mean the whole kit-and-caboodle: the overall structure, and the narrative, the pacing and focalisation, the characterisation, the dialogue, the tone. All of it. The writing is bad from the get-go. 'She managed to be pretty if not beautiful despite a nose that was overbold at best' – at *best?* How would it have been if it had been the worst? 'Gaunt cheeks and a narrow nose hid the ageless quality of the red sister's features': so 'cheeks' and 'nose' don't count as features?

> Her eyebrows climbed as she directed her gaze back to them, eyes black as her white-winged hair, a demanding stare of impatience so loud she night as well have shouted. [p. 47]

Her eyes are black, they're white, her eyebrows are escaping, her gaze is audible. This is terrible writing.

And this is the part I can't seem to get my head around: *the fans know that it's terribly written.* They know and they don't care. Why don't they care? I don't *know* why they don't care. After finishing Wotviii I Googled for some reviews, and I found a piece posted on SFSite by James Seidman:

> In the book, Jordan succeeds in carrying forward his stunning world building in this detailed story of a struggle between good and evil [...] Yet, after reading *A Path of Daggers*, I found myself wishing that Jordan had succeeded in his original goal of completing the story in eight books, rather than the current estimate of twelve. While the novel certainly advances the plot of the series, it fails to really introduce many new themes to keep the story fresh [...] I don't want to leave the impression that *A Path of Daggers* is a bad book or boring. It's a piece of excellent writing that is part of an excellent series. However, this particular piece of *The Wheel of Time*, taken by itself, seems to drag on. It seems like Jordan could have focused on progressing certain plot lines faster to give more of a sense of progress. Fortunately, several things happen at the very end of the book that suggest that the ninth book will again be refreshing and different. I would suggest that readers with enough patience wait for the ninth book to come out, then read it back-to-back with *A Path of Daggers*. This will probably hide any of the book's shortcomings and lead to a more pleasurable reading experience.

This is, I think, one of the most astonishing reviews I have ever read. Seidman describes the book as 'stunning' and uses the superlative 'excellent' twice despite conceding that the novel is stale, draggy and possessed of unpleasant shortcomings. And he does so with a straight face. He then suggests how a reader might get through the volume in such a way as to camouflage precisely those shortcomings. Assuming that 'stunning' is not being deployed in its abattoir bolt-gun sense, and putting aside the theory that 'excellent' is used sarcastically, this amounts to a reviewer saying 'vol. 8 is an *excellent* novel, although, obviously *in a shit way*, but maybe volume 9 *won't* be so shit, and *maybe*, if you swallow them both together, that as yet unwritten book will be sweet enough to disguise the shitty taste of this one.'

What to say to such a review other than: don't! Please don't! The libraries of the world are crammed with beautiful, powerful, moving, mind-blowing literature! Read some of that instead!

'I don't care!' you cry. 'I don't *want* good writing! I just want to get away to Wotworld for a while!'

Well, hey. Sure. We're all a bit ground-down by life, I know. We all want to get a little drunk, from time to time, so as to ameliorate the grind; to step through the portal to somewhere more appealing. But getting drunk doesn't have to mean sitting on a park bench with a 2-litre plastic bottle of strong cider. It is possible to get something more refined from the experience. How can I communicate this fundamental truth about art to you? Is there any point in me telling you: 'look, if you just *try* this Château Margaux 1787, you'll get all the intoxication you want but also a really beautiful drinking experience...'? Because, here's the thing; with alcohol, supermarket cider is cheaper than fine wines (that of course dictates why different people drink the one and not the other). But with books *the difference in quality is not reflected in the cover price*! Maybe it should be. Maybe it *ought* to cost £1:99 to buy a Robert Jordan novel and £45.99 to buy a Vladimir Nabokov one. But it doesn't! Amazingly, it doesn't! There is nothing stopping you going for the higher quality experience! Honestly!

9. *Winter's Heart* (2000)

So now we reach WoTix, another 'international No.1 bestseller'. So here we are. This is a book that makes explicit something about Jordan's multivolume endeavour which has been previously only implicit. This series, though it starts as a more-or-less conventional Heroic Fantasy product, has by this point metamorphosed into something much odder: a kind of anti-Fantasy, a deconstruction of the premise of Fantasy as a genre.

As Samuel Beckett's career progressed, his writing became more and more pared down, less and less verbal, increasingly approaching the asymptote that was at the heart of Beckett's bleak vision: silence. The great, productive paradox at the heart of Beckett was that one of his century's greatest verbal artists mistrusted the ability of words ever to articulate truth – not just specific arrangements of words but the whole of verbal art itself. *The Unnameable*, in that near-sublime novel, says: 'I'll speak of me when I speak no more.' For him silence is 'the only chance of saying something at last that is not false.

To step briskly *ab sublimi ad ridiculus*, Jordan's career manifests something similar. Insofar as Heroic Fantasy is a fundamentally narrative art form, to which readers go in order to experience the pleasure of following the movement of characters through time, Jordan says: no. WoTix is the closest he has yet come to a book that disperses wholly that force of narrative momentum – that great strength of the novel as a mode – into a great swarm of indistinguishable coexistent characters and non-progressions. If the traditional novel takes the shape of a quest, a linearly horizontal progression through narrative time, WoTix explodes that linearity in a bewildering near-dimensionless knot or tangle of non-progression.

Wotviii ended at the point when Egwene and her rebels laid siege to Tar Valon. The reader expects WoTix to carry the story on from that point, but instead Jordan rewinds the narratives a week or so and plays through more-or-less the same events over again. The narrative works on this minus scale, as it were, for almost the whole book; only passing through zero and into the plus for its big-gosh-wow conclusion

Or, another example of what I'm talking about: the first six chapters here concern Perrin's quest to recover his kidnapped wife Massive Fail Bashere. Is his quest successful? Unsuccessful? Do interesting things happen on it? The reader has no idea, because after chapter six this plotline vanishes completely from the novel.

Or to state it more plainly still, and at the risk of repeating myself: on the most fundamental level *nothing happens* for 620 pages of this 650 page novel. It's a bold experiment in un-narrative. It's a text worthy of an OULIPO project.

Now I did wonder, as I neared the end of this textual slab of stasis, whether Jordan slips at the last hurdle and permits narrative movement, development and interest to contaminate the pure Pollockian tangled obstruction of the whole. Because in chapter 35, Something Happens. The source of WoTworld's magic, 'saidin' has long been 'tainted' by the Dark Lord. Men can 'get at' this magic, but the use of it inevitably corrupts them and drives them mad. Until chapter 35 of this volume, that is. There, in a kind of massive good-versus-evil magical heavy-ordnance fire-fight, the Dragon himself, Rand al-Newman, manages to 'cleanse' the saidin. The scene seems at first blush very 'something-happen-y', written with Jordan's characteristic gnashing over-style: 'a huge ball of coruscating fire surrounded the other hilltop, red and gold and blue [...] a flame blacker than black, then another, another, until the dome boiled with a stygian fire. The roar of ten thousand thunders made her clap her hands over her ears and shriek soundlessly' [pp. 653-4]. Nor is it free of bathos – the magic creates a black dome that is, in Spinal Tap idiom (and not for the first time in this series) quite literally *none more black*: 'black no longer seemed to describe it. There was no term for it now, but black was a pale colour by comparison.'

So this, the cleansing of saidin, is 'the big event' of the novel. But actually it is not an event at all. It is, on the contrary, a kind of un-event. What is 'cleansed' in this interminable text is *narrative itself*: drama, plot, narrative interest. This, of course, is why the book is called 'Winter's Heart'; not because the WoTworld is in the grip of a profound winter – although it is – and not in allusion to Rand's supposedly 'wintry' heart – although some play is made of this idea. But no, actually the evident allusion is to Barthe's *Le Degré zéro de l'écriture*. This is Jordan's attempt at a Barthean masterpiece, written in a weird yet ideologically freighted 'blank' style that is achieved not by neoclassical restraint but on the contrary by hurling great quantities (we might say, by a *blizzard*) of chaff at the reader: irrelevant detail and mass-produced repetition... she tugged her braids, she smoothed her skirts. This is in a brilliantly, perversely *inverted* form *precisely the style Barthes talks about*, style which 'has always something crude about it [...] a form with no clear destination, the product of a thrust, not an intention, and, as it were, a vertical and lonely dimension of thought. Its frame of reference is biological or biographical, not historical.'

But this is only to state the obvious: that the WoT series, despite launching itself with more-or-less conventional narrative stylings, increasingly sheds its narrative momentum as it goes on. Each volume covers less ground, goes slower, dissipates so-called 'narrative interest' in a welter of pointless detail and endlessly proliferating characters. What Debord calls 'neosemioticist narrative' replaces sequential developmental progression with a frozen constellation of semiological placeholders. Now, of course, there is a temptation to read this on the level not of text but rather of author – to say, in effect: 'Jordan prolonged his series because he found it financially profitable to do so'. The zeno's-paradox of Jordan's own writing practice, turning a trilogy into (five – eight – twelve – fourteen–) many books may indeed have had a practical moneymaking aspect to it. That doesn't interest me. I'm struck, rather, by the fetishistic nature of the undertaking on a textual level.

The aim, in other words, is precisely *the necrophilic jouissance of postponement*, an endless deferral, a tantric-sex approach to narrative satisfaction. So we read:

> At [Shiane's] nod, Murellin stepped aside and motioned Daved Hanlon to enter, closing the door behind him. Hanlon was swathed in a dark cloak, but he snaked out one hand to cup Falion's bottom through her dress. She glared at him bitterly, but did not move away. Hanlon was part of her punishment. Still, Shiane had no wish to watch him fondle the woman. 'Do that later,' she ordered. [pp. 248-9]

That 'do it later' is the principle of fluid narrative deferral that, as here, is always explicitly sexualised. The text simultaneously positions us so that we watch him fondle the woman, and declares that it has no wish to watch him fondle the woman. And though this may look like a paradox, it is not: for the text's erotic investment is precisely *not* in fondling, but in *the deferral of fondling*. This is the WoT fetish: bondage. Not sensual motion, but the 'objet petit a' of *the bonds that prevent motion*. Here, for spurious reasons allegedly related to 'plot' Tylin persuades Mat to tie her up ('she pulled his head down for a kiss that curled his toes in his boots'):

> Tylin insisted on supervising her own binding. She seemed to take pride in it. She had to be bound with strips cut from her skirts, as if she had come upon him by surprise and been overpowered. The knots had to be tight, so that she could not escape however she struggled, and she did struggle against them once they were tied, thrashing about hard enough that it seemed she really was trying to get free [...] her ankles and wrists had to be tied together in the small of her back, and a leash run from her neck to one leg so she could not wriggle [...] he gently pushed one of her silk kerchiefs into her mouth [...]' [pp. 583]

A lesser writer might have been deflected from writing a scene such as this on the grounds that it 'is embarrassing', or indeed on the grounds that, 'dude, you don't need to display your lame-ass bondage fantasies like that for everyone to see' – or conceivably even on the grounds that 'Christ, Bob, if you must indulge your leering bondage daydreams then at least do so *properly*, hombre, not mincing around the edges like this.' But this would be to miss the point. These bonds, so cheesily sexualised, *are the very principle of narrative obstruction itself.* In this novel they become the totems of libidinous restriction that coalesce the essence of the series as a whole. This volume of the *World of Time* is a handkerchief stuffed in the mouth of the Muse. It is text that seeks to obstruct text.

10. *Crossroads of Twilight* (2003)

Let me see if I can boil down *Crossroads of Twilight*'s 700-pages for you.

Drivel.

There you go.

I was warned. Many people warned me. Jordan writes. He doesn't *revise* what he has written, and nobody *edits* what he has written. He writes a great fog of fretfully realised detail, very loosely bunched into clusters of pointless character interactions. Nothing else happens. Jordan writes many ill-formed and many more gangling, clumsy, clause-carcrash sentences of the 'Sashalle was no taller than she, not to speak of, but she had to hurry to keep up, as the Red glided swiftly, along wide, square-vaulted corridors' and 'Sheriam's shriek shattered the stillness in more ways than one' and 'the stream of people flowing the other way was mostly Seanchan, soldiers in ordered ranks, with their segmented armour, painted in stripes, and helmets that looked like the heads of huge insects, some marching and some mounted nobles, nobles who were always mounted, wearing ornate cloaks, pleated riding dresses and lace veils, and voluminous trousers and long coats' kind. But we're used to that from previous books.

Jordan writes: 'but then, who would have expected to see Bertholme Saighan walking peacefully with Weiramon Saniago, neither man reaching for the dagger at his belt?' [p. 81]. And we read (for reading is in part a process of interpreting writing): 'but then, who can honestly say they *remember* who Bertholme Saighan is, or why he should or shouldn't be walking peacefully with Weiramon Saniago, or whether we've ever encountered either of them before, oh god when will this end, haven't we suffered enough?'

Jordan writes: 'the odour of horse dung seemed strong.' [p. 286] Well, quite.

Is there tea? There *is* tea. Even better than that, there is *explosively detonating honey*: 'Without thinking Elayne picked up her teacup and took a sip. The tea had gone cold, but honey exploded on her tongue.

Honey! She looked at Avienda in astonishment.' [p. 351] Exploding honey would astonish me too.

Have you ever nodded to somebody? Ah, but have you ever nodded *like this*. 'After a moment, his chin moved, the vestige of a nod' [p. 541].

Oh. You have?

'Loial's ears trembled with caution, now.' [p. 553] That's a neat trick.

Towards the end, Jordan writes in a way that might even betray that most un-*Wheel of Time* quality, ironic self-awareness ('so many fabulations drifted out that telling reality from nonsense became difficult', p. 363). But no; it's all painfully earnest; he really thinks that we will be interested in all this clothing, and furnishings, and terrible, terrible sentence constructions.

This is the conclusion to which I have come: Jordan is the Fantasy-writing equivalent of a marble fanatic. He has assembled a large collection of marbles, and built a curving, angled course from wood, along which they can roll. And that's how he amuses himself, rolling his marbles endlessly, happily round and round the same track. He's enjoying himself. It's not really for our benefit (although it's performed under the polite fiction that it is). It's for his *own* benefit, and does us no harm. Can't we leave it at that?

Here's the opening paragraph I originally wrote for this review:

> The *Wheel of Time* does *not* turn, and books freeze and stall, leaving memories that become confused as to whom all these minor characters are, actually. Minor characters blur to one another, and even quite important figures are long forgotten when the series that gave them birth comes again. In one Book, called the Tenth by Jordan, a Book neither future nor past but interminably, tediously present, a wind rose at the reviewing waterfall. The wind is not the end. It is not even the beginning of the end. But it is, perhaps, the end of the beginning. The wind says: I was warned. And yet, to encounter textual stasis of quite such magnitude is a staggering experience. My God, and I thought earlier books were slow.

But riffling through some of the 1000+ www.amazon.com readers' reviews of *Crossroads of Twilight*, I found the following author review – which is the same gag, done not only first but rather better:

The *Wheel of Time* turns, and Books come and pass, leaving memories that become legend. Legend fades to myth, and even myth is long forgotten when the Book that gave it birth comes again. In one Book, called the Tenth Book by some, a Book yet to be written, a Book already burned, a yawn rose in the *Crossroads of Twilight*. The Yawn is not the beginning, there are neither beginning nor endings in the *Wheel of Time* (not if Jordan is still paid by the word.) But it is a beginning.

…which busted my flush somewhat. I also, from the same place, liked 'Time Traveller's review from the future:

Greetings Fellow Humans. I come from a thousand years in the future and have travelled back in time to tell all of you that the end is in sight and it is worth the wait. Robert Jordan, having his consciousness digitized has greatly increased his efficiency and is on Book 1452 and is now writing at a clip of 2 books per year. Each book now spans a time period of 1 minute, and he has introduced over 5 dozen new characters, none of whom (like Jordan) can die. But as I said before, the end is in sight. Robert Jordan X20485 has promised that he plans to end the series at Book 1500. So I urge all of you to stay the course. Be diligent and read the books. And finally, there is a twist in Book 438 that will simply blow your mind. It is so great that it was instrumental in brokering peace between Pakistan and India after WW4.

11. *Knife of Dreams* (2005)

I'm going to start by quoting the blurb on the back of this volume:

As the very fabric of reality wears thin all portents indicate that Tarmon Gai'don, the Last Battle, is imminent.

Not all the portents, though, surely? For instance, there's the counter-portent that we're still two-and-a-half-thousand pages away from even the *start* of the final volume. So I'm not sure 'imminent' is the word I'd use.

– and Rand al'Thor must ready himself to confront the Dark One.

He hasn't had enough time to ready himself? If eleven fat volumes don't give him enough time, I'm not sure what meaning the phrase 'enough time' can possibly have.

> But Rand must first negotiate a truce with the Seanchan armies, as their forces increasingly sap his strength.

That's a bold move, by the publishers, there. Brave. I mean, putting a reference to 'sapped strength' right there, in plain view, on the back of this book.

Otherwise, what have we got? Well, stylistically it's the same hideous jumble, the same self-parodic bloat. Jordan is a writer who writes 'this fire was not at all small, and the room seemed not far short of hot, a welcome heat that soaked into the flesh and banished shivers' [p. 343] because he is constitutionally allergic to the phrasing 'a large fire warmed the room.' He thinks the former sentence is more precise and therefore evocative. He's wrong. That's not precision, it's a finicky fussing textual Asperger's, a style that can see nothing *but* details (and, more to the point, nothing but a certain very *limited palate* of details – colours of clothing, speed of movement, types of food, gradations of heat and cold – never the telling details great writers master). It is a style wholly incapable of illuminating penetration or evocation. *Knife of Dreams* is a novel in which this havering, hesitant John Majorish 'a not un-large fire that was not un-warming' idiocy has spread into all the limbs of the novel. Quite apart from anything else – 'the fire was hot, *a welcome heat that soaked into the flesh and banished shivers*'? I ask you. As opposed to a heat that *bounces off the flesh and chills the very bones?* Because that's not the sort of heat you want from an open fire. No indeedy.

So, yes, I'm still breaking this butterfly upon the wheel.

> Romanda took a longer look, and nearly gasped herself. [p. 508]

I gasped myself the other day, actually. I've still got the red mark. Painful. What else? Well, there seemed to be an enormous amount of *gathering of skirts* in the novel, viz.: 'Amylia jumped, then gathered her bronze-colored skirts to her knees' [p. 483].

> They were disparate men, alike only in the way a leopard was like a lion. [p. 508]

So these two men were alike in that […] they both had four legs?

> Gathering her skirts, Malind jumped down and rushed out. [p. 508]

Again with the skirts!

> Naris grimaced, before gathering her skirts and darting into the corridor. [p. 343]

OK. I think the skirt gathering point has been made. What I mean is, it's not as if the novel is all gathering skirts, and nothing but gathering skirts. There are plenty of other things.

> 'That would be stealing,' Mistress Anan told him, in a lecturing tone, gathering her cloak around her. [p. 235]

See? *Cloak*.

> First came Seonid, a short woman holding her dark divided skirts up out of the mud. [p. 583]

That one doesn't even *use* the word 'gathering'! This is the kind of stylistic and descriptive variation that makes Jordan the writer he is.

> 'Fail me, and you'll regret it!' Gathering the skirts of her silk robe, she scurried away into the crowd. [p. 598]

OK. That one uses 'gathering.' I concede that. But, look, there's plenty you can do with skirts, apart from gathering them up or holding them out of the mud! See:

> Her mouth snapped shut, and she smoothed her dark blue skirts unnecessarily...

I rest my case.

> ...then the small dark woman began walking toward them slowly, holding her pleated skirts up off the damp ground. [p. 607]

Conceivably I rested my case too soon.

The small dark woman is Tuon, a Seanchan princess, and the book gives us a lot of detail, and tells us almost nothing, about her, and her relationship with Mat. There's also some business with Elayne, and a certain amount of Rand faffing about. Although, to speak truthfully, plot-wise there's not an awful lot to report here. The 90-page prologue does contain some action: tension, a duel, build-up. But it's a false dawn. The most memorable thing in the novel is that Rand gets his left-hand Luke-Skywalkered. Otherwise a summary of the novel might be: people wear clothes of varying styles and colours; people talk to people about various things; the food is all going off, but that doesn't stop people eating enormous minutely detailed meals all the time. That aside, what is there in *Knife of Dreams* but Jordan's unique prose? That prose... one last time, for the gipper?

'On the wind roared [...] shrieking over military camps near the river where soldiers and camp followers sleeping on the ground suddenly had their blankets stripped off and those in tents awoke to canvas jerking.' [p. 93] I tried canvas jerking myself, when I was younger. Painful. Or, wait... did I already do that gag?

'His scowl deepened creases on his flushed face that needed no deepening.' [p. 124]

'They slept together like puppies of necessity.' [p. 168] That's a quotation from Shakespeare, you know: 'Cry havoc and let slip/The puppies of necessity.' *Julius Caesar*, I think.

'Only Alliandre was there, lying facedown on her blankets in her collar with a damp cloth dipped in an herbal infusion over her bruised bottom.' [p. 169] If there's one thing Jordan likes more than attractive women being spanked on their bare arses, it's attractive women learning to love such abusive treatment. The word for this is: *cre-e-epy*.

'He must have a leather tongue.' [p. 176] Must he? What if he doesn't want one?

'He was studying the board, when Joline led Teslyn and Edesina into the wagon like haughty on a pedestal, smooth-faced Aes Sedai to their toenails.' [p. 240] I'm afraid I don't understand that sentence at all.

'Essande produced an ivory-backed hairbrush and removed the towel from Elayne's head.' [p. 352] Neat trick!

'Elayne trembled, hands tightening to fists on the arms of her chair.' [p. 361]

'Elayne laid one finger atop a bronze horseman less than a hand tall, standing a few leagues west of the city.' [p. 377] Another neat trick!

'His ears quivered with embarrassment yet again. He had a great deal to learn about being a husband.' [p. 414]

'The face of the man from Shadar Logoth floated in his head for a moment. He looked furious. And near to sicking up.' [p. 462]

'She tried to work moisture into her mouth, but it was thick' [p. 653]

'She showed him her teeth, hoping he did not take it for a grin.' [p. 654]

'Before you can have eyeless prisoners, you need an eyeless victory. What we've had are a string of eyeless defeats.' [p. 737] Wise words.

'Abruptly Loune seemed to recall who he was talking to. His face turned to dark wood, a hard mask.' [p. 738] And there's yet another neat trick!

I tell you what. Let's give Faile the last word:

'Faile clasped her hands together. Of course she was solid. Hoisting her robes to avoid any more washing than she absolutely had to do, she began to walk. And then to run. [p. 168]

12. Final thoughts: the Butterfly is broken on the Wheel.

At last they rode over the downs and took the East Road, and then Merry and Pippin rode on to Buckland, and already they were singing again as they went. But Adam turned to Staines, and so came back, as day was ending once more. And he went on, and there was yellow light, and fire within, and the evening meal was ready, and he was expected. And Rachel drew him in, and set him on his chair, and put little Daniel upon his lap. He drew a deep breath. 'Well, I read them,' he said.

So – what have I learned? Well, mostly I was reminded of a line from Tibor Fischer's celebrated, or perhaps infamous, *Daily Telegraph* Review of Amis's *Yellow Dog*:

The way publishing works is that you go from not being published no matter how good you are, to being published no matter how bad you are.

I can't think of a clearer illustration of that baleful truth than these novels. The first is pretty good; the last are staggeringly, stupefyingly bad. Imagine an alternative universe in which *Wheel of Time* was never published. Now imagine a new writer approaching an editor at a major publishing house with the manuscript of *Winter's Heart* or *Crossroads of Twilight*. Now imagine the editor leaping upon this unpublished manuscript with cries of joy. But, see, that last one goes beyond what can be imagined by any sane person.

This, it seems to me, has a number of deplorable consequences. One is that, since the market becomes saturated by rubbishy fat volumes issued on the strength of the authors' long corroded reputation rather than any intrinsic merit, good books get crowded out. Yes I'm talking about you sir, and you madam, and the superlative but as yet unpublished Fantasy classic sitting on your hard-drive. The people who should be reading that are instead picking up WoTx. It's a shame for you. It's a bigger shame for them, even though they don't realise it.

I'm not suggesting that publishing is entirely a zero-sum operation, and that the choice is starkly between this rubbish late WoT book and your unpublished, fresh masterpiece. But I *am* suggesting that commercial publishing works within the horizons of finite bookshop shelf space and finite reading time in customers' lives. And that, given this, it would be in everyone's interests to see more good books published and fewer bad ones.

The other consequence is even more insidious: good young writers, noting the commercial success of the series, conclude that *this is how Fantasy must be written*. Their writing becomes infected, their originality degraded, and a kind of malign self-perpetuating miasma of rubbishness settles over the whole field.

Still, let me not grow cranky. Here's The FAQ.

***

Will you be reading Brandon Sanderson's concluding three volumes? I may do. Strangely I came across a copy of *The Gathering Storm*, title-page signed by Jordan himself (perhaps from beyond the grave) in the possession of my grey-haired old mother. You need to understand that my mother reads a rhino's-weight in crime novels & whodunits every month, but never knowingly picks up an SF or F title – she doesn't read my novels, for instance. 'Mum,' I said, chancing upon the vol. when visiting last month. 'I didn't realise you were a Robert Jordan reader!' 'Robert Who?' she replied. 'This,' I said, holding up the hefty hardback. 'Oh, that,' she said, vaguely. 'Somebody gave me that. Do you think I should read it?' 'Have you read the previous eleven volumes?' 'No,' she said. 'No I haven't. What happens in them?' I sat down next to her on the sofa. 'Mum,' I said. 'Would you mind if I borrowed this?' 'Take it,' she said, opening the new Dalziel and Pascoe. 'Take it.'

Are you going to read the New Spring prequel? No. I'm reconciled to the thought that I shall go to my grave never having read the *New Spring* prequel.

From Miles, a frequent commenter on the blog whence these reviews first appeared: 'I'm trying to think of another long-running fantasy series I've read that Adam can take a whack at after he's done with WoT...' That's very kind of you. I'm touched. I will probably not be launching myself into tens of thousands of pages of Fantasy soon though.

You were supposed to be writing reviews, but all you did was slag Jordan off. This is a 'FAQ'. The Q stands for 'question'. This is a statement, not a question.

How do you explain the success of the series? Isn't it possible that you were missing something major? If the books are as bad as you say, how come they sold so well? This came up several times in the comments, and is clearly important. And, I agree: I can't argue with the series' success. Frankly I'm not sure why the books have done so well; although I'd hazard the later huge sales were more reflections of the previous books' huge sales than any actual merit in the novels themselves. But that still leaves to be explained the earlier books' huge sales. I'm not sure what the answer is.

The bottom line is that there is something, or some things, about this series has resulted not just in many people reading them, but a good number falling in love with them too. Not me, but I probably need to be more open to whatever this 'thing' or 'things' is/are. Part of me thinks it must have to do with the series' sheer length, which by a sort of textual brute force can replicate the immersiveness a more skilful writer achieves through style, worldbuilding or character. The shift (as in Star Wars) into increasingly obviously sexualised territory can't have hurt either: I can imagine readers growing up reading the series. Or, thinking a little more about this (and picking up on Larry's perceptive comment): by 'length' I suppose I mean more than just bulk of pages. I mean the immense accumulation of and attention to trivial details.

Put it this way: there's an interesting bifurcation in the 'market' – horrid term – for SF and Fantasy: on the one hand the texts themselves (as it might be: *Lord of the Rings*, *Star Wars*) which provide one sort of pleasure, and on the other immensely detailed and elongated fan encyclopaedia-style anatomies and extensions of those texts: all the *Star Wars* novelizations, all the books of ships specs and timelines and whatnot. This latter body of writing appeals to a subset of broader fandom, those SFF fans who want to know every atom of the imagined world.

Now what's happening with WoT, it seems to me, is that after a conventional opening, the series is increasingly turning into a man-and-fly-in-the-matter-transporter-together mutant melding of these two modes of text. Each instalment devotes a certain amount of energy to moving the story on, and much more to encyclopaedically anatomizing world and character.

David Moles and I once had the following exchange on this matter:

> **David Moles**: The fans aren't fans of the books, they're fans of the Platonic WoT that's revealed, dimly, through the books [...] It's not as though the pleasure provided by WoTworld is simple, or even that it's equally well-provided by a plethora of well-written books. You don't find that level of mechanical complexity very often outside of a role-playing supplement, and when you do it's likely (Donaldson, Feist) to be more or less equally badly written — let's say, sufficiently badly written – if not necessarily in the same way.

> **Adam Roberts**: Hmm. I'm not sure that the books' currency is complexity, actually. There's a fetish for minutiae, true, but that's not the same thing. I'd say the appeal is something simpler: not just that

this is a wishfulfilment world that is more colourful than ours, but that it combines an idealised nostalgic past with all present-day bourgeois creature-comforts, parlayed through honest-to-goodness melodramatic emotional intensity. Not that there's any shortage of imaginary Westworldesque themeparks in Fantasy more generally that do that, or stuff like it; although I daresay Jordan gains something from the Great Wall Of China, visible-from-the-moon scale of his undertaking.

David Moles: I'm not denying that it provides those pleasures, but I think you can't dismiss the trainspotting, stamp-collecting aspect either – the sheer plethora of implied, distinct collectable figurines and playsets, the number of possible 'which would win in a fight, X or Y?' matchups. I'm not sure there's anything in print fiction to match it.

Moles is a very clever man, and may have come close to the truth with this.

Millions of people love these books. Do you really think you're 'better' than them? What gives you the right to be so rude? You realise that by criticising Jordan's books you're criticising these fans too? It is, clearly, a ticklish business telling people who 'really really love these novels' that I think the novels are crap. Here's what I wrote a while ago on this very subject:

So, let's say, you read *The Eyes of Argon* and you love it; you're gripped, thrilled, moved and inspired. Then you read a review that says *'The Eyes of Argon* is terribly bad stuff.' Do you then:

(a) say to yourself: a different opinion to mine, how interesting, let a thousand flowers bloom and a thousand schools of thought contend, one feature of great art is that it provokes a diversity of responses. Or:

(b) say to yourself: the review, by calling this book crap, is saying that *my taste in books is crap* which is tantamount to calling me a big crappy crap-crap. **Nobody** calls me a big crap-crap and gets away with it. *Where does this motherfucker get off* calling people big crap-craps like this? Why can't he keep his offensive opinions to himself?

But of course it goes without saying that reviewers respond to the book they have read, not to the idea in their heads of the sort of people who like the book they have just read. Apart from me, I mean. Obviously when I review, I do so specifically to mock the value-systems and worth of people who read. People like you, sir. And you madam.

Beyond that, we get into the broad territory of what ultimately grounds critical judgment. Properly discussing that would take more time than I have at my disposal. I was, though, terribly interested by the Jordan fan opinion, expressed in the comments to my blog, that Jordan was a better worldbuilder than Tolkien and a better stylist than Flaubert.

I'm interested in adapting all eleven of your WoT reviews into a prog-rock opera. Is that OK? Go right ahead.

I must say I find it hard to believe that any of these are real 'questions', asked frequently or otherwise. Isn't it true that you just made them all up, now? It is.

Steel Quill Books

A new venture from multiple award-winning genre publisher
NewCon Press

Established in 2006, NewCon Press has built a reputation for delivering the very best in science fiction, fantasy, and horror, whether from established 'big name' authors or from exciting new voices.

Steel Quill Books is intended as a vehicle for showcasing high quality works that fall outside the established NewCon parameters but that undoubtedly deserve to be read. I'm delighted to begin this new chapter with *Sibilant Fricative*, a collection of reviews and critical essays from one of Britain's most forthright reviewers, Adam Roberts, all of which are available in print for the first time.

Ian Whates
Cambridgeshire,
June 2014

NewCon Press and Steel Quill titles are available to buy from
Spacewitch
http://www.spacewitch.com/publishers/newcon-press

NEWCON PRESS

Publishing quality Science Fiction, Fantasy, Dark Fantasy and Horror for eight years and counting.

Winner of the 2010 'Best Publisher' Award from the European Science Fiction Society.

Anthologies, novels, short story collections, novellas, paperbacks, hardbacks, signed limited editions, e-books from:

Neil Gaiman, Brian Aldiss, Kelley Armstrong, Alastair Reynolds, Stephen Baxter, Christopher Priest, Tanith Lee, Joe Abercrombie, Dan Abnett, Nina Allan, Sarah Ash, Neal Asher, Tony Ballantyne, James Barclay, Chris Beckett, Lauren Beukes, Aliette de Bodard, Chaz Brenchley, Keith Brooke, Eric Brown, Pat Cadigan, Jay Caselberg, Michael Cobley, Storm Constantine, Hal Duncan, Jaine Fenn, Paul di Filippo, Jonathan Green, Jon Courtenay Grimwood, Frances Hardinge, Gwyneth Jones, M. John Harrison, Amanda Hemingway, Paul Kane, Leigh Kennedy, Kim Lakin-Smith, David Langford, Alison Littlewood, James Lovegrove, Una McCormack, Sophia McDougall, Gary McMahon, Alex Dally MacFarlane, Ken MacLeod, Ian R MacLeod, Gail Z Martin, Juliet E McKenna, John Meaney, Simon Morden, Mark Morris, Anne Nicholls, Stan Nicholls, Marie O'Regan, Philip Palmer, Stephen Palmer, Sarah Pinborough, Robert Reed, Rod Rees, Andy Remic, Mike Resnick, Mercurio D Rivera, Adam Roberts, Justina Robson, Stephanie Saulter, Gaie Sebold, Robert Shearman, Sarah Singleton, Martin Sketchley, Kari Sperring, Benjanun Sriduangkaew, Brian Stapleford, Charles Stross, Tricia Sullivan, EJ Swift, Adrian Tchaikovsky, Steve Rasnic Tem, Lavie Tidhar, Lisa Tuttle, Ian Watson, Freda Warrington, Liz Williams, Neil Williamson, and many more.

Join our mailing list to get advance notice of new titles, book launches and events, and receive special offers on books.

www.newconpress.co.uk